THE ROMAN REPUBLIC

MICHAEL CRAWFORD was born in Twickenham in 1939, and educated at St Paul's School and Oriel College, Oxford. He was made a Fellow of Christ's College, Cambridge in 1964, and was University Lecturer in Ancient History from 1969 until 1986. He has been a Visiting Professor at the universities of Pavia, Milan, L'Aquila and Padua, and at the Sorbonne and the Ecole Normale Supérieure in Paris, and he was made a Fellow of the British Academy in 1980. Since 1986 he has been Professor of Ancient History at University College London. Amongst his other books are *Roman Republican Coinage* (1974), *Sources for Ancient History* (1983) and *Coinage and Money under the Roman Republic* (1985).

D0807706

FONTANA HISTORY
OF THE ANCIENT WORLD

Series Editor: Oswyn Murray

MICHAEL CRAWFORD

THE ROMAN REPUBLIC

SECOND EDITION

Fontana Press
An Imprint of HarperCollins*Publishers*

Fontana Press
An Imprint of HarperCollins*Publishers*
77–85 Fulham Palace Road,
Hammersmith, London W6 8JB

First Edition published by Fontana 1978
This Second Edition published by Fontana Press 1992
¨ 9 8

ISBN 0 00 686250 0

Set in Imprint

Printed and bound in Great Britain by
Omnia Books Ltd, Glasgow

Preface

I HAVE TRIED, within prescribed limits, both to present a balanced picture of the Roman Republic and to write an interpretative essay. I have also tried to do justice to the immense diversity of the source material for the period, sometimes by citation rather than quotation. (In this context, I should explain that my translations of the written sources are often explanatory paraphrases rather than strict translations.) The plates and figures also offer visual evidence of an importance equal to that of the written material.

The maps show the location of the most important places mentioned in the text; for the others an atlas must be used.

Dates are BC, except for a few which are indicated as AD and a few which are quite obviously so. The date chart should compensate for the fact that the arrangement of the book is only loosely chronological.

The suggestions for further reading concentrate naturally on recent work in English.

All the indices are intended to function as tools of reference and therefore provide information, not easily incorporated in the text, on sources, persons, places and technical terms.

Tim Cornell, Oswyn Murray, John North, Helen Whitehouse and Peter Wiseman have all read the manuscript and have helped to eliminate a variety of aberrations. They of course bear no responsibility for the defects of the final version. The maps and figures are largely the work of Bill Thompson, of the Museum of Classical Archaeology, Cambridge; I am gateful to British Archaeological Reports, the British School at Rome and Filippo Coarelli for illustrations. To him, Peter Brunt, Emilio Gabba, Keith Hopkins, Claude Nicolet and those already mentioned I owe thanks for many enjoyable discussions of Republican history. But my greatest debt, and with it the dedication of this book, is to my immediate colleagues in the period when it was taking shape, Jack Plumb, Simon Schama and Quentin Skinner.

* * *

In preparing a second edition, I have slightly expanded the text and altered it in places to accommodate changes of mind and some recent discoveries. I have learnt a great deal from the careful suggestions of Kai Brodersen, who oversaw the German translation of the first edition. There is now a much fuller Date Chart to provide a certain chronological framework for those who are unfamiliar with the Roman Republic. And the Further Reading is related to the Date Chart in a way which I hope will be helpful. I hope that in this as in other cases I have learnt from the kind comments of reviewers, though I have found myself unable to accept suggestions which involved wanton changes to the original texts which underly my translations. Nor do I have any regrets about the space devoted to social and economic, as well as political and institutional, factors. I continue to believe that the principal reason for the destruction of Republican government at Rome was the neglect of the legitimate grievances of the population by the governing classes, just as I continue to believe that a socialist framework offers the only eventual hope for the survival of our own world. That the Roman Republic remains for me as live and fascinating a complex of problems as it has ever been owes much to the friendship and sparkle of my fellow Republican historians at University College London, Tim Cornell and John North; I should like to associate them in the dedication of this book.

Contents

List of Illustrations

Historical Introduction

Between the sack of Rome by the Gauls in 390 BC and the middle of the second century BC, a part-time army of Roman peasants, under the leadership of the ruling oligarchy, conquered first Italy and then the Mediterranean; the loyalty of the Roman population to its leaders was assured by a share in the rewards of victory. As the empire expanded, it became harder for the lower orders to gain access to these rewards, while at the same time competition within the oligarchy became more intense. The peasant armies of Rome were drawn into the conflicts born of this competition and the Republic dissolved in anarchy.

Some parts of this story may perhaps seem unduly dramatic; I can only say that a century like that between 133 BC and 31 BC, which killed perhaps 200,000 men in 91–82 and perhaps 100,000 men in 49–42, and which destroyed a system of government after 450 years *was* a cataclysm.

Three other themes also figure largely. In the first place, it seems to me important that the prevailing ideology of the Roman governing class was one which facilitated change, including in the end the abolition of Republican government itself; for it permitted and even encouraged the justification in traditional terms of actions which were in fact revolutionary.

The Roman state was one in which *libertas*, freedom, was early identified with *civitas*, citizenship, that is to say, political rights and duties; *libertas* was therefore universally accepted as desirable and trouble only arose when the question was raised of whose *libertas* was to be defended. At the same time, great services to the state brought a man *dignitas*, standing, and *auctoritas*, influence;

and naturally both were sought after by all men of great ability or noble descent.

In the history of the Republic, appeal was made to the concepts of *libertas* and *dignitas* both by those who sought to introduce radical change, notably by appealing to popular opinion against aristocratic consensus and by attempting to increase the material privileges of the people, and by those who sought to preserve the *status quo*, both in terms of political power and in terms of the distribution of resources.

The struggles between politicians during the Republic were given free rein by the failure to develop communal institutions for the maintenance of order; thus even legal procedure often involved the use of an element of self-help, as in bringing a defendant to court. Such a state of affairs perhaps did not matter greatly in a small rural community, and the struggle of the Orders, between patricians and plebeians, was in the end resolved in the course of the fifth and fourth centuries BC. But when men turned to force in the late Republic to resolve political differences, the result was catastrophic, with armies composed of many legions rapidly involved.

Secondly, I should like to stress the innovativeness of the governing class of the Republic in a wide variety of fields, cultural as well as political. If one looks at the two centuries between the Second Punic War and the age of Cicero, the impression is of an enthusiastic borrowing of Greek artistic and intellectual skills, slowly leading to the emergence of a developed Latin culture; the central period of Hellenization of the Roman oligarchy was precisely the period when it was locked in escalating internal competition which finally destroyed the system.

Finally, I have attempted to illustrate how the sources for a particular event often adopt, consciously or unconsciously, a polemical approach and how the development of this polemic is itself part of Republican history. The sources for the history of the Republic, indeed, leave much to be desired; the works of Roman and Greek historians contemporary with the events which they chronicled have largely perished; so too have most official records; even the works of later historians who reproduced and reshaped the material in earlier historians and in official records are rarely complete. But our inadequate knowledge of what happened is partly compensated for by the possibility of observing something of how the Romans saw their past and how that vision affected their conduct.

I

The Sources

IT WAS NOT UNTIL the end of the third century BC that any interest in the writing of history manifested itself at Rome; this interest was the result of an awareness that Rome was or was becoming part of the civilized world, that is the Greek world, surrounded by states of great antiquity and with a long and glorious history. A similar pedigree was a vital necessity for Rome. Within a few years of each other, Q. Fabius Pictor, a member of the Roman nobility, set out to write in Greek a history of Rome; Cn. Naevius, a poet from Campania, composed in Latin an epic poem on the First Punic War which included a great deal of material on early Roman history; and the family of L. Cornelius Scipio Barbatus, who died about 280 BC, inscribed on his sarcophagus an account of his career in nearly four lines instead of a simple line-and-a-bit giving his names and titles (See Pl. 1).

From this point onwards there is a rich Roman historical tradition, albeit now very imperfectly preserved. Beside this tradition there is another, that of Greek historians observing Rome from the outside. The Roman tradition has certain unifying characteristics; Pictor removed history from the hands of the official priests who had been responsible for most of such records as had been kept, but since the official priests of Rome were drawn from its aristocracy and were more officials than priests he did not change its essential nature. History at Rome was almost always written at least unconsciously from an aristocratic viewpoint and was often consciously apologetic. It shows a strong tendency to simplify the dilemmas of the past; and particularly in the late Republic it tends to see the antecedents of the revolution in purely moral terms, with evil men subverting the efforts of the heroic defenders of the *res publica*.

The Greek tradition is perhaps more complex. With Rome's confrontation with and defeat of King Pyrrhus of Epirus (Map 3) in 275 and the consequent abandonment of his attempt to create an empire in the west, the Greek world began to take notice, even if Rome remained unconscious of the significance of what she had achieved. The first serious Greek historian of Rome was Timaeus. Born in Tauromenium (Taormina) and exiled as a young man by King Agathocles of Syracuse (Map 2), he spent his working life in Athens, some fifty years in all; but his interest in the west remained and led him to write a history of Sicily and a history of Pyrrhus. The contemporary defeat of a Hellenistic king by a republic may have been a congenial theme to a man exiled by a tyrant and attested as an opponent of divine honours for kings. At all events, Timaeus was led to a serious investigation of the new power in the west; and it is not surprising that Polybius in his wish to establish himself a century later as *the* historian of Rome should have devoted so much energy to attacking the credentials of Timaeus.

We are told that Timaeus narrated the early history of Rome and the Pyrrhic War; but he went beyond merely accounting for the existence of the power which had defeated Pyrrhus. He questioned native informants about the Roman *sacra* at Lavinium (Map 1); he knew of the curious Roman customs relating to the sacrifice of the October horse; he wrote of the origins of the Roman monetary system and census classes; he synchronized the foundation of Rome with that of Carthage and thus knew, unlike all his fellow Greeks hitherto, that a long period intervened between the arrival of the Trojans in Italy and the foundation of Rome.

Timaeus lived to record only the first serious encounter of Rome with a Greek state; a century later Polybius of Megalopolis (Map 3) was stimulated to record the defeat by Rome not only of Carthage in the First and Second Punic Wars, but also of one Greek state after another and the consequent emergence of Rome as the dominant power in the Mediterranean. Unlike Timaeus, Polybius was an active politician, involved as a young man in the affairs of a Greek community, the Achaean League, which was allied with Rome in the early second century BC and whose leading city, Corinth, was eventually sacked by Rome in 146. Polybius, interned by Rome as a man whose allegiance was doubtful in 167, on balance approved of the Roman victory of 146. He had in any case already established a number of close friendships with members of the Roman aristocracy and his picture of Rome is hardly that of a complete outsider (p.71).

The last great Greek historian of Rome is Posidonius; contemporary with and a friend of many of the great men of the late Republic, he wrote, apart from numerous works on philosophy, science and geography, a history of Rome carrying on from where Polybius ended, the destruction of Carthage and Corinth in 146. An admirer of traditional Roman values and contemptuous of Rome's declared enemies in the Greek east, he nonetheless devoted much space to internal stress at Rome and commented on her often deplorable approach to provincial government.

Of all the historians of Rome writing before the death of Caesar no work is now preserved complete. The histories of Polybius have fared best, but of the other Greek historians and of all the Roman historians only miserable fragments have survived in quotation by later authors, often grammarians interested primarily in rare word forms. Their works, however, lie behind and are often directly used in the histories of two men writing under the principate of Augustus, the Greek Dionysius of Halicarnassus (Bodrum) and the Roman T. Livius of Patavium (Padua). The 'Early history of Rome' by Dionysius covered the period down to the beginning of the First Punic War and is preserved complete down to 444–3, thereafter in excerpts; the 'History of Rome from its foundation' by Livy covered the period down to the defeat of Varus in Germany in AD 9 and is preserved complete down to 293 (Books I–X) and from 218 to 167 (Books XXI–XLV), otherwise in résumés made for the semi-literate reading public of the later Roman empire, in the works of later historians and compilers of collections of *exempla*, moral tales, and in occasional quotations *in extenso*.

A third ingredient in the works of Dionysius and Livy, apart from the writings of earlier Greek and Roman historians, consists of official Roman records. Although the Romans displayed no interest in the writing of history before the end of the third century BC, they had nonetheless kept from the beginning of the Republic records which were capable of serving as the bare bones of history and had also preserved certain documents important to the life of the community.

The records called the Annales Maximi appear to have been kept year by year by the Pontifex Maximus, the head of the most important of the Roman colleges of official priests, and displayed outside his house on a notice-board; there is little evidence for their content – no doubt the names of the annual officials and a jejune record of phenomena of religious import such as eclipses and of events such as major wars. The annual display of the Annales Maximi was abandoned by P. Mucius Scaevola, who became Pontifex Maximus in 130; the doubtless edited form in which they were kept after being displayed had clearly long been available for consultation at any rate by members of the aristocracy and at some point the whole corpus was worked up and published. But the annual display was presumably abandoned because by now there flourished at Rome a more literary type of history, and the publication of the Annales Maximi, whenever it occurred, fell on stony ground; the historians of the late Republic and after made almost no use of them.

More important for our purposes is the preservation of major documents. Some were already exploited by Polybius, notably the early treaties between Rome and Carthage; a wider variety can be found in Livy, ranging from the decree of the Senate on the suppression of the worship of Bacchus in the early second century BC to the records of booty brought in to the treasury by victorious Roman generals or the treasury records of building activity. The decree of the Senate on the worship of Bacchus survives also in a contemporary inscribed copy from which the substantial accuracy of the version preserved by Livy may be seen. Related to the Roman respect for tradition in religious matters is the careful recording of the foundations of temples; the historical framework implied by these records, for instance the picture of a Rome rediscovering the Greek world around 300 and borrowing Greek conceptions of the celebration of victory, is often strikingly confirmed by the archaeological record.

The historical tradition as preserved by Dionysius and Livy is marred, however, by serious deformations. This is the result of two main factors. In the first place, the early historians of Rome, whether Greek or Roman, were interested in and recorded only the relatively recent past and the very distant past; later historians, moved by a *horror vacui,* set out to fill this gap, building on the bare record of the Annales Maximi, in their unelaborated and unpublished form. What they offer may be anything from informed guesswork to patriotic fiction; it is not history.

Secondly and more seriously, however, few Roman historians were able to resist the temptation to improve the image of their own family in the history of the Republic. As we shall see, Rome was ruled by the members of an aristocracy, one of whose prime concerns was to achieve distinction in competition with their peers. This competitive ideology comes out already in the epitaph of L. Cornelius Scipio, son of the Scipio Barbatus mentioned earlier, inscribed in an archaic form of Latin around 230: 'honc oino ploirume consentiont R[omane] duonoro optumo fuise viro' – 'this one man most Romans agree to have been the best of the good.' The effects of this ideology on the writing of history are graphically described by Cicero:

> And speeches in praise of the dead of past ages are indeed extant; for the families concerned kept them as a sort of mark of honour and a record, both in order to be able to use them if anyone else of the same family died and in order to preserve the memory of the achievements of the family and document its nobility. Of course, the history of Rome has been falsified by these speeches; for there is much in them which never happened – invented triumphs, additional consulates, false claims to patrician status, with lesser men smuggled into another family with the same *nomen,* as if, for instance, I claimed to be descended from Marcus Tullius, who was a patrician and consul with Servius Sulpicius ten years after the expulsion of the kings (*Brutus* 62).

The funerals at which such speeches were delivered are characterized by Polybius from his own experience:

> Whenever any famous man dies at Rome, he is carried to his funeral into the forum with every kind of honour to the so-called Rostra, sometimes conspicuous in an upright posture and more rarely in a reclining position. Here with all the people standing

round, a grown-up son, if he has left one who happens to be present, or if not some other relative mounts the Rostra and discourses on the virtues and successful achievements of the dead man . . . Next, after the burial and the performance of the usual ceremonies they put an image (*imago*) of the dead man in the most public part of the house, placing it in a little wooden shrine. The image is a mask, remarkably lifelike, both in its modelling and in its complexion (Pl.8). When any famous member of the family dies, his relatives take the masks to his funeral, putting them on men who seem most like the original in general appearance or bearing . . . (and) he who delivers the oration over the man about to be buried, when he has finished speaking of him, recounts the successes and exploits of the rest whose images are present, beginning from the most ancient (VI, 53–54, 1).

Even for a relatively recent period, Livy remarks that the recording of the death of M. Marcellus in 208 was complicated by the version in the funeral speech pronounced by his son; similarly, one of Livy's sources omitted the consuls for 307 and 306, either by mistake or, as Livy suggests, supposing them to have been invented; and Livy comments in total despair on the impossibility of discovering the truth about a dictator of 322 as a result of the vitiation of the record by funeral speeches.

When one reflects that the historians contemporary with or close to the events they were describing and on whom Dionysius and Livy ultimately depended for much of their material were not above allowing family pride to influence their history, it is clear that any attempt to reconstruct, on the basis of the only more or less continuous sources surviving, the history even of the middle Republic from the fourth to the second centuries BC is a hazardous proceeding.

Despite this caution, the no doubt largely oral traditions of family history are not wholly to be decried. In a modern, literate society, oral traditions beyond the living generation have been found to reflect what has been read in books; but in early Rome, anchored to the *imagines* of the ancestors, traditions may have had a firmer basis. Funeral speeches may have been written down at a relatively early date and Cato (p. 81) is represented by Cicero (*de *senectute* 21 and 61) as explicitly claiming that the sight of the tombs of men long dead served to keep fresh the memory of their deeds and as quoting the epitaph of a man who was consul in 258 and 254. And there is another point; the vision of the early Republic in Livy is no doubt fanciful, but it was a vision in its main outlines shared by his contemporaries and predecessors, a fact of the highest importance for the understanding of a society as prone as the Roman to identify itself by reference to the past.

A problem of a different kind arises in connection with the account in Livy of the Second Punic War and the early second century BC. For this period Livy used Polybius for affairs in the Greek world and for other matters earlier Roman historians, who themselves depended ultimately on official records and on contemporary authors. The result is a detailed chronological narrative of a particularly measured kind, which does not exist for any later period; the narrative breathes a confidence and a degree of normality which is necessarily lacking from the sources for the late Republic and it is desirable at least to ask how far the obvious contrast which exists between the middle and the late Republic results from the different nature of the source material.

Four lesser figures pose problems similar to those posed by Dionysius and Livy and require brief mention. Diodorus of Sicily, writing in the late first century BC, is the author of a universal history from the earliest times down to his own day. His work survives only in excerpts for the period in which we are interested, but possesses one great merit: he was disinclined to do more than copy or paraphrase one source at a time and therefore preserves much good material. The other three historians who concern us all belong to the period of the renaissance of Greek literature in the second and early third centuries AD. Appian, a native of Alexandria in Egypt, wrote a series of monographs (for the most part surviving) on the wars which Rome fought during the Republic; like Diodorus, Appian faithfully reflects his source of the moment; his own comments are of a degree of naivety which sheds an interesting light on the nature of the Roman imperial administration, of which he was a member. By deciding, however, to write not only on Rome's foreign wars, but also on her civil wars, Appian came in effect to write a continuous history of the last century of the Roman Republic, from 133 to 35; moreover the first book of the

Civil Wars contains the only serious surviving account of the agrarian history of Italy.

Plutarch of Chaeronea in Boeotia was a member of the upper class of his community, a wide reader and a prolific writer; among his writings is a series of paired biographies of eminent Greeks and Romans, covering with equal verve half-legendary figures like Romulus and historical figures like Julius Caesar; they are as reliable as their sources and Plutarch's memory permit. Finally, there is Dio of Nicaea in Asia Minor, an easterner in the Roman senate at the turn of the second and third centuries AD; an acute and original historian of his own times, his account of the middle Republic survives only in the version of a Byzantine abbreviator and in excerpts; it represents, however, in some cases a tradition not otherwise preserved. Dio's account of the last generation of the Roman Republic, from 69 onwards, survives nearly intact and is of enormous value.

Fortunately there is other evidence outside the main historical tradition. In the first place, there is a great deal of evidence from contemporary sources of one kind or another which is in a sense free from contamination or distortion, the evidence of public and private inscriptions, of non-historical literature and of archaeology and coins. Outside early Roman history, archaeological evidence is particularly important in allowing us to know far more of non-Roman Italy than the literary sources reveal. At the same time, the development of Roman art under the patronage of the Roman aristocracy is one of the threads of Republican history. The production of the coinage of the Republic was entrusted to young men at the start of their political careers and the types which they chose often reflected the pretensions of their families and their own ambitions. Moreover, as time passed, the coinage of Rome circulated ever more widely, becoming eventually the coinage of a world state. That too is one of the threads of Republican history.

We also possess, for instance, twenty plays of Plautus, produced at the turn of the third and second centuries BC, which provide an extraordinarily vivid picture of Roman society and institutions. The poems of Lucilius, even in the fragmentary form in which they survive, present us with a succession of often savagely satirical vignettes of the aristocracy of the late second century BC.

Finally, Rome's involvement with the Greek world on a massive scale from 200 onwards resulted in the promulgation there of numerous decrees of the Senate and letters of Roman officials, meticulously inscribed on stone by the communities to which they were addressed; laws of the people and decrees of officials along with treaties are preserved on stone or bronze in increasing quantities as we approach the end of the Republic.

The Romans were also in some respects a highly conservative people, often preserving as fossils, especially in a religious context, institutions which no longer fulfilled any useful function; much interest was shown in them in the first century BC and antiquarians such as Varro were responsible both for recording valuable evidence of this kind about early Roman history and for attempting to elucidate it. Antiquarian evidence of this kind plays a major part for instance in any attempt to reconstruct the development of the Roman assemblies. The evidence of language may also sometimes illuminate the earlier stages of Roman history.

For the last hundred years of the Republic, the amount and the nature of the information available change radically. The voluminous writings of Cicero not only document many aspects of the period of his maturity – roughly from the 80s onwards – but also contain much information on the two generations which precede his own. Sallust, a budding politician of the late Republic, writing in retirement after the death of Caesar, composed two monographs, which survive, on a past which was to him relatively recent and for which good information was still available; they are on the Catilinarian Conspiracy and the Jugurthine War. He also wrote a history of the period from Sulla to 70, which survives only in fragments. Finally, the first book of Appian's *Civil Wars* draws on a late Republican source, sometimes identified with Augustus' acquaintance C. Asinius Pollio; this source in any case paid a degree of attention, remarkable for antiquity, to social and economic factors.

A last word. The history of the middle Republic, as presented to us in the Roman tradition, is despite its diverse origins extraordinarily monolithic; the literary material only occasionally preserves variants, such as the assertion that Remus was not killed by Romulus, or that Rome surrendered to Lars Porsenna of Clusium, or that the Capitol was taken by the Gauls; on the other hand, the epitaph of Scipio Barbatus, inscribed in the late third century BC, preserves a record of campaigns which differs from that in the literary tradition; a tomb-painting from the Esquiline Hill (Fig. 1) of the same general period records an incident unattested in the literary tradition; coin-types sometimes display an item of family history which did not manage to enter the collective tradition.

In one case, literary and archaeological evidence combine, a version of early Roman history rediscovered by the emperor Claudius from Etruscan sources being confirmed by the paintings of the François tomb at Vulci; the account known to Claudius and the paintings both deal with the adventures of Mastarna, the Etruscan name for Servius Tullius, the sixth king of Rome. This case serves to draw attention to what is perhaps the most serious loss for the historiography of the Roman Republic, the disappearance of the non-Roman tradition. Stray references enable us to perceive that apart from Etruscan, there were once Campanian, even Mamertine (p.48) histories and numerous local traditions on which Cato (p. 81), when he wrote his history in the second century BC, was still able to draw. But that history has perished apart from fragments, and the view which our sources present us is almost wholly Romanocentric. It was not always so, and in writing the history of the Roman Republic one must remember that it is the history of Italy as well as of Rome.

1 Drawing of painting from tomb of Fabii on Esquiline Hill. The second register shows a peaceful encounter outside some city walls, the third register the edge of a battle scene and a peaceful encounter between a M. Fan(n)ius and a Q. Fabius, the fourth register a battle scene; the general context seems to be the Samnite Wars. *Affreschi romani dalle raccolte dell' Antiquarium comunale*, Exhibition catalogue, Rome, 1976, 3

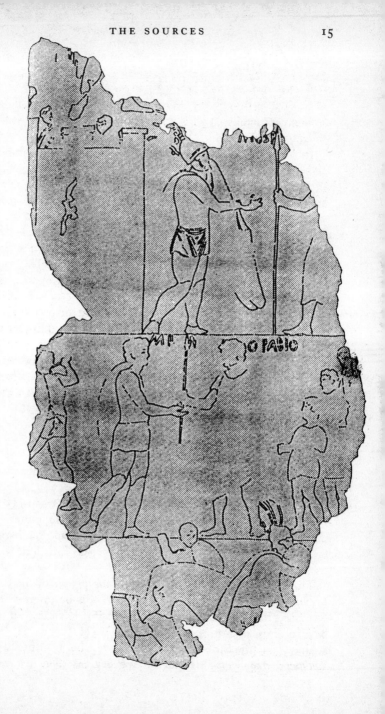

II

Italy and Rome

BY THE TIME HANNIBAL invaded Italy in 218, the whole of the peninsula was under Roman control with the exception of the Po valley, inhabited by Gauls and known to the Romans as Cisalpine Gaul. Much of the process was already complete by 280, when Pyrrhus invaded Italy from Epirus; many of the crucial steps were taken in the years immediately following 338, the end of the last war between Rome and her immediate neighbours, the other cities which were like Rome of Latin race and language.

Before turning, however, to consider the process of the unification of Italy and the nature of Roman institutions (Ch. 3), it is important to have some understanding of the diverse elements which comprise the mixture which we call Roman Italy; this not only because these various elements each influenced Rome in the period when Rome was still a small city state, but also because all of them directly affected the nature of the eventual mixture.

It is for these reasons as well as because of the distinctive nature of certain Roman institutions that if any other power had united Italy the result would have been different; though, it must be said, the view that if the Samnites, for instance, had united Italy the result would have been federation rather than domination is merely the transposition to the ancient world of modern wishful thinking.

The three main groups involved are the people of the central Italian highlands, culturally on a level with or inferior to the Romans, but ethnically related and using a variety of Italic languages related to Latin; the Greeks of the south Italian colonies; and the Etruscans. These two were both culturally more advanced than Rome, but in varying degrees alien in race and language. The Gauls of the Po valley, culturally no more advanced than the Romans and of alien race and language were in due course in effect exterminated and their culture destroyed.

There is a further reason for spending some time on the non-Roman peoples of Italy. The Etruscans, to a certain extent, and the Greeks of the south to a much greater extent, both of them in contact with other areas of the Mediterranean world, provided for the expanding Republic avenues leading to involvement with that world.

The peoples of the central Italian highlands survive in the literary record chiefly as bitter and often successful opponents of the extension of Roman control; the most prominent group, the Samnites, provided in the Romanocentric eyes of Florus (1, 11, 8) material for twenty-four Roman triumphs. The Samnites lived, as recent archaeological work shows, in settled farmsteads, cultivating cereals as well as olives and vines; for despite their height and relative inaccessibility the Appennines include numerous pockets of agricultural land; the Samnites had few cattle, but many pigs and large flocks of sheep and goats, which were no doubt moved over short distances between summer pastures and winter pastures close to the farmsteads (a technique known as transhumance); both sheep and goats provided milk for cheese, wool, and whey for pig-food, as well as meat when killed at a ripe old age. The symbiotic relationship between plain and hill which transhumance involved was clearly widespread in Appennine Italy and no doubt supported a basically similar economy throughout.

Spreading outwards from the hills, partly by way of raids, but eventually with more serious intent, the peoples of the central Italian highlands were attracted by the fertile plains of Campania, just as the Volscians farther north were attracted by the plains of Latium; the Etruscan city of Capua (see below) fell in 423, the Greek city of Cumae in 421, a Greek element in the population surviving in the case of the latter. Neapolis (Naples) remained the only Greek city in Campania, though even there infiltration took place; the Greek cities of the south came similarly under pressure from the tribes of the hinterland. In the end, the hills were conquered by the plains, but at the turn of the fifth and fourth centuries BC it was by no means an obvious outcome.

Of the three groups of people whom I wish to discuss, the

Greeks are on the whole the most straightforward. A variety of Greek cities had planted a string of self-governing foundations along the coasts of Italy and Sicily, beginning with Pithecusae (Ischia) about 775; the earliest of these colonies, as they are rather inappropriately described, was almost certainly intended to act as an entrepôt for trade with Etruria; but its own foundation on the mainland opposite, Cumae, was an agricultural community, as were the vast majority of Greek colonies both in the west and elsewhere.

Greek colonization, invariably the venture of an organized community, involved the transfer of a developed society and culture, of its political organization, religious organization, language, monetary system; the colonial experience and contact with indigenous populations might eventually lead of course to considerable transformations.

But Magna Graecia, the collective name for the Greek cities in Italy and Sicily, was very much part of the Greek world, despite alleged Athenian ignorance of Sicily prior to the mounting of the great expedition of 415; men from the west participated in the great Greek festivals and their successes were celebrated by the Greek poet Pindar in the fifth century BC. In the fourth century Timoleon of Corinth set out to rescue Sicily from Carthage and, as we shall see, a succession of Greek condottieri attempted to help Tarentum (Taranto) in her wars with the tribes of the hinterland. The last of them Pyrrhus of Epirus, fought a full-scale war against Rome, by then the major threat.

The position of a Greek city overwhelmed by its barbarian neighbours is poignantly described in the case of Poseidonia (Paestum) by the near-contemporary Aristoxenus of Tarentum:

We act like the people of Poseidonia, who dwell on the Tyrrhenian Gulf. It so happened that although they had originally been Greeks, they were completely barbarized, becoming Tuscans; they changed their speech and their other practices, but they still celebrate one festival that is Greek to this day, wherein they gather together and recall those ancient words and institutions, and after bewailing them and weeping over them in one another's presence they depart home (quoted by Athenaeus, XIV, 632a).

For most of the cities of Italy the effective choice lay between the barbarian tribes and Rome; it is not surprising that many of them chose Rome, a civilized community and in the eyes of some contemporary Greeks a Greek city; the process began with the survivors of the original population at Capua in 343 (p. 34), followed by the Greeks of Neapolis (Naples) in 326.

The Etruscans are *sui generis* and were so regarded in classical antiquity; it was a unique characteristic of their religion that it was centred on sacred writings that had supposedly emanated from supernatural sources, and they also claimed a special ability to discover the will of the gods by a variety of processes of divination. Furthermore, Etruscan society was characterized, at any rate in its upper echelons, by the relatively high status of its female members and, as a whole, by a deep division between the governing class and a serf population.

Etruscan culture evolved from the Villanovan culture of central Italy and was from the eighth century BC onwards both extraordinarily receptive of foreign influences and extraordinarily adept at integrating them in a local framework. The Etruscans borrowed most perhaps from the Greeks, from whom they imported on an enormous scale fine pottery in exchange for metal; the origin of their language is mysterious.

By the end of the eighth century BC they occupied the area bounded by the River Arno, the Appennines, the Tiber and the sea; during the sixth and fifth centuries they established an empire in Campania, probably beginning at the coast and in due course occupying Capua, according to Cato in 470; during the fifth and fourth centuries they created another empire in the Po valley; as a by-product of this process of expansion, Rome was ruled for a time by kings who were in effect Etruscan condottieri. The process of expansion was not a single national effort, but reflected the disunity of Etruria and its division into independent city units.

The Etruscans provided Rome with early access to at any rate a form of Greek culture; they also probably provided Rome with some of her insignia of office:

The ambassadors, having received this answer, departed, and after a few days returned, not merely with words alone, but bringing the insignia of sovereignty with which they used to

2   Iron model of *fasces,* axe and rods, from Vetulonia. The Romans
believed that this symbol of sovereignty, conveying the right to scourge or
put to death, came to them from Etruria.

decorate their own kings. These were a crown of gold, an ivory
throne, a sceptre with an eagle perched on its head, a purple
tunic decorated with gold, and an embroidered purple robe like
those the kings of Lydia and Persia used to wear, except that it
was not rectangular in shape like theirs, but semicircular. This
kind of robe is called toga by the Romans and tebenna by the
Greeks; but I do not know where the Greeks learned the name,
for it does not seem to me to be a Greek word. And according to
some historians they also brought (back to Rome) the twelve
axes, taking one from each city. For it seems to have been a
Tyrrhenian custom for each king of the several cities to be
preceded by a lictor bearing an axe together with the bundle of
rods (the *fasces*), and, whenever the twelves cities undertook
any joint military expedition, for the twelve axes to be handed
over to the one man who held supreme command (Dionysius of
Halicarnassus, III, 61, using the results of Roman antiquarian
research; see also Fig. 2).

More fundamentally, the Capitoline Triad of Jupiter, Juno and
Minerva is of Etruscan origin; the Roman system of nomenclature,
however, personal name (as Marcus), name of *gens*, or large family

group (as Tullius) and *cognomen*, or family name (as Cicero), is Italic rather than Etruscan in origin.

The Etruscan empire in Campania was destroyed by the Samnites (see above), the empire in the Po valley by the Gauls. Etruria itself was progressively subjugated by Rome, much aided by the fragility of Etruscan social structures; the lower orders are described by Dionysius in connection with a campaign of 480 as *penestai*, the word used to describe the serf population of Thessaly in Greece. In return for support against the lower orders, the governing classes were only too happy to accept Roman over-lordship, as at Arretium in 302 and Volsinii in 264. It was a technique that Rome never forgot.

III

The Roman Governing Classes

DOWN TO 510, Rome was ruled by kings. The monarchy was in some sense elective, though the descent of a candidate from an earlier king was not an irrelevant consideration; the office of *interrex*, the man who presided over an *interregnum* and the emergence of a successor, survived the end of the monarchy with its name unchanged and its function essentially the same, to preside over a hiatus between duly elected officials of the community.

The essence of the transition from kings to pairs of officials (called by the Romans *magistratus,* magistrates) holding office for a year is encapsulated by Livy (II, 1, 7–8), following the common opinion of his day; the truth, if different, is irrecoverable:

> One can regard the cause of freedom as lying rather in the fact that consular *imperium* was made annual than in any diminution in the regal power (inherited by the consuls); the first consuls retained all the rights and insignia (of the king); the only precaution taken was that they should not both hold the *fasces* simultaneously and thereby create a double impression of fearfulness. Brutus was the first to hold the *fasces* (for the first month), with the agreement of his colleague.

Two consuls instead of a king now stood each year at the head of the community; the assembly of adult males which elected them remaind the same,[1] as did the body of elders who advised them; this was the senate, composed in practice of former magistrates. Time and circumstance produced various modifications in the

1. See Appendix 1 for the different varieties of Roman assembly.

three elements whose interplay *was* the Roman political system, including notably the creation of a large number of lesser magistrates (pp. 69 and 71); nothing altered the central fact of Republican government, that it was the collective rule of an aristocracy, in principle and to a varying extent in practice dependent on the will of a popular assembly. This aristocracy was in one sense self-perpetuating, but it was of course one from which many families disappeared over the centuries and to which new families were admitted, while an inner core of great families persisted (see Pl.8).

It was a form of government to which modern notions of being in or out of power are almost wholly inappropriate; a particular individual held office only at rare intervals and with one unimportant exception (for the dictatorship, see pp. 24, 55) always as a member of a college of magistrates whose powers were equal. But increasing age, if coupled with a growing reputation for practical wisdom, brought with it increasing influence in the deliberations of the ruling élite. The voice of a few powerful men was often decisive.

At the same time, competition within this élite was fierce, for a consulship or other magistracy and for the recognition of primacy in practical wisdom; given the succession of wars in which Rome was involved, it is not surprising that success as a consul regularly involved victory in battle, rewarded with a triumph (p. 46); primacy in practical wisdom was rewarded with the title of *princeps senatus*, leader of the deliberative body of the Roman state.

Aristocratic attitudes to the political process emerge not only from the inscriptions on the tombs of the Scipios (pp. 13–14), but also from the record of the victory of C. Duilius over the Carthaginians in 260:

As consul he relieved the Segestans, allies of the Roman people, from the Carthaginian siege and nine days later drove the Carthaginian troops and their commanders from their camp in broad daylight and took the town of Macela by assault. And in the same magistracy as consul he for the first time had success with a fleet at sea and for the first time prepared and equipped naval forces and a fleet and with these ships defeated in battle on the high sea all the Punic fleet, including large Carthaginian

forces in the presence of Hannibal their commander, and took by
force with his allies 1 septireme and 30 quinqueremes and
triremes. (A list of booty follows). At his naval triumph he
presented the people with the booty and led many free
Carthaginians (captives in the triumph) before his chariot . . .
(*ILLRP* 319)

The history of Republican government is to a large extent the
history of competition within a group of men formally peers,
always within the framework of the overriding decisions of the
group; the ideology of collective rule in the middle and late
Republic was powerfully reinforced by stories, improving
whether true or false, of the fate suffered by men who in the early
Republic stepped out of line:

(Sp. Maelius had distributed corn from his own resources;
emergency measures were taken to deal with the threat posed by
his ambition; these measures involved the appointment of a
dictator and a master of horse as his deputy, in office for six
months with supreme power overriding that of the consuls.)
C. Servilius Ahala as master of horse was sent by the dictator to
Maelius and said 'The dictator summons you.' When Maelius
fearfully asked what he wanted, and Servilius replied that he had
to stand trial and disprove before the senate the charge laid by
L. Minucius, Maelius began to retreat into his band of followers
. . . Servilius followed him and cut him down; covered with the
blood of the dead man and surrounded by a band of young
patricians, he announced to the dictator that Maelius had been
summoned to him, but had fought off the attendant (who had
tried to arrest him) and had incited the mob, and had received
his deserts. The dictator replied 'Bravely done, C. Servilius, for
freeing the *res publica* (from the threat of a tyrant)' (Livy
IV, 13–14).

Within the Roman community, a closed group of families,
knows as patricians, had been defined already under the monarchy
by a process which is now unknowable. The group succeeded after
the overthrow of the monarchy in substantially monopolizing the
tenure of magistracies and priesthoods alike; as a result patricians

also largely filled the senate. Wealthy and ambitious families of plebeians mostly excluded from the processes of government were naturally anxious to be admitted; at the same time the poorer plebeians were anxious to reduce or eliminate the economic exploitation to which they were subjected. The two groups of dissidents combined to extort concessions, the breaking of the monopoly of office by the patricians and the alleviation of the harsh laws of debt (under these a peasant who could not pay off a loan, perhaps of seed corn from a wealthy neighbour, could be reduced to slavery). In the process, the *plebs* acquired its own assembly and legislative organ, the *concilium plebis* (Appendix 1), and its own officials, the tribunes, whose chief function was to protect citizens from arbitrary action by a magistrate. At some time they acquired the important right to veto *any* action by a magistrate or the senate. They were sacrosanct, protected by an oath of the *plebs* to kill anyone who killed a tribune.

By 342 the battle was essentially won, with the admission of plebeians to the consulate; the most important consequence was the creation of a mixed patrician-plebeian nobility, defined by the tenure of the consulship – a man who held this ennobled his direct descendants in perpetuity – and less exclusive than the patriciate (it must be remembered that in the Roman tradition even the patriciate had once admitted a new family to its membership, the Claudii). This mixed nobility established its right to supremacy by its leadership in the conquest of Italy through the second half of the fourth century BC, the rewards of which, in the form of land, were in large measure distributed to the poorer plebeians, reconciling them to the political *status quo*. The problem of debt was in fact probably circumvented rather than solved.

Aristotle observed that an oligarchy which remained united could not be overthrown; the collective rule of the mature Republican aristocracy only eventually dissolved in the last century BC when it failed to attend to the increasingly serious grievances of the poor and when individual members of the aristocracy appealed to these lower orders for support in their competition with each other, a competition whose scale and nature had meanwhile already been changed out of all recognition by the spread of Roman rule over the Mediterranean basin.

The most important feature of Roman government is the

structure created by the traditional obligation on anyone responsible for taking action to consult a group of advisers. It is apparent
everywhere in Roman society; the decision in the last resort might be
that of one man alone, but the obligation to take advice was absolute.
A *paterfamilias* might summon a family *consilium*, a politician
might summon his family and his friends (the hapless Brutus in 44
after the murder of Caesar consulted his mother, his half-sister, his
wife and his friends Favonius, Cassius and Cicero), a magistrate in
his province had to consider the opinions of his entourage; the senate
was the *consilium* of the two highest magistrates, the consuls, by the
late Republic the *consilium* for the whole world (Cicero, *Philippica*
IV, 14).

Political groupings in the late Republic may indeed be regarded as
consisting of those men whom a leading politician habitually
summoned to his *consilium*; discussion there prepared for sessions
of the senate and meetings of the assembly. Such groupings of
course sometimes followed a leader out of habit, sometimes from
conviction (see p. 29).

Possessed of certain fairly limited actual powers, the senate by
monopolizing the rôle of advising magistrates during their terms of
office in Rome and Italy effectively controlled the Roman state. The
senate's formal powers (Polybius VI, 13) were the control of finance
(total, despite Polybius' qualification) and security, the administration of Italy and the running of relations with foreign powers (except
for the actual decision for war or peace which was taken by the
people). The control of finance for campaigning was one of the
things which slipped from the senate's grasp in the late Republic (see
p. 179), with disastrous consequences.

The most crucial part of the senate's advisory rôle lay in the field of
legislation; any intending legislator was expected to consult it. The
corollary of course was that the senate was also in a position to advise
on the invalidation of legislation, a position of which it took
advantage in the turbulent years of the late Republic. The grounds
for invalidation, technical and ideological, are expounded by
Cicero, in a passage highly revealing of the unyielding mentality of
part of the Roman governing class:

Marcus Cicero: For many evil and disastrous decisions are taken
by the people, which no more deserve to be regarded as laws than

if some robbers had agreed to make them . . .

Quintus Cicero: I fully realize that, and indeed I think that there is nothing else (except a law as defined by Marcus) which can even be called a law, let alone be regarded as one.

Marcus Cicero: So you do not accept the laws of (Sex.) Titius or (L.) Appuleius (Saturninus)?

Quintus Cicero: I do not even accept those of (M.) Livius (Drusus).

Marcus Cicero: Quite right too, for they in particular were instantaneously invalidated by a single decree of the senate (*de legibus* II, 13–14, compare 31).

The domination of the Roman governing class found expression in the institution of *clientela*, clientship, an archaic form of personal dependence, which survived at Rome with undiminished relevance, in striking contrast to Athens and the Greek world in general. Cicero regarded the institution as created by Romulus (*de re publica* II, 16); it placed the client in the position of being, in E. Badian's words, an inferior entrusted, by custom or by himself, to the protection of a man more powerful than he, and rendering certain services and observances in return for this protection.

Among the services rendered was political support; a man might be helped to office by the votes of his clients and by those of his friends and associates; naturally they expected him in return to deliver the votes of his clients. The ingrained habits of dependence of clients in particular and the lower orders in general emerge with dramatic clarity from the reaction of one of the characters of Plautus to the notion of a marriage into a higher social class for his daughter:

Now if I married my daughter to you, it occurs to me that you would be like an ox and I should be like an ass; when I was linked to you and couldn't pull my share of the load I, the donkey, should drop down in the mud, while you, the ox, would pay no more attention to me than if I wasn't born; you would be above me and my own order would laugh at me, and I should have no fixed abode if we were separated. The asses would tear me with their teeth, the oxen would run me through; it's very dangerous to climb from the asses' to the oxen's set (*Aulularia* 228–35).

It is not surprising, given such subservient attitudes, that the

Roman aristocracy was able to demand economic sacrifices from its clients:

> Mucius Scaevola at any rate and Aelius Tubero and Rutilius Rufus . . . are three Romans who observed the Lex Fannia (limiting expenditure on food, see p.76) . . . Tubero for one bought game birds from those who worked on his own estates for a denarius each, while Rutilius bought fish from those of his slaves who were fisherman for half a denarius a mina . . . And Mucius fixed the value of things bought from those who were under an obligation to him in the same way (Athenaeus VI, 274 c–e; compare, e.g., Lucilius 159–60 W).

In seventeenth- and eighteenth-century England, aristocrats depended on credit demanded from suppliers who belonged thereby to a kind of client economy; the resentment felt against the English aristocracy is well documented and it is likely that a similar resentment was eventually felt against the Roman aristocracy and for similar reasons. If this is right, force is added to the suggestion of P.A. Brunt that the Roman mob in the first century BC included like the mobs in France in the eighteenth century many people of the middling sort, and a further explanation of their readiness to turn to violence emerges.

One important consequence of the institution of clientship was that the struggle of the Orders, of the patricians and the plebeians, was in no sense whatever a class struggle; the plebeian leadership was rich and ambitious and part of its support came not only from those in whose interest it was to support it, but from its clients at every economic level; the patricians were similarly supported by all their clients, the humble amongst them perhaps acting against the economic interests of their class, but nonetheless bound to their patrons by real ties of shared sentiment and mutual advantage.

It is also important to remember that the process of Roman government was not simply a matter of deploying clients and friends and relations in the pursuit of an aristocrat's turn in office and the prestige and influence which that brought. Political power, then as now, was sought for a purpose; support was directed to one man rather than to another not only because of the traditional obligations of clientship and so on, but also on a calculation of the likelihood of his achieving a desired end; his conduct had to be validated by reference to the ideas of what was desirable and the aspirations of his supporters. The general expectation of anyone on whom the Roman people conferred office was that he was capable *rem publicam bene gerere* – of managing affairs of state well. The reasons for holding this view – noble birth counted for much – may sometimes strike a modern reader as curious; but they were none the less real.

Elections were in any case serious contests; from Ap. Claudius Caecus (p.43) onwards, the lower orders sometimes successfully supported one member of the nobility against the wishes of the majority of the nobility and even brought unwanted outsiders to the consulship; at the turn of the third and second centuries, T. Quinctius Flamininus, the man who defeated Philip V of Macedon (p. 64), came to the consulship after holding only very junior magistracies, but offices which in some cases involved him in the distribution of land to the lower orders and won him popularity thereby. P. Cornelius Scipio Nasica Serapio failed in an election because he asked a farmer whether his hands were so hard because he walked on them.

Farmers indeed in the early and middle Republic formed the vast majority of the Roman electorate. The earliest codification of Roman law, the Twelve Tables of the middle of the fifth century BC, already takes for granted the distinction between the *assiduus*, the self-supporting freeholder, and the *proletarius*; Cato in the second century BC, and other writers after him, painted a no doubt idealized position of an early Rome composed of yeomen ever ready to defend their country, but the fact that service as a legionary was before 107 in principle a right and a duty of the *assiduus* alone makes it clear that early Rome was indeed a community of freeholders, for whom military service was as central an element of the citizenship as voting in the assembly. It is no accident that the variety of Roman assembly which elected the consuls was the people organized as an army (Appendix 1).

The general acceptance – barring extreme circumstances – of a hierarchical ordering of society and of the importance of traditional patterns no doubt led to a conceptualization of the political process in predominantly moral terms; but the consequent imperatives were deeply felt, despite perhaps growing cynicism. P. Cornelius

Rufinus, consul in 290 and 277, was expelled from the senate in 275 for possessing ten pounds weight of silver vessels and by this luxury breaking the moral code of the governing class; his family was submerged for four or five generations.

If I am right in arguing, however, that at all times the conduct of the Roman governing class had to be justified in terms of the Roman system of values, *a fortiori* nobles who advocated particular policies were under an even greater compulsion to validate them in terms of an existing complex of ideas; the pattern is relevant to the progress of the Roman revolution.

IV

The Conquest of Italy

I HAVE SO FAR emphasized certain structural and permanent features of aristocratic society and government in the Roman Republic; but in many respects Rome of the early and middle Republic was astonishingly innovative.

An early stage of Roman history had probably seen the admission to political rights and duties of men who were domiciled in Rome, but were not full members of the community; the struggle between the patricians and the plebeians had seen the eventual admission of the latter to secular and religious office. One may hypothesize that these bendings of the rules were the result of the interest of the Roman governing class in the display of military *virtus* which made its members peculiarly amenable to pressure from those followers on whom they depended for success in battle.

In any case, just as non-exclusiveness was ultimately characteristic of privileged groups within Roman territory, so it was also of Rome in relation to Italy. It is also worth remarking that just as Rome throughout the early and middle Republic was anxious to add new members to her citizen body, so she was also open beneath a mask of religious conservatism to the import of foreign cults, as J. A. North has pointed out. The attitude was a general one.

And we shall see that after 200 the Roman aristocracy remained just as innovative, but devoted its energies increasingly to the enormous political problems posed by contact with the Greek world, to the acquisition of Greek culture and to the pursuit of the wealth available from the east.

Rome was originally simply one of a homogeneous group of Latin cities, sharing above all a number of common places of worship, although she possessed by reason of her position, controlling a route along and a route across the Tiber, certain peculiar strategic advantages. Unlike the other members of the Latin League, Rome also came under strong Etruscan influence and under her Etruscan kings expanded at the expense of her Latin neighbours.

Already by the fall of the monarchy, the four regional units of the city of Rome, *tribus*, tribes, instituted for census purposes and for the levying of men and taxation, had been joined by fifteen regional units in the countryside around Rome.[1]

With the overthrow of the monarchy there was a Latin reaction against Roman power, defeated by Rome at the battle of Lake Regillus; Roman relations with the Latin cities were then regulated by an agreement known as the *foedus Cassianum*, the terms of which were apparently still extant in the time of Cicero. (There were also treaties with some individual Latin cities.)

The next century was characterized by battles between Rome, the Latins and the associated tribe of the Hernici on the one hand and the Etruscans to the north, the Volsci to the south (see Map 1). Largely successful wars on all fronts culminated with the Roman capture of Veii in 396. There followed almost immediately the first Gallic raid into Italy, with the Roman defeat at the battle of the Allia River, the sack of the city, the near capture of the Capitol and the departure of the Gauls only on receipt of a large indemnity.

It might seem that all lay in ruins and the impression is confirmed by the obvious patriotic fictions which the Roman tradition offers for the years after the Gallic sack. But there is impeccable evidence for the fundamental irrelevance of the Gallic sack to Roman expansion and for its negligible effect on Roman power. A mere twelve years after the sack, in 378, Livy records the building of a wall round the city of Rome:

> After a short breathing-space had been granted to those in debt, when everything was quiet as far as Rome's enemies were concerned, jurisdiction (in matters of debt) was resumed and hope was so far abandoned of relieving the burden of existing debts, that new debts were contracted by reason of the taxation

1. In 471 these regional units were chosen as the basis of a new organization of the Roman people for voting purposes, the *comitia tributa,* tribal assembly (see Appendix 1).

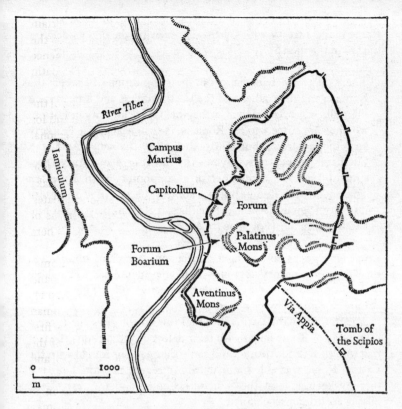

3   Map of Rome showing area enclosed by walls of 378.

levied for the wall in squared blocks put out to contract by the
censors (VI, 32, 1).

The wall is the so-called 'Servian' wall of which extensive tracts still
survive; this massive construction shows the structures of the
Roman state intact and functioning and able to deploy substantial
resources for a communal undertaking. The area enclosed (Fig 3)
is already large, and, as if to symbolize the conviction that the
Gallic sack changed nothing, the wall is built with tufa from the
territory of conquered Veii.

The Roman sphere of interest was also extending steadily
southwards. A Roman treaty with the Samnites in 354 was

followed by the first war of Rome against the Samnites. In 348 Rome made a treaty with Carthage, renewing the one made after the fall of the monarchy:

> There is to be friendship on these conditions between the Romans and their allies and the Carthaginians and Uticans and their allies . . . And if the Carthaginians take any city in Latium which is not subject to the Romans, they may keep the property and the captives, but must surrender the city. And if a Carthaginian captures anyone (in the course of piracy, presumably) who is a member of a community with a written agreement with Rome, but not subject, he may not bring him into any Roman harbour; if he does, a Roman may touch him and free him . . . (Polybius III, 24, 3)

Rome emerges as possessing a subject zone, which by implication the Carthaginians may not touch, as having an interest in the whole of Latium and as having a wider protective rôle. This nascent empire was joined by Capua in 343.

An attempt by the Latin cities to throw off the growing *de facto* hegemony of Rome failed with their defeat in 338; despite the fact that the Volsci and Aurunci and some Campanians fought with the Latins, Rome was able momentarily to secure Samnite help and thereby keep at least the Sidicini occupied and the rest of the hostile coalition preoccupied.

The settlement of 338 is crucial in the development of the forms in which Rome came to express her relationship to the rest of Italy (p.36); in the present context it is one more step on the road to hegemony.

In 328 Rome founded a colony at Fregellae; she thereby embroiled herself irrevocably with the Samnites and in the following year became involved even more closely than hitherto with the affairs of Campania. Neapolis (Naples) appealed to Rome in 327 (p.19) and a treaty was concluded in 326. An attempt to win a decisive victory over the Samnites in 321 led to the disastrous defeat of the Caudine Forks. The scale of the disaster is again indicated by the patriotic fictions reported for the subsequent years in the Roman tradition; again the check was momentary, with the Via Appia linking Rome and Campania being built in 312 (it eventually reached Brundisium (Brindisi) where the pillars marking its end may be seen a few yards from the modern steamer terminal). When peace was made with the Samnites in 304, that was for them effectively the end. Roman control of Samnium was followed in due course by the foundation of colonies at Beneventum (268) and Aesernia (263). At the same time, the establishment of Roman control over Italy opened the way for the long-distance transhumance agriculture of the second century (p. 102).

A last attempt was made to resist the rise of Rome by a coalition of Samnites, Gauls, Etruscans and Umbrians, destroyed when the Samnites and Gauls were defeated at Sentinum in 295 (an event noticed by the Greek historian Duris of Samos); thereafter it was simply a question of mopping-up. The only wars Rome fought on Italian soil south of the Po valley down to the great Italian rebellion of 91 were wars against the invaders Pyrrhus and Hannibal and very minor wars, in response to the appeal of the governing class of Volsinii in 264, and to suppress the isolated revolts of Falerii and Fregellae in 241 and 125.

The reasons for Rome's success in conquering and holding Italy are manifold. Supposed factors such as the absence of an attack on Italy by Alexander the Great are a red herring, nor does Rome's geographical position provide much help in explaining anything after the very early stages. Clearly in some cases, such as that of Neapolis, the fact that Rome was a tolerably civilized power helped and in other cases, such as that of Volsinii, the fact of her being aristocratically governed opened the way for her to intervene (p. 21). Rome's eventual neutralization of the Gallic invaders was also important, but the crucial factor is to be found in the generosity and flexibility of the ways in which she gradually bound the rest of Italy to herself and the manpower upon which she could call as a result. Furthermore, the gradual incorporation of Italy by Rome helps to explain the nature and logic of Roman imperialism. It is thereafter the success with which Rome expanded and her willingness to share the fruits of expansion which underpin her strength; this was built upon the consensus, both of the Roman political system and of the Italian confederacy, from the late fourth to the early second century.

The group of communities with which Rome was most intimately involved was, as we have seen, that composed of the

Latin cities; she and each of them were in principle equal, possessed of certain reciprocal rights, *commercium*, or the right to conclude valid contracts, *conubium*, or the right to contract marriages of which the offspring were legitimate, *migratio*, or the right to change domicile and acquire the citizenship of the new domicile, and (after 471, p.32) the right to vote in one regional voting unit chosen by lot in a community of temporary domicile.[2] These rights were no doubt mostly traditional, regulated by the *foedus Cassianum* of 493 (p.32).

Rome and the Latin cities divided up the booty and the land which they acquired as a result of joint military enterprises. Although there is no evidence for the Latin communities, we may presume that they like Rome assigned land so acquired individually, *viritim*, to members of their own citizen bodies. What also happened was that the Latin League as a body founded colonies which were additional Latin communities, self-governing and possessed of the same reciprocal rights as the old Latin cities.

With the end of the war against the Latins in 338, Rome incorporated many of the disaffected communities into her own citizen body; there remained separate, however, some of the original Latin cities and some colonies. In addition the status of *civitas sine suffragio*, citizenship without the vote, was conferred on the Campanians, and on the cities of Fundi and Formiae (Livy viii, 14, 10).

The Roman incorporation of some of the Latin communities into her own citizen body was an act which had precedents. Part of the process by which Rome achieved hegemony over Italy was the actual extension of Roman territory, *ager Romanus*, and some extension had already taken place before 338; there were two ways in which this happened and they help to explain the relative superiority of Rome over the Latins in 338.

Rome had fought the war against Veii largely on her own account, as she was later to fight her wars against the rest of Etruria and to become involved in Campania, although the Latins lay between; the consequent access of land, booty or mere influence accrued to Rome alone. Such land, distributed to Roman citizens, led to an increase in those possessed of enough land to equip

2. Much later the rule was introduced whereby the magistrates of Latin communities acquired Roman citizenship.

themselves as heavily-armed soldiers (and to an increase in the number of regional voting units, *tribus*, tribes, into which the Roman people was divided).

Rome had also increased her territory already before 338 by the incorporation (in circumstances the details of which escape us) of other communities, perhaps Crustumeria during the monarchy (for extension of Roman territory during the monarchy, see p.32), Tusculum perhaps early in the fourth century.

Civitas sine suffragio, citizenship without the vote, on the other hand, is an innovation of the settlement of 338; those possessed of this status are the original *municipes*, those who bear the burdens (of Roman citizenship), military service, *militia*, and direct taxation, *tributum*; they are never Latin speakers and were no doubt for that reason debarred from voting. Originally independent, the communities concerned came in the end to identify themselves with Rome; the process no doubt helped to create the climate of opinion to which a dual *patria*, a local community and Rome, was normal and which was one of the characteristic strengths of the political structure of late Republican Italy.

The truly revolutionary sequel, however, of the settlement of 338 was that Rome, although the Latin League had disappeared, continued to found colonies with the status of Latin cities. The first of these new, self-governing communities to be founded was Cales in 334. Their prime purpose was of course strategic; and at the same time Rome began to found small colonies of Roman citizens to act as garrisons at vulnerable points on the coasts of Italy. These were too small to possess developed organs of self-government, though someone was no doubt charged with organizing the levy when the colony was attacked.[3]

The standard Roman view of the colonies is well expressed by Cicero:

Is every place of such a kind that it does not matter to the state whether a colony is founded there or not, or are there some places which demand a colony, some which clearly do not? In this as in other state matters it is worth remembering the care of our ancestors, who sited colonies in such suitable places to ward off

---

3. A variety of *ad hoc* measures existed to provide jurisdiction for Roman citizens in colonies and scattered in individual assignations.

danger that they seemed not just towns in Italy, but bastions of empire (*de lege agraria* II,73).

The last and by far the largest group in the Italy of the turn of the fourth and third centuries was that of the allies, bound to Rome after defeat by a treaty, the central obligation of which was to provide troops for Rome.

The global result was the military levy *ex formula togatorum* – 'according to the list of those who wear the toga'; the relevant categorization of the population of Italy appears in the Agrarian Law of III in a formulation which is presupposed by a Greek inscription of the early second century and which is certainly archaic:

> those who are Roman citizens or allies or members of the Latin group, from whom the Romans are accustomed to command troops to be levied in the land of Italy, according to the list of those who wear the toga (*Roman Statutes*, no. 2, lines 21 and 50).

The relationship of command is in no way dissimulated (see also Polybius VI, 21, 4—5) and after 209 Rome dealt out severe punishment to twelve Latin colonies which claimed that they could not supply any more troops (p.53).

The levy that could be produced is described by Polybius in the context of the Gallic incursion of 225:

> But I must make it clear from the facts themselves how great were the resources which Hannibal dared to attack and how great was the power which he boldly confronted; despite this, he came so close to his aim as to inflict major disasters on the Romans. Anyway, I must describe the levy and the size of the army available to them on that occasion. (Polybius goes on to claim that the total manpower available to Rome was 700,000 infantry and 70,000 cavalry.) (II, 24)

The link between the manpower thus available and Rome's openness to outsiders was already obvious to Philip V of Macedon, a future rival of Rome, as appears from a letter written to Larisa in 217:

. . . and one can look at those others who adopt similar approaches to admission of citizens, among them the Romans, who when they free their slaves admit them to citizenship and enable them (actually their sons) to hold office; in this way they have not only increased the size of their own country, but have been able to send colonies to almost seventy places . . . (*SIG* 543 with Chr. Habicht, in *Ancient Macedonia*, 265, for date)

The admission of outsiders as a source of, presumably military, strength is also explicitly recognized by Cato in his *Origines*, talking of early Rome:

Those who had come together summoned several more thither from the countryside; as a result their strength grew (Gellius XVIII, 12, 7 = fr. 20 Peter).

The fourth century BC saw not only the emergence of what we call the Italian confederation, but probably also the progressive articulation of the Roman citizen body into the five census classes known in the late Republic; the original division of the citizen body had probably been into *assidui* and *proletarii*, members of a single class and those below it, those who served as legionaries and those who did not; *assidui* were probably simply those who could equip themselves with a full suit of armour. It may be that Servius Tullius, the sixth king of Rome, then defined *assidui* in monetary terms, but the elaborate division of these *assidui* into five different classes, defined by different levels of capital wealth, is probably a development of the fourth century BC. Pay for the army had been instituted in 406, to be funded partly by indemnities from defeated enemies, partly from *tributum*, a levy on the capital wealth of the *assidui*; it was surely this and the growing complexity of the Roman fiscal system in general which called forth the so-called Servian system in its final form. The shift from a system which singled out those who could arm themselves to one which singled out those who were wealthy is clearly an important stage in the development of the Roman state.

Quite apart from providing the manpower which Rome controlled, the organization of Italy was also a considerable source of strength by reason of the loyalty which Rome was able to inspire by its means. In the first place, the range of statuses, with full citizens at one end and allies at the other and *cives sine suffragio*, citizens without the vote, and Latins in between prevented undue polarization. Secondly, the process of conquest of course involved deprivation, of booty or land or both, for the defeated; but once part of the Roman confederacy, they were entitled to a share in the spoils of the next stage and had indeed, as we shall see, an interest in ensuring that it took place. Finally, the way in which Italy was organized meant that there were open avenues of approach to full Roman citizenship. *Civitas sine suffragio*, citizenship without the vote, came to be regarded as a half-way house, whatever its original function; and it was possible for allies to join Latin colonies and thence, eventually no doubt, for their descendants to become Roman citizens.

It is also important to remember that apart from the levy, which was normally followed by a successful campaign, Roman rule lay light on the Italian communities; even in the case of incorporated communities, local government survived, and mostly the various elements of the Italian confederacy were left to themselves to perpetuate or evolve their own peculiar political structures. P. A. Brunt has indeed shown that the levy itself could not have been conducted without considerable local government institutions.

Given the power and preponderance of Rome, however, it is hardly surprising that the different cities of Italy should have increasingly assimilated themselves to Rome. Colonies obviously had a tendency at the outset to model themselves on different aspects of the city of Rome; thus Cosa, founded in 273, borrowed the notion of a *curia*, senate-house, linked with a circular *comitium*, place of assembly, directly from Rome (see Fig. 4). Building styles in general came increasingly to spread out from Rome to the periphery. And Cicero talks of the voluntary adoption of Roman institutions by Latin cities:

C. Furius once passed a law on wills, Q. Voconius on inheritance by women; there have been countless other measures on matters of civil law; the Latins have adopted those which they wished to adopt (*pro Balbo* 21).

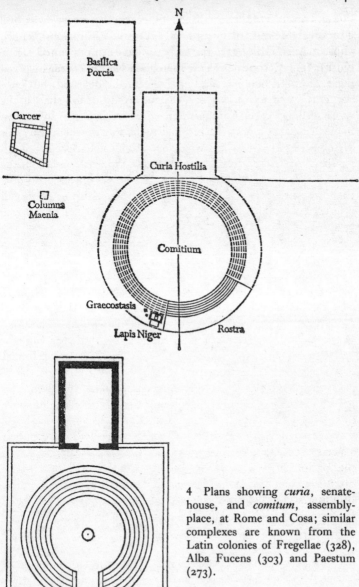

4 Plans showing *curia*, senate-house, and *comitium*, assembly-place, at Rome and Cosa; similar complexes are known from the Latin colonies of Fregellae (328), Alba Fucens (303) and Paestum (273).

The end product of the social and political process I have described is incisively delineated by Ennius, a native of Rudiae in Apulia, whose maturity belongs in the early second century (*Annales*, line 169 V): 'The Campanians were then made Roman citizens.'

V

From Italian Power to Mediterranean Power

THE REMOVAL OF the barriers against the participation of plebeians in the political and religious life of the Roman state was followed by the Roman assertion of her hegemony over Latium and then by the defeat of the Samnites and of the Gallic incursion of 295. The mixed patrician and plebeian nobility was tested and confirmed in power by the successes of those years; but it is also plausible to suppose that the opening up of avenues to power to groups previously excluded was likely to cause disturbances. The career of Appius Claudius Caecus, the earliest Roman to appear in our sources as a personality rather than the edifying stereotypes dear to the later Republic or the age of Augustus, provides evidence of such disturbances. Despite the deformation in a historical tradition often hostile to the *gens* to which he belonged, the essential outline is clear. His *elogium*, re-inscribed at Arretium (Arezzo) in the age of Augustus, is startling enough, with its frequent repetition of magistracies:

Appius Claudius, son of Caius, Caecus (the blind), censor, consul twice, dictator, interrex three times, praetor twice, curule aedile twice, quaestor, tribune of the soldiers three times. He captured several towns from the Samnites, routed an army of Sabines and Etruscans. He prevented peace being made with King Pyrrhus. In his censorship he paved the Appian Way and built an aqueduct for Rome. He built the temple of Bellona (*Inscr. It.* XIII, 3, no. 79 – contrast the original funerary inscription of Scipio Barbatus, p. 5).

The most revolutionary period of Appius Claudius' career was his censorship in 312:

Ap. Claudius had his fellow-magistrate L. Plautius under his thumb and disturbed many ancestral practices; for in currying favour with the people he paid no attention to the senate. First he built the aqueduct known as the Aqua Appia over a distance of nine miles to Rome and spent much public money on this project without senatorial approval; next he paved with stone blocks the greater part of the road named after him the Via Appia, which runs from Rome to Capua, the distance being well over 100 miles; and since he dug through high ground and filled in ravines and valleys even where substantial fill was needed, he spent all the available public money, but left an enduring monument to himself, deploying his ambition in public service.

And he changed the composition of the senate, not only enrolling the noble and eminent in rank, as was customary, but including many who were sons of freedmen; so that those who were proud of their nobility were angry. He also gave citizens the right to be enrolled in whichever regional tribe they wished and to be registered accordingly by the censors.

In general, seeing the cumulative hatred for him of the upper class, he avoided giving offence to any other citizen, contriving to gain the good-will of the masses to balance the hostility of the nobles. At the inspection of the cavalry (one of the functions of the censors), he deprived no man of the horse provided for him by the state (a way of disgracing someone), and in drawing up the list of senators, he ejected no member of the senate as unfit, unlike his predecessors. And the consuls, because of their hatred for him and their desire to curry favour with the upper class, summoned the senate not as constituted by Ap. Claudius, but as constituted by the preceding censors.

But the people, resisting these moves and sharing the ambition of Ap. Claudius and wishing to secure the advance of their class, elected as curule aedile (the election is effectively undated in Diodorus, but occurred for the year 304) Cn. Flavius, the son of a freedman, who was the first Roman whose father had been a slave to gain that (or presumably indeed any) office (Diodorus xx, 36, 1–6).

Apart from his other misdemeanours, Ap. Claudius refused to resign his censorship at the end of eighteen months according to the law and according to one tradition was still censor when a candidate for the consulship of 307. He was also remembered as the man who persuaded the family of the Potitii to make public the nature of the rites at the altar of Hercules, for which they had been responsible, and thereby invited their destruction by an angry divinity, and as the man who attacked the privileges of the sacred college of flautists (*tibicines*).

Much in all this may well be doubted, though hardly the uniqueness of Ap. Claudius among the politicians of his generation, but another act of Ap. Claudius, which may be accepted implicitly,[1] places him in the context of other innovatory activities of the turn of the fourth and third centuries. This is his building of the temple of Bellona, vowed during a battle in the course of his second consulship in 296 (the year before the battle of Sentinum, p.35); the building of this temple forms part of a whole pattern of interest in the honouring of the gods of war and victory, which shows Rome newly aware of her enormous power and, what is more, aware of the ideology of victory of the Hellenistic world. It is also interesting that the lifetime of Ap. Claudius saw Rome adopt the Greek device of coinage (see also Pl.1).

It was no doubt his awareness of the enormous power of Rome which led Ap. Claudius, towards the end of his life and in perhaps its most celebrated incident, to reject the notion of peace with King Pyrrhus of Epirus (p. 48), addressing the Roman senate thus:

> Whither have your minds in madness turned aside, which stood four-square on the path hitherto? (Ennius, *Annales*, lines 202—3 V)

We have seen that by the time of Pyrrhus' invasion, Rome controlled virtually all Italy south of the Po valley and thus possessed the power with which to defeat Pyrrhus and other enemies after him. Furthermore, the nature of Rome's control of Italy goes far to explain the nature of Roman imperialism, of interest to us, but something the existence of which Polybius took for granted. With the Pyrrhic War, Rome faced for the first time an enemy from the civilized core of the Mediterranean world and,

---

1. Records of temple foundations appear to have been preserved independently of the main historical tradition (p. 8).

with his defeat, that world began to take notice of Rome (p.6). Rome's wars of the third century and after are relatively well-attested and took her between 280 and 200 from a position on the fringe of the Mediterranean world to one from which she can be seen, with the benefit of hindsight, to dominate it. We must consider for a moment the nature of Roman imperialism and then look at the course of Rome's wars down to the defeat of Hannibal.

Roman society can be seen as deeply militaristic from top to bottom, in a way and to an extent that is not true of any Greek state, not even Sparta. Whatever the Romans said and no doubt in part believed about their fighting only just wars, the value attached to successful wars of conquest found expression in a number of central institutions. It was an ancient custom, revived by Sulla, for those who had extended Roman territory in Italy to be allowed to extend the *pomerium*, the sacred boundary of the city of Rome; the censors at the end of their term in office prayed that the Roman state might be granted greater wealth and extent, and *haruspices*, priests from Etruria, were consulted at least from the late third century to say whether a sacrifice made at the beginning of a war portended (as hoped) extension of the boundaries of the Roman people; Ennius (*Annales*, line 465 V) talked of 'you who wish Rome and Latium to grow'. That Roman territory *did* grow in extent throughout the period when Rome was establishing her hegemony in Italy is in any case obvious; the land taken from conquered peoples and used for the foundation of colonies or for individual assignation became *ager Romanus*, Roman territory, unless used for Latin colonies; its progressive extension can be plotted down to 200, after which year the pattern remained unchanged until 91. It seems in fact that the Romans supposed that success in wars of conquest was the reward for their piety and the justice of their cause.

At the level of the individual, a general who brought a war to a successful conclusion was of course rewarded with prestige, booty and the avenue to popularity which its distribution could bring, and clients among the defeated; he was also likely to be permitted to hold a triumph, an astonishing and spectacular public and religious celebration of his victory. None of this was unwelcome to an ambitious member of a competitive oligarchy; the pretensions of such a man are graphically documented by the frequency with which they are satirized by Plautus, as at *Amphitruo* 657 (compare 192 and 196):

> I routed them at the first attack by my divinely conferred authority and leadership.

or at *Epidicus* 381 (compare 343):

> I am returning to camp with booty because of the bravery and authority of Epidicus.

Another factor operated both at the level of the community and at the level of the individual, the urge to intervene far afield; faced with an appeal from Saguntum in 220, Rome could not resist hearing it, although Saguntum lay in the area of Spain which Carthage reasonably held to be within her sphere of influence; it was yet another factor which fed Carthaginian enmity towards Rome. Similarly, individual members of the oligarchy involved themselves in the internal affairs of the kingdoms of Macedon, Syria and Pergamum in the course of the second century. Again, the involvement was related to competition within the oligarchy.

Furthermore, Rome had of course suffered defeats, some of them momentarily catastrophic; but that hardly explains why a desire for security, understandable in any community, amounted in Rome almost to a neurosis over her supposed vulnerability; in 149 Rome persuaded herself that Carthage was still a threat and duly annihilated her (p.89).

Sheer greed also often played a part, overtly expressed by a character in Plautus:

> Yes, you both go in, for I shall now summon a meeting of the senate in my mind, to deliberate on matters of finance, against whom war may best be declared, so that I can get some money thence (*Epidicus* 158–60).

But perhaps more important than any of these factors was the nature of the Roman confederation in Italy; Rome drew no *tributum* from any of her associates (other than from the *cives sine suffragio*) or allies, but demanded from them manpower. The origin of the institution is intelligible enough in a world in which Rome and Latium and the Hernici lived under permanent threat of invasion from marauding upland tribesmen; but the consequence of the institution was that the only way in which Rome could derive benefit from her confederation was by summoning troops. The only way in which she could symbolize her leadership, a factor of at least as great importance in an empire as its practical benefits, was by placing the troops of the confederacy under the command of the consuls. And then – what else but war and conquest?

The Roman involvement with Pyrrhus came about because of the difficulties of Tarentum. Under increasing pressure from the barbarian tribes of the interior in the latter half of the fourth century, Tarentum turned to the Greek homeland and to the help of a series of Greek condottieri, Archidamus of Sparta, Alexander of Epirus, Acrotatus of Sparta, Cleonymus of Sparta (in Italy from 304 to 299) and finally Pyrrhus of Epirus (in the west from 280 to 275); this last general was summoned to help not against the barbarian tribes who were neighbours to Tarentum but against the expanding power of Rome.

After a series of successes and an expedition to Sicily, Pyrrhus was finally defeated by the Romans at Beneventum and abandoned the Tarentines to their fate. The confrontation with Rome was in a sense marginal to the career of Pyrrhus; but it was a confrontation between Rome and a successor of Alexander the Great and marked the definitive emergence of Rome into the Greek world (see p.5).

Not long after the defeat of Pyrrhus, Rome found herself in 264 led to intervention outside Italy for the first time:

The Mamertini (Italian mercenaries settled in Messana and under threat of attack from Syracuse) wanted, some of them, to appeal to the Carthaginians (the other great power apart from Rome in the western Mediterranean and known to the Romans as Poeni, Phoenicians, whence Bellum Punicum, Punic War) and to hand over themselves and the acropolis to them, others to send an embassy to Rome, handing over the city to them and asking them to help them as being men of the same race. The Romans were in a quandary for a long time because the illogicality of such help seemed absolutely obvious; for shortly before they had inflicted the supreme penalty on some of their own citizens for illegally seizing Rhegium; now to seek to help the Mamertini, who had behaved in much the same way not only towards Messana, but also towards Rhegium, involved misconduct hard to condone. The Romans did not ignore any of these factors, but they realized that the Carthaginians had not only subjugated Africa, but also much of Spain (Polybius or his source here exaggerates), and controlled all the islands in the Sardinian and Tyrrhenian seas; and the Romans were worried lest if the Carthaginians became masters of Sicily they would be overpowering and dangerous neighbours for them, surrounding them and threatening all parts of Italy. It was clear that they would rapidly subjugate Sicily, unless the Mamertini received help; for if Messana were handed over to their control, they would rapidly conquer Syracuse, being already masters of almost all the rest of Sicily.

The Romans foresaw all this and thought that they must not abandon Messana and allow the Carthaginians as it were to acquire for themselves a stepping-stone over to Italy; they debated for a long time and eventually the senate did not pass the motion (to help Messana), for the reasons I have just outlined; for the illogicality of helping the Mamertini balanced the advantages to be derived from helping them.

But the assembly took a different line; the people had been worn out by recent wars and badly needed a change for the better in their circumstances; in addition to the arguments I have just outlined on the desirability of the war from the point of view of the state, the generals-to-be spoke of the clear and considerable advantage (in terms of booty) which each individual might expect; the people voted to help the Mamertini (Polybius 1, 10, 1–11,2).

After some successes, including the acquisition of Hiero of Syracuse as an ally, Rome found that the war had reached a position of stalemate, with the Carthaginians masters of the sea, the Romans masters of Sicily apart from a few fortified places. As capable of innovation in the technical sphere as elsewhere, the Romans took to the sea:

When they saw that the war was dragging on for them, they set to for the first time to build ships, a hundred quinqueremes and twenty triremes. And since the shipwrights were totally inexperienced in building quinqueremes, none of the communities of Italy then using such ships, their project caused the Romans considerable difficulty. All this shows better than anything else how ambitious and daring the Romans are as policy-makers. (Using a wrecked Carthaginian ship as a model the Romans duly built a fleet and put to sea.) (Polybius 1, 20, 9–11)

The war was settled by Roman persistence, a characteristic which had already helped to defeat Pyrrhus and which was to help defeat Hannibal, the chief Carthaginian general in the Second Punic War; Rome built one more fleet than Carthage was capable of building and in the peace imposed in 241 made Carthage withdraw from Sicily and pay a large indemnity. By a piece of what even Polybius regarded as sharp practice, Rome acquired Sardinia and Corsica shortly after.

Not altogether surprisingly, there were those in Carthage who did not regard the verdict of the First Punic War as final; the creation of an empire in Spain and the acquisition thereby of substantial military and financial resources were followed by Hannibal's invasion of Italy in 218 (the Roman tradition attempted to make the entirely justified attack on Saguntum by Hannibal into the *casus belli*, in order to salve its conscience over the failure to respond effectively to the appeal by Saguntum to Rome, p. 47). By a curious irony, the decisive confrontation between Rome and Carthage came at a moment when trading links between the two communities were greater than ever before – a large part of such fine pottery as Rome exported in the third quarter of the third century went to Carthage and her neighbourhood (Fig. 5).[2]

Hannibal's initial success was electrifying; invading Italy with 20,000 infantry and 6000 cavalry, he defeated the Romans in a succession of battles; at the River Ticinus and the River Trebia in the Po valley in 218, at Lake Trasimene in Etruria in 217 and at Cannae in south-east Italy in 216. Given his small forces, it was inevitable that he should seek to supplement them with such allies

2 It is also interesting that at some time the Romans acquired the word *macellum*, market, from a Phoenician source.

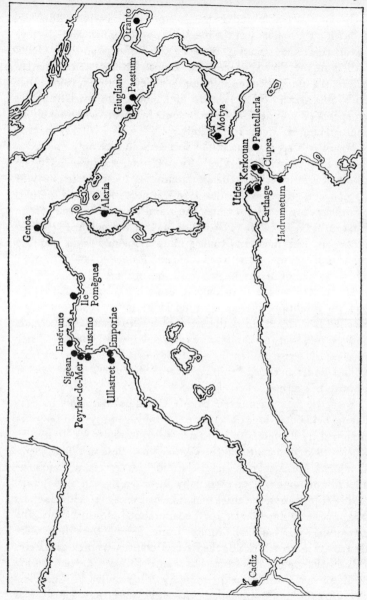

5   Map showing places to which Roman fine pottery was exported in the middle of the third century BC

as became available and indeed ultimate success depended on detaching the majority of the members of the Roman confederacy. Given the secular enmity between the Romans and the Gauls settled in the Po valley and the Roman attempts immediately before 218 to plant colonies in the Po valley, it was inevitable that the Gauls should be anxious to join him, quite apart from the prospects of plunder. Their adhesion, however, was unlikely to endear Hannibal to the rest of Italy.

Hannibal's spectacular initial successes in fact only masked a deeper long-term failure. The battle of Cannae was followed by the revolt of a number of Italian communities and conspicuously of Capua, some eager to abandon Rome, others constrained to do so by military force; Hieronymus, the grandson of Rome's ally of the First Punic War, Hiero of Syracuse (p. 49), was persuaded to join Carthage. But most of Rome's allies remained loyal and the community of interest between them and Rome remained the most important factor in deciding the outcome of the war.

It was clear in the immediate aftermath of Cannae that Rome had no intention of ever surrendering; given that, her allies recalled her leadership in the series of battles against Gallic raids and the fact that the Gauls were now allied with Hannibal. They recalled the sense of identity which Rome had created for an Italy united under her leadership. Above all they recalled the shared rewards of success.

Syracuse was recaptured by M. Claudius Marcellus in 211, having held out so long only because of the ingenuity of the engines designed by Archimedes (who was killed in the sack). In 209 P. Cornelius Scipio captured the Carthaginian base in Spain, Nova Carthago. Meanwhile in Italy, Hannibal was forced to watch the superior manpower of an essentially unshaken Roman confederacy slowly subjugating the cities which he had won over and which he was unable to defend. In 207 he summoned Hasdrubal and the remaining Carthaginian forces from Spain, but they were destroyed in a battle beside the River Metaurus in north-east Italy. Hannibal's departure from Italy and ultimate defeat in 202 at Zama by a Roman expeditionary force under P. Cornelius Scipio, as a result surnamed Africanus, were only a matter of time.

The measure of Rome's control over her allies is her response to the plea in 209 of twelve of her Latin colonies that they could neither provide more men nor pay for them:

> There were then thirty (Latin) colonies; twelve of these, when representatives of all were at Rome, informed the consuls that they no longer had the resources to provide men or money . . . Shocked to the core, the consuls hoped to frighten them out of such a disastrous state of mind and thought that they would get further by rebuke and reproof than by a gentle approach; so they claimed that the colonies had dared to tell the consuls what the consuls would not bring themselves to repeat in the senate; it was not a question of inability to bear the military burden, but open disloyalty to the Roman people . . . (The remaining colonies produced more than their quota; the delinquent colonies were temporarily ignored and later severely punished by the imposition of additional burdens.) (Livy XXVII, 9, 7)

Just as the rewards of success kept her confederacy loyal to Rome despite occasional rumblings, so they held the lower orders loyal to the rule of the oligarchy, again with occasional rumblings. The career of the *novus homo*, a man without ancestors who had held office, Manius Curius Dentatus, undoubtedly depended on popular support. Consul in 290, he defeated the Samnites and the Sabines, and celebrated two triumphs, and he then distributed land taken from the Sabines among the Roman needy. Not surprisingly he went on to hold command again, against a Gallic tribe, the Senones, in the 280s; he then held office yet again, to inflict defeat on Pyrrhus in 275. A final consulate in 274 was his reward.

But the most serious clash before the second century between the will of the oligarchy and a representative of the people was provoked by C. Flaminius, tribune in 232, who carried in that year against the opposition of the senate a law by which individual allotments were made to Roman citizens in the Ager Gallicus and Ager Picenus. The bitterness of the oligarchy against C. Flaminius was conveyed to Polybius in the middle of the next century by his aristocratic sources:

> The Romans distributed the so-called Ager Picenus in Cisalpine

Gaul (the Po valley), from which they had ejected the Gauls known as Senones when they defeated them; C. Flaminius was the originator of this demagogic policy, which one may describe, as it were, as the first step at Rome taken by the people away from the straight and narrow path (of subservience to the oligarchy) and which one may regard as the cause of the war which followed against the Gauls. For many of the Gauls, and particularly the Boii, took action because their territory now bordered on that of Rome, thinking that the Romans no longer made war on them over supremacy and control, but in order to destroy and eliminate them completely (Polybius II, 27, 7–9).

The reasons for senatorial opposition to the proposal of C. Flaminius are not hard to guess – not any theoretical concern with the effect of an extension of Roman territory on the functioning of the city-state, but simple apprehension of the rewards awaiting C. Flaminius in terms of prestige and clients.

Nor was the law of 232 the only thing which alienated C. Flaminius from the senate:

(He was) hated by the senators because of a recent law, which Q. Claudius as tribune had passed against the senate and indeed with the support of only one senator, C. Flaminius; its provisions were that no senator or son of a senator might own a sea-going ship, of more than 300 amphoras' carrying capacity; that seemed enough for the transport of produce from a senator's estate; all commercial activity seemed unsuitable for senators. The affair roused storms of controversy and generated hostility to C. Flaminius among the nobility because of his support for the law, but brought him popular backing and thence a second consulate (Livy XXI, 63, 3–4).

The law was without practical consequences, since a senator could engage in commercial activity through an intermediary, as the elder Cato, that upholder of traditional values, discovered; rather, the law accurately expressed a fundamental belief of the Roman governing class, that a gentleman should live off the land, or at any rate seem to do so. The chief importance of the law was that it involved public recognition of the senate as the governing council of the Roman community (and indeed of a senator *and* his son as belonging to a distinct Order in society); the law insisted that its members should be above worldly considerations.[3] The law also provided evidence of the willingness of the people to legislate for the conduct of their leaders; *that* was its offence – an offence that came to be repeated more than once as the revolution of the late Republic unfolded.

The second consulship which his support for the Lex Claudia brought C. Flaminius was that of 217; defeat at Lake Trasimene cost him his life and provided further material with which the oligarchy could blacken his memory. But he was not the last leader whom during the Hannibalic War the people brought to office against the wishes of the oligarchy. C. Terentius Varro, one of the consuls for 216, came to office partly as a result of popular dissatisfaction with the oligarchy's conduct of the war (Livy XXII, 34, 8, is also a plausible reconstruction of part of the ideology of his supporters); the policy associated with the name of Q. Fabius Maximus, of avoiding battles with Hannibal, was supposed to involve prolongation of a war which could easily by won outright. C. Terentius Varro took the Roman legions down to the greatest defeat of the war at Cannae.

Despite his failure, the rumblings continued. Not surprisingly, one reaction of the oligarchy to crisis during the Hannibalic War was to authorize a consul to name a dictator, in office for six months with supreme power. This emergency office was reduced to a nonsense in 217 when the people elevated M. Minucius Rufus to a dictatorship alongside Q. Fabius Maximus; ironically, the senate itself weakened the position of Maximus by quibbling over his access to finance for ransoming prisoners. The people again nominated a dictator in 210; and in that year tribunician interference with the activity of a dictator was allowed for the first time. The office fell into desuetude and its function was taken over when need arose by a very different institution (p. 122); the office itself was revived in a very different form by Sulla and Caesar.

3. It is unreasonable to suppose with some scholars that the law was motivated by the desire of men of business to eliminate competition from senators.

But the most remarkable product of popular feeling during the Hannibalic War was the emergence of a charismatic leader who for the moment avoided any overt challenge to the collective rule of the oligarchy, but whose example had nonetheless the most sinister implications for the future, P. Cornelius Scipio. Carried by popular fervour to the command in Spain, he there found himself hailed as king by some native Spanish troops; he turned the embarrassing compliment by creating the title *imperator* for them to use. The title was initially monopolized by members of his family and then competed for in the escalating political struggles of the late Republic. The victory over Carthage at Zama then gave Scipio the title of Africanus and a degree of eminence over his peers never before achieved. He even claimed a special relationship with Jupiter. Also symptomatic of the degree of eminence which an individual could achieve in this period is the cult offered to Marcellus, the captor of Syracuse, by that city (we do not know whether in his lifetime or posthumously). For the moment, however, senatorial control was unchallenged; the astonishing thing is not that the assembly in 200 refused initially to vote for another war, with Philip V of Macedon, but that it was persuaded so readily to change its mind. Such was the grip of the oligarchy on the Roman state.

VI

The Conquest of the East

ROMAN POLITICAL involvement east of the Adriatic began with the First Illyrian War in 229, an event as crucial to our understanding of Roman expansion as to that of Polybius, with his Hellenocentric view of the 'world' conquered by the Romans. According to Polybius, the Illyrians (Map 3), long in the habit of molesting ships sailing from Italy, did so even more when in the course of the reign of Queen Teuta of Illyria they seized control of Phoenice; a Roman protest led to the murder of L. Coruncanius, one of the Roman ambassadors, on his way home and war was declared. Roman distaste for a queen who could not or would not control her subjects' piracy is intelligible enough and one can compare the Roman punishment of their troops who seized Rhegium in 280; but the strategic threat posed by Illyria with its capital at Rhizon on the bay of Kotor should not be underestimated. 'Whoever holds Kotor, I hold him to be master of the Adriatic and to have it within his power to make a descent on Italy and thereby surround it by land and sea' remarked Saint-Gouard in 1572. Of the power of Illyria after the seizure of Phoenice Rome had tangible evidence in the shape of the pleas of those who suffered.

In the course of the war against Queen Teuta, Corcyra (Corfu) expelled its Illyrian garrison, surrendered when invited to do so into the *fides* of the Romans and was accepted into their *amicitia*; Apollonia, Epidamnus, the Parthini, the Atintanes and Issa are explicitly attested by Polybius as following suit. Roman sensitivity to the diplomatic niceties of the Hellenistic world emerges very clearly from her actions. After the final victory over Teuta and the imposition of tribute, envoys were sent to announce the victory to Aetolia and Achaea, whither the victims of the Illyrians had also appealed, and to Athens, spiritual capital of Greece, and to Corinth, where the Isthmian games were in progress; the Romans were admitted to the games. Even at this early date, there is nothing casual about the Roman handling of public relations with the Greek world.

The political configuration of that world (Map 3) was the result of the conquests of Alexander the Great. When he died in 323 he controlled an empire which stretched from Macedonia to India and to which were attached in awkward symbiosis the notionally free cities of Greece. A generation or two of fighting after his death left three stable monarchies, the kingdom of Macedon, the empire of the Seleucids, who controlled Syria and much of Asia Minor, and the empire of the Ptolemies, who controlled Egypt. In the course of the third century BC the kingdom of Pergamum was carved out of Seleucid territory in Asia Minor. Apart from administering, taxing and protecting their vast territories populated by peasants living in villages and deprived of political rights, the Hellenistic monarchs engaged in intermittent wars with each other and made continuous attempts to woo the Greek cities, who tended to claim, and sometimes actually possessed, free status. The war between Athens and Sparta between 431 and 404 had had as its proclaimed aim the freeing of the Greek cities from the Athenian yoke and the successive collective peace treaties of the fourth century BC had all paid lip service to the notion of the autonomy of the cities. The result was that no Hellenistic monarch could afford not to present himself as a champion of the freedom of the cities, particularly since a city discontented with his patronage could often turn elsewhere for support. And, in fact, the monarchs managed to divide the Greek world into a patchwork of protectorates. Into this world, with its stable political structure and its ideology of autonomy for the Greek cities, came the Romans.

After the First Illyrian War, Rome left Demetrius of Pharos in an influential position in Illyria, a position which he converted to one of dominance. In 220 the Romans chose to suppress him, no doubt fearing for their eastern flank in the impending war with Carthage; the grounds alleged were Demetrius' subjection and destruction of Greek cities in Illyria (an area described by Polybius as placed under the Romans) and his piracy in the Aegean, which of course involved breaking the ban on sailing south of Lissus imposed on Illyria after the First Illyrian War; it is hard not to suppose that Rome had at least one eye on Greek public opinion.

Demetrius was forced to flee to Philip V of Macedon and Rome again withdrew her forces from east of the Adriatic, but Philip V was now clear that the Romans were *de facto* rulers of part of Illyria (compare Polybius' description of the cities attacked by Demetrius of Pharos as placed under the Romans) and observed with distress their intervention soon after on behalf of his enemy Scerdilaidas. After an abortive naval expedition to the Adriatic in 216, he chose the moment of Roman weakness after Cannae to ally with Hannibal in an attempt to reverse the situation. Ironically, it was not Roman intervention east of the Adriatic itself which embroiled Rome with Macedon, but Philip V's reaction to the effects of that intervention.

He undertook to help Carthage, Carthage in return undertaking to see that any peace with Rome embraced Macedon, protecting her from assault and leaving Rome no longer ruler of Corcyra, Apollonia, Epidamnus, Pharos, Dimale, the Parthini and the Atintanes.

Threatened by Philip V and at the same time unable to detach significant forces from Italy, Rome turned to Aetolia and in 212—211 negotiated an alliance, one group of the provisions of which is preserved on a fragmentary inscription from Thyrrheium:

> . . . the magistrates of the Aetolians shall make war against all these (enemies) immediately, as the Aetolian people thinks fit. If the Romans take by force any cities belonging to these people, the cities and their territories shall, as far as the Roman people is concerned, belong to the Aetolian people; anything the Romans get hold of apart from the cities and their territories shall belong to them. If the Romans and Aetolians operating together take any of these cities, the cities and their territories shall, as far as the Roman people is concerned, belong to the Aetolians; anything they get hold of apart from the cities shall belong to them jointly. If any of these cities go over to or join the Romans or the Aetolians, the Aetolians may, as far as the Roman people is concerned, take the inhabitants and the cities and the territories into their league . . .
> . . . autonomous . . .
> . . . peace . . . (*IG*IX, I², 2, 241)

The whole text provides eloquent testimony to the Roman anxiety not to get involved in Greece. But the emphatic provisions relating to movable booty, promptly implemented, went a long way to destroy the good name of the Romans in the Greek world. The capture by Rome of Anticyra and of Aegina echoed through the Greek world. Precedents for the provisions relating to booty may be found in both the Greek and the Roman worlds, but in view of the Roman need to avoid involvement in Greece and of the fact that the version of the treaty in the inscription was translated from a Latin original, we may accept that the provisions were inserted at the behest of the Romans. Certainly they were later applied when Rome and Attalus of Pergamum captured Andros and Oreus. And in a Greece where obsession with movable booty was known as an Illyrian characteristic, it was not a principle likely to make the Romans popular. Polybius' brilliant and bitter account of the Roman sack of Nova Carthago in Spain in 209 will reflect the Greek view of Rome at that period:

When Scipio thought the number of those who had entered the city adequate, he despatched the majority of the troops against those in the city, according to the Roman custom, instructing them to kill anyone they met and to spare no-one, and not to start plundering before the signal was given. The purpose of this Roman custom seems to me to be to instil terror; for one can often see in cities taken by the Romans not only the bodies of human beings, but dogs cut in half and the severed limbs of other animals (the remains of a deliberately dismembered human corpse have been found in the excavations of Morgantina in Sicily, sacked by the Romans in 211). On this occasion indeed there was much of this kind to be seen because of the number of people in the city (x, 15, 4–6).

Possessed of no better reason for war than when they had accepted peace with Philip V in 217, hated for their association with Roman conduct in the war, perhaps advised that Rome would turn on Greece when her hands were free in Italy if she had an opening, and inadequately supported by Rome in 207, the Aetolians made peace with Philip in 206; the Romans followed suit in the same year.

Five years later Rome and Philip were at war again; it was a war which marked the beginning of Roman involvement in the Greek east on a massive scale and which raises in its acutest form the problem of Roman imperialism. It is therefore desirable to establish its proximate causes, but in the present state of our knowledge this is an almost impossible task. Nonetheless, the attempt is worth making.

For Livy, there was no great problem; both Philip V and Rome had included a number of their allies in the terms of the treaty of 206, Rome most notably Athens; in 203 an embassy from 'allies' of Rome in Greece complained of attacks by Philip (and brought news that the Macedonians were helping Carthage). Rome finally went to war in defence of Athens, the assembly first rejecting war, then accepting it, at the very beginning of the consular year in March 200.

The trouble is that if Polybius is to be believed, Rome was still not at war when M. Aemilius spoke to Philip at Abydus, which Philip was besieging, later in 200:

For the Romans had heard firm news in Rhodes about the siege of Abydus, and wishing to address Philip personally according to their instructions, deferred their project of going to see the other kings and sent off Marcus Aemilius Lepidus. Meeting the king near Abydus he informed him that the Senate had passed a decree, begging him neither to make war on any of the Greeks nor to lay hands on any of Ptolemy's possessions. He was also to submit to arbitration the question of the damage he had done to Attalus and the Rhodians. If he acted thus he would be able to remain at peace, but if he did not readily obey he would find himself at war with Rome. When Philip wished to point out that the Rhodians were the aggressors, Marcus Lepidus interrupted him and asked, 'What about the Athenians? What about the Cianians? And what about the Abydenes now? Did any of these attack you first?' The king was enraged and said that he forgave him for speaking so arrogantly for three reasons, first because he was young and inexperienced in affairs, next because he was the handsomest man of his time – and this was a fact – and chiefly because he was a Roman. 'My principal request,' he said, 'to the Romans is not to violate our treaty and not to make war on me;

but if nevertheless they do so, we will defend ourselves bravely, calling on the gods to help us.' (Polybius XVI, 34, 2–7)

Nor is this yet a declaration of war; it is only a report of a decree of the senate, warning Philip not to make war on Greeks and not to attack the possessions of Ptolemy V of Egypt and to accept arbitration of the claims of Attalus and Rhodes against him. The eventual formal *casus belli*, injuries to Attalus and Rhodes, is perhaps here adumbrated; they could with some plausibility be regarded as allies of Rome, had certainly suffered from Philip and were in a position to urge action on Rome. The reply of Philip to M. Aemilius Lepidus implies the still existing possibility of peace, as does the Achaean attempt to reconcile Rhodes and Philip immediately after the fall of Abydus.

But it has also to be asked why Rome went to war with Philip at all, only a few months after the conclusion of peace with Carthage, a problem which seems not to have exercised Polybius. Reacting against the notion of a plot to annex the east, M. Holleaux argued that it was news of a pact between Philip V and Antiochus III of Syria to divide the realms of Ptolemy V of Egypt which pushed Rome to decide on war. An elaboration of this theory by A. H. McDonald and F. W. Walbank had it that the news arrived after the first assembly of 200 had rejected war and impelled the second assembly to accept war. But there is little likelihood that there was any long interval between the two assemblies; and the extent of Roman knowledge of the east at the end of the third century (p.67) makes it most unlikely that the senate could have been so ignorant as to be pushed into precipitate action by such a pact.

In my view the senate regarded the peace of 206 as provisional and was always determined to pursue the war with Philip as soon as opportunity arose, a determination no doubt congenial to Attalus and Rhodes; the stab in the back after Cannae could not be regarded as revenged by the peace of 206. It also seems to me likely that individual ambitions, attested by Polybius as affecting Flamininus' conduct a few years later, now aroused by a wish to outdo Africanus, also played a part. And it is perhaps permissible to speculate that some senators saw a successful war in the east as a solution to the pressing financial problems which were the legacy of the long war with Carthage. It may well be that the refusal of the first assembly to vote for war was occasioned by the fact that the formal grounds advanced for war were very weak, the real grounds having to be decently veiled.

The chief objection to this view and the chief prop to support the view that Rome decided on the war with Philip only at the last moment is the alleged rejection by Rome of an approach by Aetolia at some stage apparently not long before the autumn of 200, perhaps in the winter of 201-0; this is held to show Rome devoid of interest in securing the support of a potential ally against Philip. But as we shall see, it was in the Roman interest from 197 onwards to present a consistent picture of Roman coldness towards Aetolia as a result of her separate peace in 206, and an alleged rebuff in 201-0 is a very flimsy peg on which to hang any view of the outbreak of war in 200.

At all events, the election in the autumn of 201 of P. Sulpicius Galba, who had already served in Greece, as one of the two consuls for 200 marks in my view the emergence of a majority in the senate for war with Philip; the subsequent assignation of Galba to the command in Greece rather than his colleague could no doubt be achieved by manipulation of the lot, an easy job, as Thomas Gataker remarked in 1627. The real interest of the following years lies in the astonishing skill with which Rome formulated and executed a policy of winning over Greek public opinion and in the way in which that public opinion came over to Rome despite earlier Roman conduct in the Greek world. The involvement of Rome in the Greek east on a massive scale after 200 was not simply an indispensable prerequisite for the increasing Hellenization of the Roman aristocracy during the second century BC; the emergence of political philhellenism in the course of that involvement had an important part to play in the process.

The campaign of persuasion began during the winter of 201—0 at Athens, which had recently been attacked by Macedonian troops and ships and been rescued as a result of the initiative of Attalus and Rhodes. A Roman embassy arrived, followed by Attalus in person, who consulted with the Roman ambassadors and discovered that they were ready for war with Philip. Attalus and a Rhodian embassy which was also in Athens then persuaded Athens to vote for war against Philip.

Not altogether surprisingly, Philip's general Nicanor then raided Attica. The Romans asked him to inform Philip that Rome asked him 'to make war on no Greek community' (and to submit his dispute with Attalus to arbitration); only so could he expect to keep the peace with Rome. Nicanor departed to Philip, the Romans left to announce their *démarche* to the Epirotes, Amynander of Athamania, the Aetolians and the Achaeans. The ideological basis for Roman intervention in Greece was already established. There is from this point absolute continuity of policy, through the message of M. Aemilius Lepidus to Philip at Abydus to the peace with Philip V after his defeat at Cynoscephalae, the proclamation at the Isthmus and the declaration of war against Antiochus III.

The exigencies of a policy based on the championing of the freedom of the Greeks come out most clearly from the Roman dealings with the Aetolians after the victory at Cynoscephalae.

The treaty of 212–211 between Rome and Aetolia states quite clearly (p. 59) as its last preserved clause that any city which went over to the Romans or to the Aetolians could be absorbed by Aetolia; the fact that the same procedure applied whether a city went over to one or other of the allies makes it evident that no meaningful restrictions could have been placed on the process of absorption, and the various attempts by modern scholars to make the inscription say something other than what it says are a waste of human ingenuity.

In 197, the Romans were of course perfectly entitled to regard the treaty as having lapsed because of the separate Aetolian peace of 206; and when the Aetolians appealed to the treaty, Flamininus took this line. But that was not enough; he was in fact prepared to go by the treaty as a working rule and surrender Phthiotic Thebes to Aetolia because it had resisted; but in order to make the Roman position as champion of the freedom of the Greeks credible it was necessary to assert that any city which came over to the Romans was entitled to freedom. So Flamininus at a conference at Tempe blandly denied the existence of the last clause of the treaty of 212–211:

When those with Phaeneas were indignant and said that in the first place the Aetolians should, as they had fought with the

Romans, now get back the cities which had formerly been members of their League, and that in any case the same should be the consequence of the terms of their original alliance, according to which the possessions of those captured in war belonged to the Romans and the cities to the Aetolians, Flamininus said they were mistaken on both points. For the alliance had been dissolved, when, deserting the Romans, they made peace with Philip; and even if it still existed, they should get and occupy not the cities which had surrendered to the Romans of their own free will, as all the Thessalian cities had now done, but only those which had fallen by force of arms (Polybius xviii, 38, 6–9).

The Aetolians had in fact in their presentation of their case simplified the terms of the treaty, precisely as Polybius and Livy do elsewhere; Flamininus went out of his way to allude to the last clause of the treaty and to deny its existence. That he was unscrupulous enough to do so need not be doubted; he was apparently prepared to make peace with Philip in 198, if his command against Philip was not to be renewed, and to connive at the murder of the anti-Roman Brachyllas. The Aetolians had of course given the Romans ground for anger, with their separate peace in 206, their boasting about their part in the victory of Cynoscephalae and their eagerness to plunder after the battle; but the lie of Flamininus served a major Roman purpose, the furthering of the policy which gave Rome the moral advantage in the war against Philip and was to do so in the war against Antiochus.

Already at the conference of the Aous in 198, Flamininus had demanded that Philip withdraw his garrisons from Greek communities and make restitution to those whose cities and lands he had ravaged; at the conference of Nicaea, during the following winter, Flamininus demanded that Philip withdraw from the whole of Greece, *before* going on to talk vaguely of territory seized in Illyria and from Ptolemy V of Egypt; Philip's envoys at Rome were asked whether he would surrender the fetters of Greece – Corinth, Chalcis and Demetrias. The lie of Flamininus at the conference of Tempe served a policy which the senate had initiated in the winter of 201–0, which he had consistently upheld and which the senate had just re-iterated.

But it was also no doubt pronounced by Flamininus with one

eye looking over his shoulder; Antiochus of Syria was on the move.

The senate duly instructed the ten commissioners sent to help Flamininus to see to the freedom of the Greeks and a decree of the senate freeing all the Greeks in Europe and in Asia was despatched. The decree included instructions to see to the liberation of Cius by Prusias of Bithynia. The proclamation of Greek freedom by Flamininus at the Isthmian Games followed and an attempt by the commissioners to give Oreus and Eretria to Eumenes II of Pergamum (who had succeeded to Attalus as king) was thwarted by Flamininus. When Rome wished to put Antiochus in his place, she was able to acquire an instant moral advantage by ordering him to leave alone the cities of Greece and the free cities of Asia and those formerly under Philip and Ptolemy V.[1] The purity of Roman motives was emphasized by the withdrawal of all troops from Greece in 194. In 193, in the presence of embassies from the Greek world, the senate ordered Antiochus to leave the Greeks in Asia free and to evacuate Europe; the second part of the order was apparently backed by the threat of military force.

War actually broke out when the Aetolians, resentful of their treatment by Flamininus, seized Demetrias in the interest of Antiochus and summoned him over. The attempt to turn the notion of freedom of the Greeks against the Romans failed miserably; Antiochus was easily driven out of Greece and the Aetolians left to face Rome alone. Roman policy in Greece remained consistent; the Aetolians in the final settlement were not allowed even to recover cities which had been captured let alone befriended by the Romans.

In Asia, before coming to grips with Antiochus, the Romans offered terms which they perhaps expected to be rejected, that Antiochus must not only free the cities of Aeolis and Ionia, but also abandon the territory west of the Taurus Mountains. In the settlement after the battle of Magnesia in 190, the area west of the Taurus was divided into two parts, with Lycia and Caria in general going to Rhodes, the rest apart from some areas of the interior in general going to Eumenes II of Pergamum. The cities which had paid tribute to Attalus were to pay it to Eumenes, those which had paid it to Antiochus were to be freed of it.

1. Perhaps inconsistently, Rome apparently proposed to return to Ptolemy V the cities which he had held.

In the event, any cities which had been free before the defeat of Antiochus remained free. Of those cities which had paid tribute to Antiochus only those which had committed themselves to Rome before the outcome was certain were freed of tribute and joined the existing group of free cities (Livy XXXVII, 56, 2 and 6; Polybius XXI, 45, 2). Much of Caria was *not* placed under Rhodes – Miletus, Heraclea, Myndus, Halicarnassus, perhaps Pedasa nearby; probably Iasus and Bargylia, perhaps Euromus, certainly Mylasa, probably Alabanda, presumably also Alinda; perhaps in Roman eyes the most obviously Greek part of the area attributed to Rhodes was left free. As in Greece after the defeat of Philip, those were freed who deserved to be freed; gratitude to Rome was evoked also by the destruction of the power of the Gallic tribes settled on the central plateau of Anatolia.

The basing of Roman policy in the east after 200 on the championing of the freedom of the Greeks does not stand alone; the Romans channelled a great deal of skill and energy into the whole process of finding out about the Greek world and presenting themselves and their institutions in terms which the Greek world understood. In A. D. Momigliano's words, the command of a foreign language meant power to the Romans; Polybius and Posidonius looked to the old Roman virtues for the explanation of Roman success, but the Romans had acquired power by innovation rather than conservatism.

We possess copies of letters of Flamininus to Chyretiae in Thessaly of 197–4, of M. Valerius Messalla to Teos of 193, of P. and L. Scipio to Heraclea ad Latmum of 190, all illustrating the process. The last emphasizes the Roman virtue of *fides*, trustworthiness, care:

L. Cornelius Scipio, general of the Romans, and P. Scipio, his brother, send greetings to the council and people of Heraclea. Your envoys (a list of names follows), excellent men, met us and gave us a copy of your decree and themselves spoke in support of the terms of the decree, showing every trace of enthusiasm. We are well disposed towards all the Greeks and shall try, now that you have placed yourselves in our care, to exercise appropriate foresight on your behalf, in general always producing some benefit. We grant you freedom, as to the other cities which have placed themselves in our care, so that you may have in your control the whole organization of your community according to your laws and shall in other respects try to indulge you and always produce some benefit for you. And we accept the honours which you offer and the assurances of loyalty and shall ourselves try to make a fair return. And we have sent Lucius Orbius to you, who will look after the city and its territory, so that no-one troubles you.

Farewell (Sherk 35).

Apart from underlining Roman *fides*, the Romans were also careful to discount any suggestion that they were motivated by greed; they always fought just wars, in defence of their allies (Polybius, fr. 99) or as revenge for wrongs received (the topicality of *rerum repetitio*, demand for restitution, at the turn of the third and second centuries BC is shown by its take-off at Plautus, *Amphitruo*, 205–10). The Romans were a model of piety; their conduct as victors was marked by moderation. The skill and adaptability of the oligarchy, confronted with the political problems posed by contact with the Greek world, are astonishing.

In other important ways also, however, the closing years of the third century BC and the opening years of the second century are years of experiment and change. The Hannibalic War and the wars which followed mark the emergence *de facto* of the Roman professional army, although no formal change was yet made in methods of recruitment or terms of service; it is no accident that the emergence of the charismatic leader, with P. Scipio Africanus (p. 56) as the archetype, falls in the period when a new type of army had to be enlisted and led.

Even more important is the formalization of the Roman attitude to the world outside Italy. The spread of Roman control in Italy had been marked by the conclusion of *foedera*, treaties of alliance, and the foundation of colonies, where control was necessary. In Sicily in the First Punic War and for a time thereafter, Rome had in my view concluded treaties of alliance with a city or declared her friendship or recognized the free status of a city casually and at random, as circumstances dictated and perhaps often at the instance of the other party. From 200, the treaty of alliance was a privilege rarely granted and communities outside Italy which were associated with Rome were entered on a *formula amicorum*, list of friends; the standard means of access to this status was a recognition by Rome of free status, though a defeated enemy such as Philip of Macedon also became a friend. At the same time, colonization as a means of control was not extended outside Italy and a governor and *de facto* standing army were used instead. In all this, the Roman oligarchy showed the same flexibility which it had already shown in increasing the number of magistrates to deal with the needs of a growing community and its imperial responsibilities.[2]

2. A praetor was first elected for 366, to relieve the consuls of the administration of justice; he was joined by a second praetor about a century later, the first thereafter concentrating on jurisdiction between citizens, the second dealing with lawsuits involving foreigners. Two quaestors were first elected for 446 and the number grew steadily thereafter; they dealt with financial matters. The plebeians (p. 25) had their own aediles, administrative officials, from very early; two curule aediles, patrician counterparts, were first elected for 366.

VII

The Consequences of Empire –
The Governing Classes

THE POLICY OF CHAMPIONING the freedom of the Greeks, adopted by Rome for the sake of an immediate tactical advantage, of course ruled out any annexation of territory east of the Adriatic after 200; Rome was in any case faced with the need to re-assert her control over the Po valley, tentatively asserted immediately before the invasion of Hannibal and then lost, and to organize her provinces in Spain, inherited unquestioningly from Carthage.

The wars which resulted led to increasing Roman involvement in Spain and helped in the end to bring about the serious discontent of the lower orders which lay behind the tribunate of Tiberius Sempronius Gracchus in 133 (p. 95); but meanwhile the absence of direct rule by Rome over the Greek world did not mean in any way an absence of involvement. Just as it had been clear to Philip V that Illyria was subject to Rome, so it was now clear that Rome was the power to which much of the Greek world had to look. Even though Rome after 190 had no consistent policy towards or interest in Asia or Syria, from the cities of Greece, Asia and Syria alike there came to Rome a constant stream of embassies; they came as earlier analogues had come to earlier ruling powers, Persia, Macedon and the Hellenistic monarchies.

At the same time the Roman governing class, made confident by success and now exposed to the full impact of the Greek world, turned much of its energy not simply to solving the political problems posed by contact with the Greek world, but also to the acquisition of Greek culture and to the pursuit of the luxurious and ostentatious life-style available as a result of contact with the Greek world and access to its material resources; the process was encouraged by the existing ethos of aristocratic competition.

The consequence was a progressive disturbance of the equilibrium within the governing class, a phenomenon on which Polybius reflected, though in general terms, without explicit references to developments at Rome in the second century:

> For when a state has survived a period of great danger and then reaches a position of unchallenged supremacy, it is clear that when the state also achieves considerable prosperity, life-styles become more extravagant and men become unduly keen for offices and other objects of ambition (vi, 57, 5).

Polybius went on to talk of popular resentment of the mighty and support of the ambitious against them; the Roman oligarchy's awareness of a deteriorating balance within the group and of a growing involvement of the people in political struggles is clear from the action which they took to reverse these trends; it is hard not to suppose that Polybius is reporting the views of his Roman friends.

It is important to notice first of all that the mere spread of Roman hegemony was in itself the cause of increased competition within the Roman élite. The number of praetorships had been increased in 227 from two to four (p.69) and in 197, with the need to organize the provinces in Spain, the number was further increased to six. The result was that from that year six men reached the penultimate rung of the ladder every year, while the top rung, the consulship, continued to have room for only two; the consulship was in any case already eagerly sought after by the ambitious, as the careers of Africanus and Flamininus make clear, and the spectacular nature of those very careers of course made the consulship even more desirable.

In 181, a law passed by M. Baebius Tamphilus as consul enacted that there should be six and four praetors in alternate years. The law was soon abrogated, despite the opposition of Cato. For the alternative to six praetors every year was worse; if Rome did not have enough new magistrates every year to cover her imperial responsibilities, she had to prorogue, or prolong in office, existing magistrates and this process was itself frequently a bone of contention. Furthermore Flamininus had perhaps been prepared to neglect the public interest and tailor his attitude to Philip of

Macedon according to whether he was to be prorogued or not (p.64).

In another way also the demands of empire were in themselves a source of instability. Like many other early empires, Rome operated with an exiguous number of permanent officials and *needed* the personal relationships between members of her own aristocracy and notables in provincial communities in order to organize her supremacy; such personal relationships of *amicitia* and *clientela* were indeed one of the chief ways in which Roman rule was mediated to the provinces under her control. But the possession of such *clientelae* brought enormous prestige to the individuals concerned; it was one of the things which served to distance some members of the aristocracy from their peers. Foreign clients could also provide favourable testimony in case of prosecution for misgovernment (for which see p.76) and exotic animals for display to the Roman people; in the age of revolution they raised armies for the dynasts. At the same time, the pattern of *clientelae* was gradually moving areas of government from public into private hands; the advice of Aemilianus to Jugurtha was timely – and unheeded:

> After the destruction of Numantia, P. Scipio decided to dismiss the allied troops and himself return home (in 133); after honouring Jugurtha and praising him lavishly in public, he took him aside into his headquarters and then in secret warned him to cultivate the friendship of the Roman people publicly rather than privately and not to get into the habit of making presents to individuals; it was dangerous to buy from a few what belonged to many (Sallust, *Bellum Jugurthinum* 8, 2).

The growth of the empire brought with it, then, increased competition within the aristocracy and increased prestige for those members most heavily involved overseas; apart from expressing its concern over the number of praetorships and perhaps also, if the attitude of P. Scipio Aemilianus may be taken as typical, over the links between men such as Jugurtha and leading Romans, the Roman aristocracy took a number of steps which may be seen as attempts to police its own conduct.

Firstly, it introduced measures to regulate the holding of office.

T. Quinctius Flamininus had been a candidate for the consulship of 198 without having been praetor or aedile, thus evoking public disapproval (Livy xxxii, 7, 8); his colleague and one of his successors had not been praetor. After this, all men who became consuls had already been praetor (except for Africanus who when he became consul for the second time in 194 had already been consul); presumably an unattested law of 197 enforced this check to ambition.[1] In 180, L. Villius as tribune passed a law regulating the legal age for certain offices and imposing a two-year interval between them; henceforth a man could not be aedile before 36, praetor before 39, or consul before 42. This progress through the different magistracies, all held after the quaestorship, which was the most junior regular magistracy and which had actually been held by Flamininus, is known as the *cursus honorum*. In one sense it represents simply a formalization of a career structure which had doubtless become conventional and which reflected the relative importance of the different magistracies; in its context, the law is yet another attempt to regulate aristocratic ambition.

The last attempt in the period before Tiberius Gracchus to regulate the tenure of magistracies falls probably in 151. In 152 M. Claudius Marcellus was consul for the third time; such dangerous eminence could not be permitted and a law was passed forbidding iteration of the consulship[2] – attested by its suspension in order to enable P. Scipio Aemilianus to be elected consul for the second time in 134.

Secondly, measures against bribery: the year 181 saw the first securely attested enactment against bribery, passed by the two consuls, *ex auctoritate senatus*, by the authority of the senate. Despite this the tradition records bribery for 166; in 164 Cato (p.81) repeated an earlier claim (*ORF* 8, XLIV, 173): 'I have never distributed my money or that of our allies in bribery.' Cato clearly assumed that such practices were widespread; he also highlighted the source of much of the wealth which was making bribery and other disturbing developments possible – the empire.

Roman expansion in Italy was marked by the acquisition of

1. It was impossible to enforce tenure of the aedileship, since there were only four aediles a year and, after 197, six praetors a year.
2. A ten-year gap between successive tenures of the same magistracy had already been imposed in 342.

booty as well as land, but the only continuing obligation on communities under Roman control was to provide manpower (p.47), though Sicily from 241 and Sardinia and Corsica from 238 provided tribute in cash or kind. From 197 onwards, however, Rome imposed tribute in cash, beginning with the two Spanish provinces, whose revenues, ironically, were organized by Cato. In addition, cash from indemnities now flowed into Rome chiefly from Carthage, Macedon and Syria, on a scale which dwarfed the indemnities of the third century. The wars themselves continued of course to provide booty on a vast scale, as a fortunate by-product of the pursuit of *gloria*. The financial resources of the Roman state evoked the impassioned admiration of the author of I Maccabees (8, 1–4) and of Polybius, as later of Posidonius (both of these commenting on the Spanish mines). *Tributum* (p.37) was not levied after 167. Much of this wealth passed from public into private hands, *in part* no doubt quite legitimately, as (perhaps generous) reimbursement for expenses to magistrates and as payment to contractors outside the senatorial order. By the second half of the second century, the treasury was regarded as a source of wealth (Lucilius 456–7 W, compare 1016 W): 'As for me, I need a quaestor or supplier, who will supply me with gold from the state money-bags.'

Some indication of the scale of the resources available to Rome in the second century may be drawn from the fact that Athens spent the equivalent of 12,000,000 denarii on the Parthenon, the cult statue of Athena and the monumental entrance to the Acropolis; Rome spent in the 140s and 130s 45,000,000 denarii simply on an aqueduct, the Aqua Marcia. The public buildings of the second century BC transformed the city of Rome (Pl.2).

Besides all this, generals and governors abroad had almost limitless opportunities for illegitimate self-enrichment. P. Cornelius Scipio Africanus never rendered precise account of 18,000,000 denarii received from Antiochus for the upkeep of the Roman army in Asia after the battle of Magnesia in 190. The continuation of the remarks of Cato (p.73) illustrates the range of possibilities:

I have never placed garrison commanders in the towns of your allies, to seize their goods and their families. I have never divided booty (compare fragments 98 and 224–6) nor what had been taken from the enemy nor spoils among a few of my friends, so as to deprive those who had won it of their reward. I have never granted permits to requisition at will, so that my friends might enrich themselves by exploiting such authorization. I have never distributed the money for the soldiers' wine (compare fragment 132) among my attendants and friends, nor made them rich at public expense.

Again, one can indicate the scale of private wealth in this period: when L. Aemilius Paullus, who put an end to the kingdom of Macedon in 167, died, he was worth 360,000 denarii, at a time when a legionary was probably paid 108 denarii per year. Paullus was regarded as poor, within the Roman aristocracy.

A further law against bribery was passed in 159: despite this, Polybius, probably writing this part of his work in the late 140s, felt able to say (VI, 56, 4): 'Among the Carthaginians, people openly bribe to gain office, but among the Romans death is the penalty for such conduct.' The Roman aristocracy would have been decimated.

Towards the end of his life, however, Polybius was not so sure about the immunity of Romans to bribes (XVIII, 35, 2; compare XXXI, 25, 3,): 'Now (in contrast to earlier times) I should not dare to assert this of everyone; but I *should* be able to say of many particular individuals that they can keep their hands clean.'

It is significant that stories about the immunity of Romans of earlier times to bribery, such as that about Manius Curius Dentatus and the Samnites, circulated already in the second century (Ennius, *Annales*, line 373 V). Such stories no doubt served as in other contexts to reinforce the official ideology, but to no avail. The context of Polybius' remarks is precisely bribery of Romans by foreigners; it was probably used by Cotys of Thrace in his dispute with Abdera, certainly by the Syrian satrap Timarchus in 161. The alternative advice given to Jugurtha at Numantia in 133 was *Romae omnia venalia esse*, that at Rome everything was for sale; in 123 the likelihood of bribery by foreign potentates was taken for granted by C. Gracchus (*ORF* 48, XII, 44).

Thirdly, sumptuary laws; it may seem astonishing to modern

readers that Rome persistently and frequently, from the second century to Augustus, attempted to limit by legislation expenditure on, *inter alia*, private entertainment or individual dress. The attempts are intelligible if seen in the context of the urgent need of the second-century aristocracy to preserve the cohesion of the group.

The Lex Oppia of 215, intelligible as an emergency measure of the Second Punic War, was repealed in 195; but already the repeal attracted the opposition of Cato, and from 181 onwards there are five separate measures in the space of forty years, the Lex Orchia of 181, the Lex Fannia of 161, a senatorial decree of the same year, the Lex Didia of 143, the Lex Licinia of 142 or 141. All of them were attempts to prevent conspicuous consumption and display by members of the group, the consequent envy and resentment of the rest and the resort to an attempt to go one better.

Fourthly, the triumph (p. 46); the years after 200 saw an unprecedented flood of triumphs by men who had held only the praetorship (some of them were fobbed off with the *ovatio*, a less prestigious celebration now revived after long disuse); many of the triumphs and *ovationes* were from Spain and the pattern reflects the need to control a new area and the need to use others than consuls for the purpose. But the development was clearly regarded as dangerous and from the mid-170s the senate was able to restore a substantial degree of limitation of the triumph to those who had held the consulship.

Fifth, provincial government; not only did much of the money used in conspicuous display and for bribery come from extortion in the provinces (see above), it was also necessary for Roman rule to be responsible for more fundamental reasons, otherwise resentment could threaten that rule itself. It would also threaten those in both east and west who accepted and identified with Roman rule; Greek notables urged moderation on Rome, Spanish and other notables with touching faith brought their complaints to Rome. Polybius, reflecting on the desertion of Carthage by her Spanish allies, perhaps also points a moral for Rome:

The Carthaginians supposed that Spain was firmly under their control and treated the natives badly, with the result that they made enemies of their subjects instead of allies and friends.

Naturally – for they supposed that there was one way of acquiring an empire and another of keeping it and did not realize that the best way to preserve pre-eminence is to stick as closely as possible to the principles by which domination has been achieved (Polybius x, 36, 3–5; compare III, 4, 4–6).

The problem was not an easy one, for it was essential not to weaken in any way the *imperium* of those who held command in the provinces; a relatively easy step was taken in 182, when the senate passed a decree regulating demands by magistrates for contributions from allies towards the cost of games which they put on; and on a number of occasions in the first half of the century complaints evoked an *ad hoc* senatorial procedure and sometimes restitution for the injured, more often absolution for the accused. In 149 the Lex Calpurnia introduced a standing procedure, with a *quaestio* (court) staffed by senators; a novel feature, perhaps borrowed from the Greek world, was the fact that the praetor who presided had to give his verdict according to the majority of the votes. Hitherto a magistrate had been bound in jurisdiction to consult his *consilium* (p. 26), but not to take a majority vote as binding.

In general the Lex Calpurnia changed little. There was still no penalty, simple restitution alone was at stake. Petitioners still had to plead through senatorial *patroni*, who might be reluctant to press charges against members of their own order, and cases could be adjourned endlessly, till the petitioners gave up. It was left to C. Gracchus to institute a stiffer procedure and to introduce a penalty.

One interesting probable senatorial decree of this period, however, enabled Aemilianus to display his outstanding virtue. The decree probably prohibited a governor from purchasing a slave except as a replacement, since his power could allow him to influence the price; on his tour of the east, Aemilianus went one better than the rule and sent home for a replacement for a dead slave (he had already displayed his modesty by only taking five with him in the first place).

In addition to attempting to police itself, the oligarchy also attempted to devise various methods of controlling the lower orders, involved increasingly in the political arena by the factors outlined by Polybius (p. 71).

The ill-attested Leges Aelia et Fufia belong in this context; they laid down, presumably restated, the grounds for preventing or subsequently vitiating proceedings in assemblies. The grounds were mainly religious and no doubt of great antiquity; their usefulness as modes of social control is obvious. The laws probably also prohibited the holding of legislative assemblies between the proclamation and the holding of electoral assemblies; such legislation, dispensing him from the provisions of the Lex Annalis (p. 73), had made possible the election of Aemilianus in 148 and the restriction was presumably introduced soon after. It was another means of controlling the assembly and preventing it from supporting undue ambition.

The early ballot laws are also to be regarded as attempts by the oligarchy to prevent malpractice; the Lex Gabinia introduced the secret ballot for elections in 139, perhaps in an attempt to reduce intimidation, such as is alleged to have occurred at the elections of 185, and bribery. The extension of the secret ballot to the extortion court by the Lex Cassia of 137 was certainly a response to the bribery used by L. Aurelius Cotta to secure his acquittal in the previous year. The Lex Cassia was certainly approved of by Aemilianus (Cicero, *de legibus* iii, 33; *Brutus* 97), perhaps also the Lex Gabinia; it is unclear whether the suggestion of Cicero that the ballot, although secret, was *optimatibus nota*, known to the leading men of the community, is more than wishful thinking. Certainly the secret ballot did not in the end deter bribery, it merely encouraged delayed payment; and later ballot laws, extending or reinforcing the secret ballot,[3] were regarded as passed against the wishes of the oligarchy.

There is also evidence which allows us to glimpse an important debate going on at Rome in the early second century over the composition of the Roman citizen body and over that of its governing élite. First, the debate over the inclusive or exclusive nature of Roman citizenship; we have seen that the openness of Rome to outsiders was one of the sources of her strength in Italy and that this fact was recognized both by Philip of Macedon and by Cato (p. 38). But the attitude to be taken to freedmen was a source

3. The Lex Papiria of 131 or 130, extending the secret ballot to legislative assemblies, and the Lex Coelia of 107, extending it to treason trials. The Lex Maria of 119 attempted to minimize interference with voters (see Pl.7a).

dissent; they were confined to the four urban voting tribes, less prestigious that the 31 rural voting tribes, probably by the census of 230–29. Perhaps in 174 a more open policy was adopted of allowing freedmen with a son (a small group since slaves were mostly freed only in old age and children born to a slave couple remained slaves) or with the property of the first *classis* to register where they wished. In 169 the ruling was reversed over the first category, though not retrospectively, and indeed Ti. Sempronius Gracchus, the father of the tribunes of 133 and 123, attempted, though without success, to disfranchise all freedmen except those in the first *classis*. The same exclusive outlook may *perhaps* be seen at work in the gradual shift from the founding of Latin colonies to the founding of Roman colonies.

An analogous debate can be detected over the composition of the governing class. M. Cato, perhaps during his censorship of 184, attempted unsuccessfully to increase the number of those who were provided with a horse by the community to enable them to belong to the cavalry (Appendix 3) and the definition of the capital wealth which qualified a man to be considered for a horse perhaps took place in the same general period. A similar concern with broadening the base of the state at the top end also emerges from the probable lowering of the capital wealth needed to qualify a man for the first *classis* from 120,000 to 100,000 asses. It is also possible that in 179 the assembly which was organized on the basis of the *classes*, the *comitia centuriata*, was made more democratic (Appendix 1).

So far in the second century, the oligarchy appears as alert and ready to innovate; similarly, at any rate to begin with, in the field of foreign policy; but there signs of increasing intolerance appear, which can also be documented in internal affairs in the years before the tribunate of Tiberius Gracchus.

VIII

The Imperial Power

THE ROMAN OLIGARCHY of the second century BC, has emerged as
alert and innovative, at least in the field of internal reform; the same
attitude appears in the context of cultural borrowing from the Greek
world. By 167, there was a substantial Greek community in Rome,
whose views on Roman policy towards Rhodes were recorded by
Polybius. Soon after 167, Polybius was able to tell P. Scipio
Aemilianus that there were plenty of Greeks in Rome to whom
Aemilianus could go to learn of things Greek; these Greeks would
not have been in Rome unless there had been a demand for their
skills and it is evident that contact between the Greek and Roman
worlds in the early second century BC was accompanied by a desire
on the part of many Romans for at any rate some of the things which
the Greek world had to offer. This desire then created a market not
only for the skills of respectable Greeks whose views Polybius
thought worth recording, but also for those of educated slaves.

There is, equally, little doubt that many Romans not only
patronized Greeks with skills they wished to learn, but also wanted
to be seen as men of Greek *paideia*, education and culture; this fact is
of far greater importance than the largely unanswerable questions of
how deep acquaintance with Greek culture really was or of how
sincere was its pursuit. Already in 211, M. Claudius Marcellus had
made at Syracuse slight, but increasing efforts to mitigate the full
horrors of a Roman sack (for which see p. 60) and had been rewarded
by the establishment of a Greek festival in his honour (see p. 57). T.
Quinctius Flamininus, who took over and developed the framework
for Roman diplomacy in the Greek world established at the
beginning of the Second Macedonian War (see p. 64), of course
spoke perfect Greek; he further took the trouble in dedicating some

shields at Delphi to accompany them with a Greek epigram and to acquire a statue at Rome with a Greek inscription. When M. Fulvius Nobilior in 186 held the games vowed during the Aetolian War, he went so far as to bring actors from Greece (who came *honoris eius causa*, to honour him, presumably as a friend of the Greeks) and introduced athletic competitions to Rome for the first time. Actors are also attested as coming from Greece for games held by L. Scipio; the story is probably false, but its invention testifies to the image of himself to which a Roman noble might attach importance. A similar concern to create an image of himself as someone with access to the cultural goods of the Greek world appears in the case of L. Anicius; he too imported Greek performers for his games, but allowed them to be pushed into some very undignified activity by an audience which found their basic repertoire too refined. In another sphere, P. Scipio Africanus, who had already displayed his knowledge of the Greek world by inventing the process of imperatorial salutation while in Spain, wrote to Philip V in Greek; Ti. Sempronius Gracchus showed off by addressing the Rhodians in Greek; the son of Africanus wrote a history in Greek.

In the midst of all this, M. Porcius Cato occupied a highly ambiguous position. The fullest expression of his antipathy to things Greek is preserved by Pliny in the context of a discussion of the medical profession:

Greek literature is worth only a nodding acquaintance, the Greeks are *nequissimum et indocile genus*, a most wicked and intractable race, their literature will corrupt Rome, their doctors will ruin Rome; in fact the Greeks have taken an oath to kill all barbarians by means of medical ministrations and include Romans among barbarians, going so far as to call them Opici (= Osci, the traditional Greek name for the non-Greek barbarian inhabitants of Italy) (*Naturalis Historia* xxix, 14).

Cato is also attested as having described philosophers as winding-sheets and as having assimilated poetry to nakedness and luxury.

The reality is not so simple. It can be shown that Cato was very well acquainted with things Greek from the internal evidence of his own writings and from the contemporary observations of Polybius. Thus Polybius tells us that Cato compared him to a man who proposed to return to the Cyclops' cave to recover his hat when he proposed to ask the senate for further concessions in addition to the repatriation of the Achaeans interned by Rome in 167 (p. 6); Cato also quoted the *Odyssey* in prophesying that Aemilianus would destroy Carthage. Given these two quotations, there is no difficulty in supposing that when in 191 Cato repeated the Persian stratagem at Thermopylae he did so in full knowledge of the account of Herodotus; and it is perhaps reasonable to hypothesize that when Cato described a monarch as a *zoon sarkophagon*, a flesh-eating animal, he did so in parody of Aristotle's famous description of a man as an animal who lived in cities, a *zoon politikon*. It also seems possible that the procedure whereby Cato allowed his slaves access to sexual gratification as a reward was a savage caricature of Plato's system for rewarding the brave among the guardians of his ideal state.

Cato emerges therefore as both influenced by Greek intellectual achievements and as capable of expressing hostility to them. It then comes as no great surprise to discover that he developed in his historical writing a view shared by Polybius. His historical writing provides indeed further evidence for Cato's position both in opposition to and within a Greek intellectual tradition and provides a starting point for an assessment of that position.

The *Origines*, written in Latin, belong to the last period of Cato's life, Books II–III being written after the battle of Pydna in 168, Book VII just before Cato's death in 149; they are in one important respect unlike any earlier, Greek, historiography on Italy and Rome and for that matter unlike any later historiography in either Greek or Latin, in their interest in Italy and in the willingness of their author to listen to local traditions on the past instead of inventing them.

But not only did Cato, like his predecessor Fabius Pictor, attach importance to the supposed Greek element in the composition of the population of early Italy; the title of his history, the *Origines*, is an echo of the works of Greek historians, Timaeus and others, including a study of origins; his preface is an echo of that of the *Symposium* of Xenophon; and the history as a whole, concentrating on the Regal period and then on the relatively recent past, is the direct successor of the works of Timaeus and Fabius Pictor, and of Naevius and Ennius, both intellectual cousins of Pictor. In following this pattern and in allowing a Greek element in Roman origins, Cato implicitly accepted that it was with reference to a Greek world that Rome needed to be identified and characterized.

Cato then, seeking to place Rome in an area of which the intellectual map had been substantially drawn by the Greeks, and Polybius, coming from the Greek world and attempting to explain Rome's meteoric rise to power, came to hold the same view of the governing principle that underlay the development of Republican institutions and the unfolding of Roman history. This governing principle, that the Roman Republic depended on the *ingenium* not of one person, but of many, is expounded by Cicero at the beginning of Book II of his *de re publica*, explicitly acknowledging the debt to Cato and certainly drawing on the *Origines*; a trick of narrative style made these indeed embody a *reductio ad absurdum* of the principle, the decision not to name commanders by name, but simply to refer to them as *imperator Romanus* and so on. The same governing principle is formulated by Polybius, like Cato explicitly contrasting the Roman system with the Spartan.

We have already seen Cato to be deeply distrustful of monarchy as a form of government and have now seen him to have held along with Polybius a distinctive and influential view of the basic principle according to which Roman society had developed. Although one would not wish to regard Cato's and Polybius' account as providing a total explanation of the development of Republican institutions, it is clear that they have grasped one essential feature of the Republican system, that it was a system which depended on collective rule by the oligarchy and which was perpetuated by a powerful ideology of the supremacy of the group. It is, I think, no accident that the concept was apparently formulated in the period when collective rule and the ideology which supported it were under attack; and the process of formulation of the concept goes far to explain Cato's ambivalent attitude to things Greek.

The dangerous distancing of some members of the Roman nobility from their supposed peers from the late third century onwards requires little documentation. P. Scipio Africanus had been hailed as king by the native troops serving with him in Spain and had turned the compliment by inventing the new title of *imperator* for them to use (p.56); he had then gone on to defeat Carthage and supposed as a result that he was entitled to ignore the niceties of constitutional conduct; T. Quinctius Flamininus had defeated Philip V of Macedon and had been offered cult in his lifetime by cities grateful for their deliverance. The enormous power wielded by Roman magistrates operating far from senatorial oversight led to grave abuses; the wealth acquired from office by some members of the oligarchy separated them spectacularly from the rest and enabled them also to bribe their own way or that of other members of their family to further office.

The oligarchy showed that it had the wish, if not always the will, to deal with all of these threats to collective rule; it passed *leges annales* to regulate the rapidity of a political career; it attempted to control and punish misconduct in the provinces; it passed sumptuary laws to prevent conspicuous display breaking the cohesion of the group and endeavoured to take action against electoral corruption.

With many of these measures Cato is associated and it is overwhelmingly likely that his view of the governing principle in the development of Roman institutions was formulated in response to the growing threat to those institutions posed by the dangerous eminence of certain individuals. His theoretical discussion and his opposition to the pretensions of Africanus are two sides of the same coin. His attitude to Greek culture is part and parcel of the same story.

There is an element in the first place simply of finding guilty by association; it was the Greek world which had raised Flamininus to his position of eminence, it was the Greek world which provided much of the new wealth of some members of the Roman oligarchy, it was the Greek world whence came a number of social and sexual habits felt to be at odds with traditional Roman behaviour; it was easy to condemn the high culture of the Greek world in one sweeping judgment. But there is more to it than that. The assimilation of Greek culture was one of the factors in the escalation of competition within the aristocracy, its possession functioning as one of the things which distanced some men from their peers, its skills ready to hand to serve the ends of political competition.

Just as the Roman oligarchy had always been relatively rich, so it had always been to a certain extent exposed to Greek culture and in a position (to put it crudely) to perceive what Greek culture had and what Roman culture did not have. The conquest of the Greek east from 200 onwards provided ready access to Greek artistic and intellectual skills and techniques and to wealth on a staggering scale. The interests of the oligarchy, given the nature of peer-group competition, did the rest; just as when one member of the oligarchy had acquired wealth the rest had no serious alternative but to attempt to follow suit or lose face by comparison and run the risk of losing status, so the process of Hellenization involved in part examples once set being followed by other members of the group.

The group as a whole and Cato in particular both showed a wish to do something about the excesses to which aristocratic competition was leading and combined to condemn many of the manifestations of Greek influence; Cato differs from his colleagues primarily in his effectiveness as a publicist of himself as epitomizing the spirit of Roman institutions and in the extent of our knowledge of his own utterances; a first-generation member of the Roman aristocracy, he encapsulates its dilemma in the second century – Hellenized while being worried by Hellenization, an ambitious, aggressive and successful politician (though unlike Africanus he held the consulship only once) while being anxious about the consequences of aristocratic ambition, a believer in Roman peasant traditions while at the same time inexorably pushed into 'modern' capitalist farming, a usurer and man of business while asserting that the land was the only proper source of wealth. The attitudes of Cato and his colleagues reflect clearly enough the crucial developments, Hellenization included, of the second century; their search for weapons in their internal conflict ensured the continued progress of Hellenization.

Willingness to experiment and innovate can also be documented in the field of foreign policy, but there the eventual impression, created as the second century wears on, is one of rigidity in the face of defiance and of resistance to change; and in the end the same refusal to yield to pressure from social or political inferiors within the community is perhaps the most characteristic attitude of the oligarchy on the eve of the tribunate of Tiberius Gracchus in 133. At the same time, ever more mental and physical energy is devoted to the pursuit of wealth and prestige and to the borrowing from the Greek world of skills useful in competition within the group. As the profits of empire become increasingly the reward of a few, the likelihood grows of an outburst both among the Roman poor and among the Italian allies.

The first real challenge to Roman dominance in the east after the defeat of Antiochus III came in 172; in that year Eumenes II of Pergamum came to Rome to warn the senate against the designs of Perseus, son and successor of Philip V of Macedon:

> Beginning then from the plans of Philip, he recounted the death of his son Demetrius, an opponent of war with Rome; he spoke of the Bastarnae summoned from their own lands, with the hope that they would provide help for the crossing to Italy; Philip, with these plans in mind, had been overtaken by fate and had left the kingdom to the man he felt to be most hostile to the Romans. And so Perseus had inherited a war left by his father and had taken over the war along with the throne and was even now plotting to bring on and carry out the war. (Eumenes goes on to underline Perseus' strength, his popularity with the other kings and with the various republics and his sundry misdemeanours.) (Livy XLII, 11, 4–5)

The trouble had actually begun two years earlier still. After the end of the war with Antiochus, in which Philip had loyally supported Rome, the senate had left Macedon very much to her own devices; there is no evidence that the demands made by the senate gradually drove Macedon into increasing hostility, nor is there any reason to accept the view of Polybius that Philip, like Carthage after the First Punic War, planned for revenge from the moment of his defeat.

It was in fact no doubt Roman indifference which led Perseus to suppose that it was possible for him to resume in 174 one of the traditional rôles of a Hellenistic king as a friend of the Greek cities:

> Nor was he satisfied to win over the minds of those peoples alone through whose territory he was to journey; he sent out ambassadors or letters more generally, asking people to forget the quarrels which they had had with his father; for these had not been so grave that they were incapable of being resolved with

him, as was proper; as far as he was concerned the slate was clean and he was ready to enter into true friendship with them. Perseus was in fact most anxious to find a way of winning the favour of the Achaean League (Livy XLI, 22, 7–8).

Polybius and Livy (xlii, 5, 1) of course viewed Perseus' attempts to regain the friendship of the Greek cities as one more stage in the grand design of revenge on Rome; but his reaction when faced with the prospect of war with Rome makes it clear that he did not want that war, and his moves in 174 were almost certainly innocent. But the senate not only saw itself as *the* champion of the freedom of the Greeks, from 200 onwards; it had become used in the period after the end of the war with Antiochus to having the Greek cities bring all their problems to Rome for resolution; at the same time many members of the aristocracy were exploring with increasing interest the cultural goods of the Greek world.

Perseus' attempts to win the friendship of the Greek cities no doubt appeared both as a threat to the political order established by Rome in the east in the years after 200 (Appian, *Macedonian Wars* II, 1) and as a move likely to reduce the importance of the Roman aristocracy, Hellenized but not Greek, as patrons of the Greek world.

The Greek world in due course rallied to Rome, more on a calculation of the likelihood of a Roman victory than from any enthusiasm for the prospect of increased Roman power; the lukewarm feelings towards Rome in the Greek world, after twenty years or so of Roman protection of the freedom of the Greeks, are perhaps a measure of the threat which Perseus did in fact represent to the Roman world order. The Roman attitude towards Rhodes after the war (see below) is certainly a measure of the extent to which Rome felt endangered.

The eventual victory, however, now as in the past, was that of the Roman legions, who defeated the army of Perseus convincingly at the battle of Pydna in 168; no power in the east now stood between Rome and the execution of her will. The Macedonian monarchy was eliminated and the territory of Macedonia divided up into four republics (Illyria was treated similarly); the decision marks a step away from one approach to the organization of the east, the acceptance of existing institutions, towards a different approach, the imposition of Roman institutions. The four regions were deprived of the right of intermarriage and citizens of one region were forbidden to acquire land or house in another; Rome was clearly thinking in terms of Latin institutions – *conubium* and *commercium* (see p. 36) were the characteristic reciprocal rights of the Latin cities – and was indeed reproducing a penalty imposed on the Latins in 338, removal of *conubium*. The settlement of 167 is a turning-point in another respect also; although it was decided initially not to exploit the Macedonian precious metal mines, it was decided to impose tribute (at a rate half that paid to the Macedonian monarchy, to allow for the expenses of local government). For the first time in an eastern context Rome imposed a money tribute (also on Illyria), to be levied in perpetuity.

Roman self-assertiveness can be seen also in the decision to lay Epirus waste and to enslave its inhabitants and in the anger at what seemed disloyalty on the part of Rhodes, the offer to mediate between Rome and Perseus at a moment when the war seemed not to be going well for Rome. Rhodes was deprived by Roman command of the territory granted by Rome after the defeat of Antiochus; some more long-standing possessions were also freed by Rome from Rhodian control. Delos was attached to Athens and declared a free port, thereby attracting traffic away from Rhodes and drastically reducing Rhodian revenue from harbour-dues. There were even those at Rome who wished to go to war against Rhodes, but they were deterred by the authority of Cato. Nor was Rhodes the only Greek state to suffer humiliation: the senate refused to admit to Rome Eumenes of Pergamum, who wished to remove the suspicions of disloyalty which fell on *him*; Antiochus IV was brutally ordered out of Egypt, which he had invaded, by C. Popillius Laenas; and Achaea and other communities were summarily ordered to surrender men of doubtful loyalty to Rome, among them Polybius. Soon after this the ethnic ROMA begins to disappear from the Republican coinage; the issues of the imperial power did not need identification.

At the same time, however, the senate can be seen as reacting flexibly to a changed situation; the earlier decision to leave the Macedonian monarchy intact had not worked and a new approach was needed. Moreover the decision not to exploit the Macedonian precious metal mines can be seen in part as parallel to measures taken at Rome to limit the deleterious effects of the increase in wealth.

After the flurry of excitement, the Roman attitude to the east reverted to a more normal one of passive involvement when prompted. But Roman mastery of the world was undisputed, casually obvious to Rome, painfully obvious, and demanding explanation, to Polybius. Interned in Italy, he had ample time for reflection, and ample opportunity to observe the victors at close quarters. His fellow Greeks turned more and more to Rome for arbitration of their disputes; the expectation of subservience which the practice created was not in the end conducive to a tolerant handling of the crisis of the early 140s (see below). Meanwhile, there was perhaps a trace of exasperation when Polybius asked:

> For who is there so worthless or lazy that he would not wish to know how and under what kind of government the Romans have brought under their sole rule almost the whole of the inhabited world, in less than fifty-three years; for nothing like this has ever happened before. Or who can be so devoted to any other subject of study that he would regard it as more important than the acquisition of this knowledge? (1, 1, 5–6)

In 149, the Romans suddenly saw the world begin to blow up in their faces; the Carthaginian reaction to their defeat in the First Punic War had been to acquire an empire in Spain; their reaction to defeat in the Second Punic War was to take over more of the African interior, at least in part in order to pay the Roman indemnity. Rome no doubt felt apprehensive about the resources which would be available to Carthage when the indemnity was paid off in 151 and Cato notoriously was so impressed with Carthaginian potential that he urged the destruction of Carthage in the interests of Roman security.

The opportunity was presented by an act of Carthaginian defiance; as a reward for his services in the Second Punic War, the Numidian King Massinissa had been rewarded by Rome with an extensive kingdom bordering on the territory of Carthage. His border quarrels with Carthage were brought to Rome for arbitration, in a manner which parallels the behaviour of the states in the east; Rome regularly decided for Massinissa, and her decisions were regularly accepted – until 149, when Carthage finally resisted.

The effect of sudden defiance on a power accustomed to arbitrate at will may easily be imagined: war was declared. Terrorized, the Carthaginians offered to surrender; they were instructed to hand over their arms and then told that they would have to move their city inland. Such terms were intolerable and the Carthaginians resolved to arm and fight till the end. It was not till 146 that P. Scipio Aemilianus was finally able to capture and sack Carthage. Africa was annexed as a new province.

In 148, the Macedonian republics opted for monarchy and rebelled under the leadership of a pretender named Andriscus. In 146, the Achaean League attempted the impossible and defied Rome, like Carthage over a problem arising ultimately out of arbitration.

Macedonia was rapidly annexed as another new province, the Achaean League was defeated, Corinth sacked, and Greece placed under the general supervision of the governor of Macedonia.

Again the oligarchy emerges as both inflexible in the face of opposition and as willing to try a new solution, in this case annexation, when an earlier one had failed. Their real testing ground was Spain: increasing preoccupation with Spain goes far to explain the intermittent nature of Roman interest in the rest of the Mediterranean world; it is also in Spain that stubbornness rather than innovativeness emerges as the dominant characteristic of the Roman oligarchy, and it was Spain which more than any other single cause fed the internal crisis which lay behind the tribunate of Ti. Gracchus.

The first half of the second century saw the successful extermination or terrorization of the Ligurians and the Celts of the Po valley. The Spaniards were tougher. The honeymoon period arising out of their liberation from Carthage by Rome over, they rebelled in 197, according to Appian taking advantage of Roman preoccupation in the Po valley and in Macedon (*Iberian Wars* 39, 158). In 195, Cato was sent out as consul, rather than a praetor, a lesser magistrate, being sent out, a measure of the seriousness of the problem; but despite his successes warfare continued on a considerable scale for the next fifteen years.

Ti. Sempronius Gracchus, father of the tribunes of 133 and 123, was able, as praetor in Hither Spain in 180 and pro-praetor in 179–8, to bring about a peace settlement; the two provinces of Hither Spain and Further Spain could even sometimes be combined in the years following the settlement. But in 155 or 154 war broke out again in both provinces; *this* emergency led to the moving of the beginning of the official year back from 15 March to 1 January, to enable magistrates to reach their province earlier. Consuls were despatched once more to Hither Spain, Q. Fulvius Nobilior in 153, M. Claudius Marcellus in 152, and L. Licinius Lucullus in 151. Opposition to Rome came principally from among the Celtiberi, and opinion at Rome gradually hardened in the direction of regarding nothing less than their unconditional surrender as acceptable; the result was the disaster at Numantia in 137, a measure both of the reluctance of the oligarchy to compromise with opposition and of the difficulties it now faced in the military enforcement of its will.

An inadequately trained army under C. Hostilius Mancinus attacked Numantia, failed, attempted to retreat and was trapped; Ti. Sempronius Gracchus, son of the praetor of 180 and future tribune in 133, negotiated a surrender on terms and a compromise agreement between Rome and Numantia. But the senate chose to repudiate the agreement and offered to Numantia as a scapegoat C. Hostilius Mancinus, naked and bound; Numantia understandably claimed that either the Roman army which had escaped should be put back in their power or the agreement should be honoured.

The oligarchy got away with its repudiation of the agreement; P. Scipio Aemilianus came to a second consulship in 134 and destroyed Numantia in the following year. But the refusal of the oligarchy to compromise with Numantia and its willingness to surrender one of its own number did not bode well for its reaction to the problems posed by the military weakness of Rome; and in 137 that weakness was plain for all to see.

The reluctance of the oligarchy to compromise can be documented in two other ways for this period. Perhaps during his consulship in 140, C. Laelius, the friend of P. Scipio Aemilianus, proposed that land be distributed to the needy in order to bring them up to the property qualification needed for legionary service and thereby improve the recruiting base of the Roman army. The proposal anticipated that of Ti. Gracchus:

> C. Laelius, the friend of Scipio, made an attempt to remedy the situation; but the powerful voiced their opposition and he was frightened at the outcry and abandoned the attempt; (he was called Sapiens, wise, as a result) (Plutarch, *Tiberius Gracchus*, 8).

One may perhaps recall the apparent reluctance of Rome to provide land, as early as 201, for the troops of Africanus; but in general, as G. Tibiletti pointed out, colonization and viritane settlement were routine matters in the early years of the second century BC, in striking contrast to the later situation.

Similarly in the field of *provocatio*; it was an article of faith at least by the time of Polybius that Roman citizens were and always had been immune within the city from arbitrary action by a magistrate, by means of a process of appeal, though the precise working of the mechanism is now obscure; various steps were taken in the course of the second century to extend this immunity to the provinces and to an area where it had not previously operated, military service. The reaction of the oligarchy was to devise a form of institutionalized lynching as a substitute for punishment by a commander:

> The punishment of *fustuarium* is managed like this: (once a man has been found guilty of an offence) a military tribune (an officer) takes a baton and simply touches the condemned man with it; as soon as this is done all those in the camp beat the man or stone him; they usually kill him before he gets out of the camp (Polybius VI, 37, 1–3).

To Polybius, despite the possibility that he listened to the worries of Cato and others about the loss of cohesion within the oligarchy and despite occasional hints that he knew not all to be well at Rome, the social control exercised by the oligarchy, mediated through religion, appeared to be complete:

> The most distinctive excellence of the Roman state seems to me

to lie in its attitude to the gods; for I think that something which is a matter for reproach among other men, namely superstition, holds the Roman state together. For this department of their activity is full of pageantry and is more prominent, both in private and in public life, than anything else. This may well surprise many people, but my own view is that the Romans' aim is to control the people (Polybius VI, 56, 6–9; he goes on to highlight Roman honesty as a result).

One may not share Polybius' belief in the superiority of Roman religion (see also Cicero, *de natura deorum* II, 8; *de legibus* II, 23) and one need not suppose that Roman contemporaries shared his cynicism (or later Romans that of Cicero, *de divinatione* II, 70; *de natura deorum* I, 3; III, 5); but his remarks are eloquent testimony to the satisfying nature of Roman religion in the mid-second century BC and to its effectiveness as a means of securing social solidarity. They also provide incidental evidence of the relative passivity of the Roman people. Some doubt about that passivity may be found in Lucilius (1017 W): 'They pass laws, a people disobedient to those very laws.'

The ambition of members of the aristocracy perhaps seemed a more serious threat to the rule of the group. P. Scipio Aemilianus was elected to the consulship in 147, having held neither the praetorship nor the aedileship, and again in 134, when second consulships had been made illegal (Cicero, *de imperio Cn. Pompei* 60, romanticizes his position). Ap. Claudius Pulcher defied the senate in 143 and triumphed, evading a threatened tribunician veto (on behalf of the will of the senate) by taking with him in the triumphal chariot his daughter, who was a Vestal Virgin. In the same general period, the types of the coinage of the Republic came to reflect primarily the interests and aspirations of the individual magistrates who produced it. The ambition of Ti. Gracchus and his determination in the face of opposition had their precedents.

IX

The Consequences of Empire –
The Governed

THE TRIBUNATE OF TIBERIUS GRACCHUS in 133 was seen in retrospect by Romans of the age of Cicero as marking an irrevocable breach with the past; Gracchus, a tribune of the Roman people, was lynched by a group of senators and their attendants, led by the Pontifex Maximus, P. Cornelius Scipio Nasica Serapio, who had been consul in 138.

> This was the first occasion in the city of Rome when the blood of Roman citizens was shed and recourse was had to the sword, in both cases without fear of punishment. Thereafter law was overwhelmed by force and greater respect was accorded to greater power, and civil strife which in the past had been resolved by agreement was settled by the sword (Velleius II, 3, 3).

For the moment Rome drew back from the brink (p. 112), but with the benefit of hindsight it could be held that the slide into anarchy and civil war from then on was continuous and progressive.

There was of course a large measure of accident and misunderstanding in the sequence of events which actually led up to the death of Ti. Gracchus; the prelude to and early phase of his tribunate involved in part political activity of a perfectly traditional kind; and precedents can be found earlier in the second century BC for many aspects of the tribunate of Ti. Gracchus. But these precedents themselves add up to a process which is nothing other than a recovery by the tribunate of the potentially revolutionary rôle played by it during the struggle of the Orders. The opposition to the candidacy of Flamininus for the consulship of 198 (p. 73) was mounted by two tribunes, fulfilling their rôle as *mancipia nobilium*, the servants of the nobility. The tribunes of the second century continued of course to be drawn from the nobility and their political activity continued to relate to traditional aspirations, but they showed an increasing tendency, however selfishly motivated, to champion the discontents of the lower orders against the collective rule of the nobility.

It is less easy to grasp the substantive reasons which impelled Ti. Gracchus and his associates to action, the precise nature of the pressures which were building up and above all the relationship between actuality and its perception. Attempting in retrospect to explain the disaster, oligarchic sources argued that Ti. Gracchus was motivated by pique at the invalidation of the treaty with Numantia (p.91); one might suppose rather that the disaster at Numantia impressed on him the shortage of good recruits for the army. C. Laelius had also seen this (p.92) and the poor themselves scribbled graffiti urging Ti. Gracchus to act.

His younger brother recorded that he had been struck while travelling through Etruria on the way to Numantia by the absence of free men and the cultivation of the land by slaves (Plutarch, *Tiberius Gracchus* 8). Something of the same concern comes across in the record of a speech said to have been made by Ti. Gracchus:

> Tiberius Sempronius Gracchus as tribune spoke at length about the Italians, about their bravery in war and their kinship with the Romans, and about how they were being reduced to poverty and declining in numbers without any hope of revival. And he complained about the slave population, about how it was no use in war and was no longer loyal to its masters, citing the recent disaster which had befallen the masters in Sicily at the hands of their slaves, who had there also been increased in numbers in order to exploit the land; he cited also the war fought against the slaves by the Romans, neither easily nor quickly won, but long-drawn out and involving many different hazards (Appian, *Civil Wars* 1, 9, 35–6).

There is no reason to suppose that either Plutarch or Appian provides other than a selection from what was said or reported; and the measure actually proposed by Ti. Gracchus had as its core the re-settlement of landless Romans (p. 107). But the factors at work in Italy in the second century BC doubtless affected Romans and Italians alike and to these factors we must now turn.

The most immediate evidence available to Romans of the second century BC was that of their own census figures; these figures were doubtless always to a certain extent inaccurate (perhaps most obviously as a result of under-registration of the very poor, who presumably did not pay *tributum* and did not normally serve in the legions):

233	270,713
208	137,108
204	214,000
194	143,704
189	258,318
179	258,294
174	269,015
169	312,805
164	337,452
159	328,316
154	324,000
147	322,000
142	328,442
136	317,933
131	318,823
125	394,736

These figures call for some comment: that for 233 is broadly confirmed by the figure given by Polybius for the levy of 225, that for 208, during the Second Punic War, is clearly meaningless and probably wrongly transmitted; in 204 special care was taken to record soldiers serving abroad (Livy XXIX, 37, 5) and the figure is presumably accurate and reflects losses during the Second Punic War; the figure for 194 is clearly either wrongly transmitted or the result of massive under-registration; the figure for 189 reflects the registration of the Campanians for the first time since their rebellion in 215 (Livy XXXVIII, 36, 5). Thereafter the figures rise erratically till 164, then decline erratically till 136; the dramatic rise in 125 is presumably the result of the very poor now registering in order to ensure eligibility for Gracchan land distributions.

It has been suggested by P. A. Brunt that these figures, if accurate, mask a much more drastic decline in the number of *assidui*, the group within the total citizen body possessed of the property qualification necessary to serve in the legions. There were presumably figures available at the time to document this decline also. In any case, even if wildly inaccurate as a result of careless registration, these and related figures were what Ti. Gracchus and others had available to go on; and other evidence suggests that there *was* a shortage of *assidui* – for example the growing proportion of Italians recruited into the Roman armies as the second century BC wore on (p. 127) and the progressive lowering of the property qualification of the *assidui*. Once 11,000 asses, it was probably reduced first to 4000 asses, at a date which is unknown, but which belongs before the mid-second century BC, and then to 1500 asses between the period of Polybius' observation of Rome and 141, when asses ceased to be an official unit of account.

The most obvious evidence of shortage of *assidui* which presented itself to Ti. Gracchus and others was probably that furnished by difficulties over the levy, even if to us complementary explanations of this phenomenon may seem possible. Roman expansion had been fed by an army of part-time farmers, part-time soldiers (p. 29); after 200, Rome found herself forced to keep troops outside Italy on a permanent basis. The result was reluctance, at times considerable, to be conscripted, reluctance which was perhaps bolstered by an increase in the incidence of conscription as a result of declining numbers of *assidui*. The full narrative of Livy down to 167 provides intermittent examples of reluctance to serve or anxiety to stop serving. There was also sometimes controversy between a man leaving his province, anxious to win *gratia* by discharging his troops (and to provide evidence of the pacification of his province), and his successor, anxious to have as many troops as possible under his command. The controversy presupposes a general background of distaste at any rate for too much military service.

From 151 onwards, our miserably inadequate literary record provides much evidence of distaste for military service; the consuls conducting the levy were sometimes imprisoned by the tribunes acting in protection of the potential recruits. All of this evidence relates to the difficult and unrewarding chore of service in Spain and it may be that there was no real shortage of *assidui* and that the Roman oligarchy was deluded when it stepped up recruitment of Italians and lowered the property qualification of *assidui* and that the decline in the total citizen body shown by the census figures is illusory. But in the well-documented period covered by Livy, there was some distaste for military service even in the relatively easy and certainly rewarding campaigns in the east. I think that the number of *assidui* was indeed declining from the middle of the second century BC onwards and that, given the reasonable assumption that in normal times the extent of non-registration was constant, the total citizen body was declining also. Polybius regarded it as a matter of common knowledge that the Romans could not in his day man fleets of the size of those of the period of the First Punic War (1, 64, 1). Since fleets were manned by *proletarii*, men below the property qualification for *assidui*, the size of the total citizen body is presumably assumed to be declining.

The immediate problems over the levy in the years after the middle of the second century BC were, then, partly caused by the unpopularity of the kind of war the oligarchy was waging, but they were also surely caused by the kind of economic exploitation of Italy which the oligarchy was increasingly practising. If the numbers of *assidui* and of all citizens were both declining, this was presumably the result in the first case of the loss of a holding of land adequate to provide the necessary property qualification, in both cases of the loss of a livelihood adequate to support a family. Both phenomena are associated with the growing estates of the rich and with the exploitation both of those and of public land which they controlled, by means of slave labour; this had presumably always existed in Italy, even outside Etruria (p. 21), but now became much more widely used.

It was a widely held belief at Rome that once upon a time all Roman families had held just enough land to support themselves and had themselves worked this land (the belief was of course incompatible with the belief in an early division of the *assidui* into five different property classes). The story of Cincinnatus called from the plough to save Rome exemplifies this belief and Cato's representation of himself as working *with* his slaves is an attempt to preserve something of the ideology involved. Whatever one may think of the aristocracy, the citizen body as a whole of the early and middle Republic clearly did scrape along on a plot just large enough when supplemented by the use of public land (see below) to support a family. The labour input needed was less than that available from the year's work of a peasant family, whence the part-time army of the early and middle Republic and whence also the fact that anyone who acquired a holding larger than a peasant plot could still work it with the labour of one family and thereby generate a surplus. The wealth which flowed into Rome especially from the beginning of the second century BC onwards encouraged, as we shall see, the development of large holdings; even if a large holding was still worked by the family who owned it, the result was the dispossession of another family. In fact, large holdings could also be worked by tenants or hired labourers, who were alike propertyless and not eligible as *assidui*, or by slaves (or indeed by a combination of free and slave).

The general development may be seen as the spread of great estates, *latifundia* (the word is not attested before the imperial age), provided one remembers that one man's large holding may be composed of a number of scattered components.

Some concentration of land holding no doubt occurred as a result of simple purchase; Rome or some of the other Italian towns no doubt came increasingly to seem paved with gold as the second century BC progressed, encouraging a peasant to sell up and move. Some Italians perhaps used the capital acquired from the sale of their land to set up as petty hucksters and try to make a fortune in the east. But pressure to sell no doubt shaded off into more violent expropriation; rural violence was endemic in Italy in Cicero's day and a poor man stood little chance of resisting the land hunger of a rich one. When the father of a family was away on a long war overseas, expropriation was of course even easier.[1]

Expropriation of freeholds was not, however, the only factor affecting the pattern of agrarian settlement in Italy in the second century BC; the rich were also engaging in the exploitation of increasing areas of *ager publicus*, public land. Much of what existed after 200 could be taken over without causing any further dislocation; for instance, in Lucania the great native urban centres did not survive the Second Punic War and much land there was no doubt simply waste.

But elsewhere, the owners of peasant plots needed *ager publicus* to survive. The figures attested for the areas of land actually owned by men settled individually or in colonies are often such that they could not have supported a family from their own property; common land available to the community, known as *ager compascuus*, is an attested phenomenon and in any case a necessary assumption.

By 167, pressure already existed at Rome to occupy (on a long-term basis) more than the permitted maximum of 500 *iugera* of *ager publicus* and to keep more than the permitted maximum of animals on other areas of *ager publicus*:[2]

> Is any law so harsh as to say that if someone wished to do something, he is to be fined half his estate, less one thousand (asses); if someone wished to have more than 500 *iugera*, the penalty should be so much; if someone wished to have a larger number of animals (pastured on *ager publicus*), the fine should be so much? We all want to have more, but we are not punished for it (Cato, *ORF* 8, XLII, 167).

The assertion of Roman control over Italy after 200 encouraged the development of long-distance transhumance, for instance between the winter pastures of Apulia and the summer pastures of the central Appennines; the need for winter pastures in particular led

1. It is sometimes argued that long absence of a man rendered his farm unworkable; given the nature of peasant farming in antiquity this is implausible, though a man's family might give up the unequal struggle in his absence.

2. The date of enactment of the law specifying these maxima is uncertain – fourth century or early second century BC.

both to the expropriation of peasant plots and to the occupation of *ager publicus* near peasant settlements (peasant plots and *ager publicus* near towns could of course also be profitably used for luxury cash crops).

Occupation of *ager publicus* then tended to make peasant plots unviable and combined with expropriation to hasten the flight from the land; the first process, like the second, was observed by contemporaries. The second century BC historian Cassius Hemina, discussing the struggle of the Orders, but no doubt seeing things in terms of the politics of his own day, talks of those who have been ejected from *ager publicus* because of their *plebitas*, because of their being mere plebeians (fr. 17 Peter). The celebrated speech of Ti. Gracchus, on the destitution of those who actually fight for Italy (Plutarch, *Tiberius Gracchus* 9 = *ORF* 34, I, 13), is clearly talking about veterans, who once were *assidui*, but now have no land. The first process, unlike the second, was also in part reversible – and it is that on which Appian concentrates:

The Romans gradually conquered Italy and regularly confiscated some of the land and either founded colonies or settled their own citizens on individual lots in the territory of existing cities. They regarded these settlements as garrisons. And of the land which came to them by right of conquest from time to time, the cultivated land they either distributed to these settlers or sold or rented out, the uncultivated land belonging to them by right of conquest, of which there was much, they offered for exploitation on a temporary basis to anyone who wished, in return for a proportion of the annual income, a tenth of the sown crops and a fifth of the produce of fruit trees; for they did not have the time to organize distribution of the land. And there was a rate of levy on those who pastured large or small animals.

The whole treatment of *ager publicus* was designed to increase the Italian race, which they regarded as extremely tough, in order to have allies who were kin. But things did not turn out that way. For the rich took over the bulk of the undistributed land and assumed in due course that no one would take it away from them; and they went on to take what other land there was which belonged in small plots to the poor and which adjoined their own, either by persuading them to sell or by forcing them out. So they came to farm great estates instead of small farms, using slave farmers and shepherds, to avoid free men being carried away to fight instead of farming. (Appian is here guilty of some anachronism, since propertyless men were not in theory at this stage eligible for military service.) This kind of exploitation brought the rich much wealth also from slave breeding, since the slave population increased undisturbed by military service (the argument is implausible, but may go back to contemporary fantasies).

So the powerful became very rich and slaves spread all over

1   Sarcophagus of L. Cornelius Scipio Barbatus, Musei del Vaticano, Rome. The elegant and sober decoration, adopting a classical Greek style, exemplifies the taste of the Roman aristocracy at the turn of the fourth and third centuries BC.
Deutsches Archäologisches Institut Rom

2   Round Temple in Forum Boarium, Rome. The earliest marble temple in Rome now surviving, the building exemplifies the transformation of Rome by the wealth which poured in during the second century BC

3   a & b 'Altar of Domitius Ahenobarbus', Musée du Louvre, Paris. The relief portrays a Roman census.
Deutsches Archäologisches Institut Rom

4   'Altar of Domitius Ahenobarbus', Staatliche Antikensammlung, München. The relief of Neptune, associated with that on the previous plate to form a single monument, shows the quality of the work which was being executed for members of the Roman aristocracy in the late Republic and was perhaps commissioned by L. Gellius Poplicola, who was censor in 70, and claimed descent from Neptune, as Caesar claimed descent from Venus (T.P. Wiseman, *Greece and Rome* 1974, 153).
Deutsches Archäologisches Institut Rom

CORNELIVS

CORNELIVS·LVCIVS·SCIPIO·BARBATVS·CNAIVOD·PATRE
PROGNATVS·FORTIS·VIR·SAPIENSQVE—QVOIVS·FORMA·VIRTVTEI·PARISVMA
FVIT—CONSOL·CENSOR·AIDILIS·QVEI·FVIT·APVD·VOS—TAVRASIA·CISAVNA
SAMNIO·CEPIT—SVBIGIT·OMNE·LOVCANA·OPSIDESQVE·ABDOVCIT

(a)

(b)

3

4

Italy and decline and shortage of manpower affected the Italians, worn out by subsistence farming and taxation and military service. And the only relief from this combination of ills was idleness, since the rich held all the land and used slaves instead of free to exploit it (*Civil Wars* I, 7, 27–31).

I have spoken so far as if the processes I have been describing were new to the second century BC; and to a certain extent they were. Long absence of peasant soldiers on military service made it easier to expropriate their land and to usurp communal rights over *ager publicus*, and the increase in the wealth of the oligarchy in the second century BC was so enormous (p. 74) as to represent a new factor. It was precisely that wealth, deriving from Rome's wars, which *had* to be invested somewhere, and, given the values of the Roman aristocracy, land was the only real possibility. It was also Rome's wars of the second century BC which provided slaves in almost unlimited numbers, from Sardinia in 177, where 80,000 were captured or killed, or from Epirus in 167, where 150,000 were captured. In due course, such numbers, increased by the development of the slave trade from the 140s onwards, brought about first brigandage and then the great slave wars of the period from 135 to 70; and by feeding the flight from the land they made the Roman revolution possible.

The hunger of the Roman aristocracy for land, in this case pasture-land, can be documented outside Italy; the waste land of Epirus was in due course grazed by the flocks of Atticus, friend of Cicero, presumably the successor to a line of *latifondisti* stretching back to 167; and in 155 Rome dealt with:

Delminium, once a great city; but the Roman commander reduced it to a village and made the plain round about into sheep pasture, because of the unruliness of its inhabitants (Strabo VII, 5, 5).

This (highly convenient) unruliness had involved attacking Rome's allies and killing her ambassadors.

Expropriation of peasant plots and occupation of *ager publicus* had probably long been endemic in Italy; the land hunger of the aristocracy may be reflected already in their opposition to the proposals of C. Flaminius (p.54). But as long as there was an ongoing programme of colonization and settlement, it mattered less that a peasant was forced off or abandoned his farm; he could go to a colony or settlement, become an *assiduus* once more and raise children.

Our literary record for the second century is of course incomplete; but even making all due allowance for the absence of Livy after 167, it still looks very much as if colonization and settlement were pursued with much less vigour after the reinforcement of Aquileia in 169. The reason is not hard to imagine. Colonies in particular served a strategic purpose and ceased to be founded in Italy because the strategic need for them had disappeared; outside Italy, Rome adopted a totally different mode of control, where control was necessary: a governor and a standing army (p.68). There was constant opposition at Rome to colonies outside Italy, which became in the end a *popularis* cause; the few colonies outside Italy during the Republic which were not *popularis* foundations were for the most part the result of the grant of colonial status, notably in Spain, to existing quasi-military settlements (themselves the result of the existence of a standing army).

The dangerous developments of the second century BC were then in large measure the result of the growth of Rome's empire, providing the oligarchy with wealth which had to be invested, making it easy for them to acquire extra land, providing them with slaves to work it, offering no alternative land elsewhere to those dispossessed. A part-time peasant army conquered the Mediterranean; that conquest then facilitated its destitution.

Three problems remain, the association of increasing use of slave labour with increasing unemployment of Roman peasants, the fate of the peasants forced to leave the land and the ways in which the aristocracy sold the produce of their growing estates and thereby derived income from them. The answer to the problem of the creation of a slave economy, as opposed to an economy in which slavery existed, at a time when free labour was available, no doubt slavery existed, at a time when free labour was available no doubt lies partly in a reluctance of former peasants to tie themselves wholly to wage labour and partly in the incredible cheapness of slaves. The last two problems are interconnected. Some peasants no doubt hung on in the vicinity of their former farms, surviving in distitution on casual labour at peak agricultural seasons – the Roman agricultural writers regularly assume the availability of casual labour and we shall see that much of the support for Ti. Gracchus was *resident* in the country. Some dispossessed peasants no doubt slipped into the army even before C. Marius abolished the property qualiication altogether, and accepted a life as a professional soldier, perhaps to be followed by settlement in the area of service; some men presumably emigrated to the east in the search of profitable employment in the areas controlled, if not ruled, by Rome. Others drifted into the towns of Italy in general and into Rome in particular where they provided for a wage services similar to those provided by the growing slave population of the city of Rome.[3] Unlike that slave population, they possessed a vote and one may surmise that some of the services they provided were of a political nature.

With the money they earned they provided a market for some of the produce of the estates of the rich. But they can hardly have absorbed more than a part of it and one needs urgently to envisage how the rich sold the rest of their produce, particularly in view of the apparent dominance of herding among their agricultural activities (documented by the dictum of Cato[4] recorded by Cicero, *de officiis* II, 89). Where did they sell the wool or meat?

Southern Italy had long been a major source of woollen goods (Tarentine sheep appear in Plautus, *Truculentus* 649) and the Roman aristocracy no doubt to a certain extent took over traditional markets; but I suspect that to a very substantial extent woollen and leather goods were sold to the contractors supplying

4. Artisan activity in Rome perhaps benefited from the decline of Capua after her revolt in the Hannibalic War; but Cato in his *de agri cultura* lists a number of towns where agricultural equipment could be purchased.

5. Cato is also the author of the *de agri cultura*, a rather ill-organized treatise on the new style of cash-crop agriculture, using slaves as the most important element of the labour force.

the Roman army, in other words that the Roman aristocracy used the produce of its estates as yet another way, this time indirect, of profiting from the revenues coming in from the empire.

X

Reform and Revolution

THERE WAS NO novelty in attempting reform (C. Licinius Crassus proposed unsuccessfully in 145 that the choice of priests be entrusted to a process of election rather than co-option); what marks out the tribunates of Tiberius Gracchus in 133 and his younger brother Gaius in 123 is in the case of both of them a degree of determination which aroused bitter opposition and led in the end to their violent deaths; and in the case of Gaius Gracchus a range of reforming interest which is unparalleled in any earlier figure.

The core of Ti. Gracchus' proposed agrarian law was the re-enactment of an earlier prohibition (p. 102) on the holding by an individual of more than 500 *iugera* (312.5 acres) of public land; sons were allowed to hold a further 250 *iugera* each; a commission of three men was to distribute land resumed by the state to the landless peasants in the countryside. Neither the contents of the proposed law nor its promulgation were frivolous; Ap. Claudius Pulcher, who had been consul in 143 and censor in 136 and was *princeps senatus* from 136, P. Mucius Scaevola, who was consul in 133, and P. Licinius Crassus, who was to be consul in 131, were all supporters of Ti. Gracchus; other more shadowy well-wishers appear in the sources.

The landless poor of the countryside came eagerly to Rome to vote for the law (Appian, *Civil Wars* i, 10, 38; Diodorus XXXIV–XXXV, 6, 1–2); the fate of C. Laelius' proposal (p. 92) induced Ti. Gracchus to take *his* proposal straight to the *concilium plebis* without consulting the senate. It was his right but it was not customary; in the face of such determination, the only course left open to the opposition was to persuade another tribune to veto the proposal and one of the ten was persuaded to do this.

Faced with the veto of his colleague, Ti. Gracchus had him deposed by vote of the *concilium plebis*; the measure was unprecedented, but again hardly illegal. It exposed, however, a fatal source of conflict in the Roman political system, which emerges even more clearly from the events surrounding Ti. Gracchus' death: if one accepted the principle of popular sovereignty, it was undoubtedly the right of the people to take away what it had given; equally, the blocking power of a magistrate within a college of magistrates and, by a process of assimilation, of a tribune within a college of tribunes, was a basic working rule, equivalent to a principle, of the Republic.

The law was eventually passed and the commission of three men set up consisting of Ti. Gracchus, his brother and Ap. Claudius; but opposition continued in the form of law-suits over the status of land claimed as public by the commissioners. A further law was passed conferring judicial powers on the commissioners. Their troubles, however, were not over:

The powerful were angry at everything which had happened and feared the increase in the influence of Tiberius (Gracchus); so they behaved insultingly towards him in the senate, using as an occasion his customary request for a tent to be provided at public expense for him when engaged in land distribution; despite the fact that others had often had such a request granted on slighter grounds, they refused it to him and fixed a daily expense allowance of nine asses (three asses for each commissioner, probably the daily wage of a Roman soldier) ... At this moment Eudemus of Pergamum brought to Rome the will of Attalus III who had died, in which the Roman people was named as the heir of the king; Tiberius (Gracchus) at once as leader of the people introduced a bill which provided that the royal treasure should be brought to Rome and be available to those citizens receiving land in the distributions, for equipment and stock for their farms.[1] (Plutarch, *Tiberius Gracchus* 13–14; the Livian tradition, that a gift of money was to be a substitute for land, is certainly tendentious.)

1. An illegitimate son of Attalus III, Aristonicus, tried to claim his heritage. His campaign, misleadingly and Romanocentrically called a revolt, was only put down in 129; it involved towards the end an interesting and ill-documented attempt to raise the lower orders against Rome.

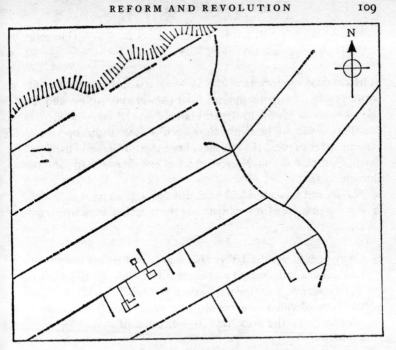

6. Plan of centuriation north-east of Luceria (Map 2)
The plan shows centuriation on two alignments, one perhaps dating from the foundation of the colony, one perhaps reflecting Gracchan assignations; internal divisions and individual farms appear within the main blocks of land; excavation shows the farms to have occupied the sites of earlier settlements and in some cases to have cultivated vines and fruit-trees.
Antiquity 1949, 67, Fig. 2

The commissioners finally began their work (see Fig. 6) and the opposition began to talk of vengeance on Ti. Gracchus in person when he became once more a private individual and liable to prosecution:

And when his friends seeing the threats made against him and the gathering of his enemies expressed the view that he should hold further tribunates in the future, he sought the favour of the people once again by promising other laws . . . (The actual proposals attributed to Ti. Gracchus here are almost certainly retrojections from the programme of his brother.) (Plutarch, *Tiberius Gracchus* 16)

The original supporters of the agrarian law had returned to the countryside to earn money from labour for the harvest and Ti. Gracchus was forced to depend largely on the votes of the city dwellers. Even so, he might have been re-elected; his opponents attempted to prevent the conduct of two assemblies and finally, led by P. Cornelius Scipio Nasica, attacked and killed the tribune and his supporters.

Nasica and Gracchus had been divided over an issue on which, given the premises from which they started, they were irreconcilable:

> (Why does Q. Aelius Tubero not ask) why there are in one state two senates and almost two peoples? For, you see, the death of Ti. Gracchus and indeed earlier the whole conduct of his tribunate divided one people into two parts (Cicero, *de re publica* 1, 31 – the work has a dramatic date of 129).

To Nasica, a breach of the principle of annual magistracies was an attempt at *regnum*, an attempt at sole rule, to Gracchus, it was the people's right to bestow the tribunate on whom it wished.

Other retrospective reflections suggest themselves also. The course of the tribunate of Ti. Gracchus exposed to full view the consequences of the dispersal of Roman citizens over the Italian peninsula. Roman citizens had been settled *viritim*, on individual plots, rather than in organized colonies, increasingly far from Rome, and Roman colonies had been founded which were not as in the past mere garrisons on the coast but were, rather, substantial settlements, often far from Rome. This latter development is reflected by the institution in Roman colonies early in the second century of a structure of full local government in the form of *duoviri*, a two-man board of magistrates; the rather distant communities of *cives sine suffragio*, Arpinum, Fundi and Formiae were given the vote in 188, but continued to possess full local self-government.

Citizenship which was in theory full citizenship had become detached from the *de facto* possibility of voting at Rome; the result was that the level of participation of the Roman citizen body as a whole in the process of government was reduced and the representativeness of a normal meeting of the assembly was diminished. This latter fact emerges from the disappearance of much of Ti. Gracchus' support once the agrarian law had been voted. The whole process is a sad consequence of something which as a whole had originally been a source of strength to Rome, her method of organizing Italy (p.35).

The tribunate of Ti Gracchus is also important as marking a step in the Hellenization of the Roman aristocracy; it is likely that the appeal to the principle of popular sovereignty over the deposition of a tribune was made in full knowledge of the existence of Greek discussions of the problems of politics. Not, of course, that Greek philosophy was necessarily a major influence on Ti. Gracchus; but it surely provided him with ammunition useful in the political battle in Rome: in the same way and in the same period, Greek literary skills continued to serve the aims of the Roman aristocracy, and Greek artistic skills were increasingly used to advertise its pretensions.

But perhaps the most important reflection which the tribunate of Ti. Gracchus can provoke is an attempt to estimate the true symbolic importance of the passage through the assembly of the bill making available to the agrarian commissioners the legacy of Attalus III of Pergamum (p. 108); support for Ti. Gracchus came in the first instance from men allowed decreasing access to the rewards of the empire which they had helped to win; a direct *mainmise* on some of those rewards is hardly a surprising reaction.

It was in fact the empire which made possible *largitiones*, disbursements of public money with political ends in view, and with them the *popularis ratio*, the political approach which sought support by enhancing the well-being of the people. There is from the time of the Gracchi onwards a recurrent link between *popularis* leaders and building programmes, and the readiness of Ti. Gracchus to use the resources of the empire was echoed by his successors. The colonization of Narbo in 118 and the proposed colonies of L. Saturninus involved the use of provincial land; revenue from Cyrene was used for corn-distributions in the 70s, the proposed agrarian settlement of Rullus in 63 again involved the use of provincial land, the younger M. Cato and his enemy

P. Clodius alike used the resources of the empire for corn-distributions.

For the moment, the Roman Republic drew back from the brink; despite some persecution of Ti. Gracchus' immediate humble or alien associates at the hands of P. Popillius Laenas, the agrarian commission was allowed to go on functioning, and P. Scipio Aemilianus, who had allowed himself a savage quotation from Homer to express his approval on hearing the news of Gracchus' death, found that he was not allowed to monopolize the senate:

> The detractors and denigrators of Scipio, taking their cue from P. Crassus and Ap. Claudius even after the death of these two keep part of the senate hostile to you (who think as Scipio), under the leadership of (Q.) Metellus (Macedonicus) and P. Mucius (Scaevola) . . . (Cicero, *de re publica* 1, 31 – highly tendentious, picking up the passage on p.110)

The attitude of P. Scaevola is particularly striking. He had refused to countenance the use of force to prevent the re-election of Ti. Gracchus, while being deeply worried about the possibility, and he now associated himself with Macedonicus, not previously a political ally, to save the essence of the Gracchan reform, which he had originally favoured; the absence of personal animus against Aemilianus emerges particularly clearly in the case of Macedonicus, who instructed his sons to carry the bier when Aemilianus died of disease in 129. Scaevola was both one of the earliest and one of the greatest of Roman jurists; the concern of a lawyer for the rule of law still held.

XI

Rome and Italy

THE *popularis ratio*, once formulated, was too attractive to be ignored by ambitious members of the Roman élite and the example set by Ti. Gracchus found ready imitators. But the awfulness of the way in which the tribunate had turned out had meanwhile politicized the normally passive majority of the senate and produced a climate of opinion hostile to gradual reform.

Yet the late second century saw the identification of two areas of government which urgently needed attention, the relationship of Italy to Rome and the organization of Roman rule in the Greek east. Some of the problems of both were of course touched on by traditional methods and by *popularis* politicians, often directly; but much energy was devoted to the futile manning of the battle lines between *optimates*, traditionalists, and *populares*. At the same time, the period of relative quiet overseas which followed the capture of Numantia in 133, the end of the Sicilian Slave War in 132 and the suppression of the forces of Aristonicus in 129 (p. 108) was broken by the outbreak in 112 of a war in Africa (which dragged on until it was ended by C. Marius as consul in 107 and proconsul in 106–105), and by the shattering defeat of Q. Servilius Caepio and Cn. Mallius Maximus by the Cimbri and Teutones at Arausio (Orange) in 105; that defeat was only avenged by the victories of C. Marius and Q. Lutatius Catulus in 102 and 101.

Despite Roman attempts to do something both about the east and about Italy, in 91 Italy went to war with Rome and in 88 Mithridates invaded Asia.

The measures of C. Gracchus during his two tribunates of 123–112 are partly developments of his brother's agrarian programme, partly minor enactments provoked by particular aspects of his brother's experiences; but they form also an attempt to shift radically the distribution of power within the Roman state and include an attempt to deal with the Italian problem, highlighted by certain consequences of the programme of 133; the roots of the problem, however, lie much deeper.

After the defeat of Hannibal, Rome had severely punished communities which had remained loyal, but which had been unable to meet their military commitments to Rome (p. 53); the treatment of communities which had rebelled was even more severe, ranging from destruction to deprivation of land or rights and the imposition of some additional burdens. The immediate corollary was that, for the generation after the Hannibalic War, the armies which fought for Rome included a higher proportion of non-Romans than of Romans; it is not surprising that there were complaints in 187 and 177 from certain Latin communities about loss of population by migration to Rome and in 177 from certain Italian communities about loss of population by migration to the Latin colony of Fregellae.

The effectiveness of Roman control over Italy, however is shown by the ruthlessness with which the decision largely to suppress the worship of Bacchus in Italy, taken in 186 after the peace with Syria, was put into effect; the spread of Dionysiac worship was perturbing for a number of reasons and its repression no doubt therefore particularly violent. Its adherents were organized, in a way which could be seen as constituting an alternative to, and therefore a threat to, the state; the unconventional morality associated with the cult was also no doubt a form of revolt. The form which the repression took provides a striking contrast with the pattern of witchcraft trials in early modern Europe, where popular hysteria generated a self-feeding process. In Italy in 186 the entire movement against the Bacchanals was articulated by the state and came to an abrupt end when security was assured. It may be doubted whether the spread of Dionysiac worship can be seen as the result of an enthusiastic response by outcasts of one sort or another to the availability of a religious escape; rather the spread was the result of a gradual and (until the Roman state took exception) uncontroversial take-over of a new outlook.

Seeds of stress, however, there undoubtedly were in Italy in the early second century; for the moment the senate was in control.

As the century progressed, the planting of colonies and the making of viritane assignations of land increasingly interspersed Romans among the non-Roman population of Italy; the resulting patchwork was a powerful force for the gradual Romanization of the peninsula, particularly combined with the fact of Roman government.

Meanwhile, substantial emigration from Italy to the Greek east had begun, of those anxious to exploit the opportunities offered to men of business; they included no doubt Romans and Italians dispossessed of land by the spread of great estates, with or without compensation, but increasingly as far as we can tell of Italians leaving voluntarily, seeking by private enterprise the rewards of empire which came automatically to the imperial people. Once abroad, Romans and Italians were regarded alike as *Romaioi* by Greeks and mingled on a basis of equality; thus also, the distinction between Roman and Italian came to seem less important in practical terms and its juridical perpetuation in the end came to be resented.

Appian persistently asserts that Italians were intended to, and did, benefit from the agrarian law of Ti. Gracchus; whereas according to Cicero:

(The enemies of Scipio) are not prepared to allow him to offer his help in such a dangerous situation as this (in 129), although he is the only person capable of doing anything; the allies and the Latins have been roused to anger, treaties have been broken, the commissioners are disturbing everything and devising something new every day, all worthy citizens are in a state of anguish (*de re publica* 1, 31 – picking up the passage on p. 112).

and even more forcefully:

(Ti. Gracchus) was steadfast in helping citizens, but ignored the rights and treaties of allies and Latins (*de re publica* iii, 41)

The dilemma may in fact be resolved by arguing that some humble Italians benefited, but that the Italian aristocracies objected to the threat to their control over their clients and also to their own loss of access to public land. It emerges from the epigraphically preserved agrarian law of 111 (largely winding up the Gracchan programme) that the Italian rich, like the Roman rich, had occupied public land and the commissioners in due course set out to resume and distribute this; some land had also been sold (to Romans) or distributed (to allies), and to much of this the legal title was now obscure.

At the instance of Aemilianus, jurisdiction was transferred from the commissioners to one of the consuls; it was then perhaps transferred back again after the death of Aemilianus. The extent and seriousness of allied agitation may perhaps be inferred from the emergency measure of 126 excluding aliens from Rome.

In 125, M. Fulvius Flaccus, one of the consuls of that year, proposed that citizenship be offered to the Italians, with the option of *provocatio* (p. 92) for those who did not want citizenship; the proposal came to nothing and the Latin colony of Fregellae rebelled and was destroyed. A more systematic assault on the problem was needed; it was one of the things to which C. Gracchus addressed himself in his tribunates of 123–122.

Even if the accusations against C. Gracchus reported by Plutarch, that he had encouraged the allies of Rome to revolt and had been involved in the affair of Fregellae, are no more than inventions intended to blacken his name after his death, it is likely that the problems relating to the Latins and the Italians, raised by the tribunate of his brother and highlighted by the revolt of Fregellae, were very much in his mind when he stood in 124 for the tribunate of 123. The rights of the Latins and the Italians and Roman abuses in Italy indeed bulk large in the surviving fragments of his speeches, though this may in part result from the fact that the measure to give Roman citizenship to the Latins and Latin rights to the Italians (p. 121) was the issue over which C. Gracchus fell from influence during his second tribunate in 122.

It would, however, in any case be wrong to suppose that the other measures of C. Gracchus were designed merely to orchestrate support for this measure. A man prepared after 125 to grasp the nettle over the rights of the Latins and the Italians may be expected to have been attracted by bold solutions to other problems.

Certainly the range of the problems with which he grappled is astonishing – and almost certainly was even greater than we can now perceive. Two measures of major importance are known to us only from a single source in each case, elsewhere the sources are frequently inadequate and in hopeless conflict. What is perhaps worse, they provide no firm chronology for the measures of his two tribunates and thus obscure any development in his thought which may have taken place.

Two proposed laws clearly spring from the experiences of his brother, one enacting that magistrates deposed by the people be debarred from further office (this measure was withdrawn), the other re-enacting the traditional view (Polybius vi, 16, 2) that courts capable of passing capital sentences could not be established except by the people (this was applied retroactively to P. Popillius Laenas, who had dealt with the supporters of T. Gracchus). Two other laws carry further the basic intentions of Ti. Gracchus, another agrarian law, probably involving consequential arrangements for road-building,[1] and a law establishing colonies, including one on the site of Carthage:

> I should regard as the most pernicious aspect of the legislation of C. Gracchus the planting of colonies outside Italy (actually only one). Earlier generations had carefully avoided this, since they saw that many colonies had become more powerful than their mother cities, Carthage than Tyre, Massalia than Phocaea, Syracuse than Corinth, Cyzicus and Byzantium than Miletus, and had always insisted on Roman citizens (temporarily abroad) returning to Italy from the provinces for the census. But Carthage was the first colony founded outside Italy; Narbo Martius was founded immediately after in the consulship of Porcius and Marcius (118) (Velleius ii, 7, 6–8).

We have seen that, after the Hannibalic War, Rome adopted a new mode of control, magistrates and standing armies, for the overseas territories which she acquired, in contrast to the mode of control used in Italy, colonies and viritane assignations (p. 68). By the age of Velleius (writing under the emperor Tiberius), overseas colonies had become unremarkable; his diatribe must go back to contemporary or near-contemporary arguments against C. Gracchus and provides an interesting example of the use of facts

1. The arrangements made by C. Gracchus for the upkeep of side roads perhaps involves, as do others of his measures, borrowing from Greek experience.

5   Triumphal monument of Sulla, Musei del Campidoglio, Rome. The helmeted head of Rome symbolizes the claim that the victory of Sulla was that of the *res publica*.

6   Triumphal monument of Sulla, Musei del Campidoglio, Rome. The eagle is the bird of Jupiter, supreme deity of Rome; the two Cupids, holding a plaque, no doubt once possessing a painted inscription, reflect Sulla's personal relationship with Venus.

7(a)   Denarii (Fitzwilliam Museum). Denarius issued by moneyer P. Nerva, 113 or 112 BC, reverse. 'The law of (C.) Marius indeed made the bridges (over which the voter passed) narrow (to prevent interference).' (Cicero, *de legibus* III, 38) The scene shows one voter receiving a ballot from an attendant below and another dropping his ballot into the box; the placard above bears the initial letter of the tribe involved.
M. H. Crawford, *Roman Republican Coinage*, Cambridge, 1974, no. 292

7(b)   Denarius issued by quaestor C. Fundanius, 101 BC, reverse. The scene shows C. Marius as *triumphator*, with his son riding on one of the horses, according to custom.
M. H. Crawford, no. 326

7(c) Denarius issued by the Italians, 90—89 BC, reverse. The representation of the bull trampling the wolf symbolizes the destruction of Rome by Italy.
Historia Numorum I, forthcoming, 'The Social War'

7(d)   Denarius issued by moneyers Kalenus and Cordus, 70 BC, reverse. The type portrays the reconciliation of Rome and Italy; but it is the former who has her foot on a globe as an indication of world rule.
M. H. Crawford, no. 403

7(e)   Denarius issued by moneyer Q. Pomponius Musa, 66 BC, reverse. The type is one of nine which portray the nine muses, in punning allusion to the name of the moneyer; the issue is also an example of artistic activity under the patronage of the Roman élite.
M. H. Crawford, no. 410/2

7(f)   Denarius issued by moneyer L. Aemilius Buca, 44 BC, obverse. The issue provides the earliest known portrait of Caesar.
M.H. Crawford, no. 480/6

8   Barberini statue, Musei del Campidoglio, Rome. The statue portrays a Roman aristocrat with the portrait busts of two ancestors. Helbig⁴ II, 1615 (Mansell Collection)

drawn from Greek history in the quarrels of the Roman aristocracy.

There were by the end of 123 few areas of the government of Rome left untouched by C. Gracchus. A *lex frumentaria* provided for the storing of corn and the sale of a limited amount in Rome at a fixed and no doubt to a certain extent subsidized price. The growth of Rome had presumably made it impossible for private enterprise to deal adequately with the provisioning of the city and some evening-out of the fluctuations of the market price had become necessary; the measure no doubt drew on Greek precedents. Now or later, C. Gracchus attempted to alleviate the problem of debt. A *lex militaris* enacted that soldiers should be provided with their clothing free and that no-one under the age of seventeen should be recruited; both facets of the measure illustrate the desperate state of the recruiting base of the Roman army, paupers who needed every *quadrans* of their pay and mere boys. The need for agrarian legislation had not become any less pressing in the decade between 133 and 123.

In the field of provincial government, C. Gracchus both established a general procedure for the annual distribution of provinces and arranged that the collection of the tax of the new province of Asia (created out of the territory of the kingdom of Pergamum) should be entrusted to the *publicani*, tax-farmers; the step was no doubt taken, as E. Badian remarks, in the interests of efficiency and perhaps included the levying of new harbour dues in Asia. Certainly a preserved fragment of a speech of C. Gracchus attests a concern with maximizing Roman revenues; it is a speech against a Lex Aufeia (Gellius XI, 10, 1–6), which is in my view most plausibly to be taken as a law giving much of Phrygia to Mithridates V of Pontus as a reward for the help given to Rome in suppressing the 'revolt' of Aristonicus. A retrospective Greek view of the change in the method of collecting the tax of Asia is brief – and bitter:

> By surrendering the provinces (actually only one) to the arrogance and greed of the *publicani*, he provoked a just hate of the Roman empire among the subject peoples (Diodorus XXXIV–XXXV, 25, 1, probably from Posidonius).

Rome reaped the result of that hate when Mithridates VI of

Pontus invaded Asia in 88. Yet that cannot have been C. Gracchus' intention. He had the senate return to the cities of Spain the cost of grain levied by the governor and sent to Rome (no doubt in an attempt to bid for popularity in opposition to the *lex frumentaria*) and part of his speech to the people after his return from serving as financial officer, quaestor, to the governor of Sardinia is reminiscent of the speeches of Cato:

> And so, Quirites, when I set out for Rome, I brought back from the provinces empty those money-belts which I had taken out full of silver; others brought back home amphorae full of silver which they had taken out full of wine (the story provides interesting evidence for the inadequacy of the *vino locale* of Sardinia in the eyes of the Roman aristocracy) (*ORF* 48, V, 28).

It is consonant with this attitude that C. Gracchus should wish to reform the procedure for trials for provincial misgovernment introduced in 149 (p. 76). His extortion law provided that those who heard such cases were to be jurors, concerned to pronounce on guilt, rather than *recuperatores*, concerned simply to assess damages. The jurors were to be chosen not from among senators, but from among *equites equo publico* (p. 200); the object was presumably to exclude senators as being biased in favour of their peers.[2] Under the new procedure, the praetor, the presiding magistrate, had no influence on the course of the trial; the jurors decided the case by a simple majority in a secret ballot. A penalty of double what had been extorted was prescribed. Provincials themselves could prosecute and need not rely on senatorial *patroni*.[3]

C. Gracchus' general interest in judicial procedure is also attested by a law against judicial conspiracy to procure a

2. It is unreasonable to suppose that in this or the preceding piece of legislation C. Gracchus was attempting to acquire the support of the *equites* as a group, let alone that a supposed new class of businessmen aligned itself with the opposition to the nobility after C. Gracchus. Few *equites* were *publicani* (p. 200) and few *publicani* were likely to sit on the new juries for the extortion court; the votes of the *equites* as a whole were presumably influential in the assembly which voted to acquit L. Opimius (p. 122).

3. The precise position over the permissibility of adjournment (which favoured the defendant) in this and subsequent laws is obscure.

conviction, but his extortion law is one of the most controversial elements of his legislation. It permitted moral collusion between *publicani* in a province and *equites* in Rome; for a governor who feared prosecution before a jury of *equites* was perhaps more likely to turn a blind eye to abuses by *publicani* (see p. 135). The measure was deeply resented by the senate as *lèse-majesté* and the composition of the juries of the extortion court and, by association, of other juries was bitterly contested for the next 50 years or so. C. Gracchus was accused, probably falsely, of saying that he intended to attack the position of the senate.

The extortion law clearly achieved a certain shift in the balance of power within the Roman state. A more radical proposal failed; it was to draw by lot the order in which the *centuriae* voted in the *comitia centuriata* (p. 168), thereby removing the automatic influence acquired by the wealthy in the *centuriae* of *equites* and of the *prima classis*, when they voted first.

The most radical proposal of all also failed, the proposal to give citizenship to the Latins and Latin rights to the allies; in a speech described by Cicero as *bona et nobilis*, good and noble, C. Fannius, consul in 122 and once a friend of C. Gracchus, played on Roman feelings of exclusiveness:

> If you give citizenship to the Latins, then, do you imagine that you will have space in the assembly as you now have, or that you will be able to attend games and festivals? Do you not think they will take up all the space? (*ORF* 32, I, 3)

C. Gracchus failed to carry the day and lost influence as a result; M. Livius Drusus was then emboldened to make a systematic attempt to erode his support overall; he was already tribune and

> proposed laws, with the one aim and intention of outdoing C. Gracchus in gratifying and pleasing the masses, like one of the rival demagogues in the *Knights* of Aristophanes . . . The senate had accused Caius of demagogy for proposing two colonies (Plutarch seems here to select the two particularly contentious colonies of Capua and Carthage) and opening them to citizens who were well-off (presumably among others), but co-operated with Drusus in his proposal for twelve colonies and the

settlement in each of 3000 citizens who were destitute; the senate was hostile to Caius as someone who curried favour with the masses because he distributed land to the poor while insisting that each settler paid rent to the treasury, but Drusus' proposal to abolish the rent paid by the settlers was acceptable to them; Caius' proposal to give citizenship to the Latins was anathema to the senate, but they abetted Drusus when he promulgated a law forbidding the flogging of a Latin with rods even on military service (see p. 93). And indeed Drusus himself when speaking before the people always asserted that he was making his proposals with the agreement of the senate, which *really* cared for the people (Plutarch, *C. Gracchus* 9).

The senate did not need instruction in the methods of diverting revolutionary support.

C. Gracchus failed to be re-elected tribune for a third term in 121; he knew how his brother had ended and, rather than see his measures repealed, armed his supporters and turned to violence. He, M. Fulvius Flaccus and their followers were summarily killed, after the senate had passed the so-called *senatus consultum ultimum*, a decree conferring moral backing on the consuls in whatever measures they might take and devised because the disappearance of the dictatorship (p. 57) had removed one possible way of meeting an emergency. L. Opimius, who took a leading rôle in the pogrom, was acquitted by the people when put on trial the following year; the victory of the oligarchy seemed complete.

XII

The End of Consensus

THE EARLY YEARS of the first century BC not only saw Italy and the east blow up in the face of Rome, they also saw two periods of civil war within the original Roman citizen body, preceded in the year 100 by an outburst of violence unthinkable even twenty-one years earlier. Then, the Roman oligarchy had once more drawn back from the brink. The quarrels of the years after 121 were pursued in the courts, but their bitterness increased rather than diminished as members of the oligarchy sought to exploit the political armoury made available by Ti. and C. Gracchus. At the same time the gradual abandonment of a programme of agrarian settlement prepared the way for the development of the personal army which L. Sulla used to inaugurate the First Civil War in 88.

L. Opimius was prosecuted by P. Decius Subulo and acquitted in 120 and on the strength of this success P. Popillius Laenas (pp. 112, 117) was recalled from exile. The fortunes of the following year were mixed: Subulo was himself prosecuted and acquitted, C. Marius as tribune succeeded in passing a law which prevented informal supervision of the 'secret' ballot (see Pl. 7a), but failed to prevent the passage of a law which wound up the programme of land distribution and offered distributions of cash to the people as a sop (see below; Plutarch, *Marius* 4, misunderstands his motives); an attempt to prosecute C. Papirius Carbo, who had abandoned his association with C. Gracchus, likewise failed. C. Marius and Subulo came to the praetorship together in 115, the former behaving himself, the latter not:

(A consul) ordered P. Decius Subulo as praetor, who had remained seated as he passed, to rise; (when he refused), he had his official dress torn and his chair of office smashed; and he decreed that no-one should go to him for legal decisions (*de viris illustribus* 72).

A childish incident, one might suppose, but a mark of the dissolution of the oligarchy, perhaps. Hysteria in a different context is apparent in the following year, with the revival of the institution of human sacrifice in connection with the denunciation of three Vestal Virgins for unchastity; human sacrifice had only previously taken place at Rome in connection with the military crises of the late third century BC.

The major source of strife within the Roman oligarchy, however, was the war against Jugurtha, a Numidian kinglet who stepped out of line and against whom Rome declared war in 112. Allegations of treason, venality and incompetence in the Roman campaign provoked the establishment in 109 of a *quaestio* by the tribune C. Mamilius Limetanus; it was staffed by *equites*, the 'Gracchan jurors' of the *quaestio* dealing with provincial misgovernment after 123. Resentment at their severity permitted in 106 a short-lived removal of this latter *quaestio* and any other special *quaestio* established on its model from the control of the *equites*,[1] a success much facilitated by the oratory of L. Licinius Crassus:

> Rescue us (senators) from our suffering, snatch us from the jaws of men whose savage lust can only be satisfied with our blood; do not let us owe homage to anyone, except to the entire Roman people, to whom homage is both possible and right (Cicero, *de oratore* I, 225).

But the people also voted C. Marius his first consulship, for 107, to deal with Jugurtha, in the course of which he both laid the foundations for his future prominence and took a step which marked the open acceptance of the failure of the programme of agrarian settlement initiated by Ti. Gracchus and continued by his brother:

1. The change was reversed probably by 104 and certainly by 101, by a law of C. Servilius Glaucia, in due course an associate of L. Saturninus. There is no reason otherwise to suppose that the two courted the *equites*.

So the revolution initiated by the younger Gracchus ended thus; and a law was passed not long after permitting those who had been assigned *ager publicus* to sell it, over which there had been dispute earlier; for the elder Gracchus had already legislated against this; and immediately the rich bought from the poor or forced them out under the cover of a simulated purchase. So things got even worse for the poor, until Sp. Thorius as tribune (in 111, by a law much of which is preserved on a bronze tablet, *Roman Statutes*, no. 2) introduced a law that no more *ager publicus* should be distributed, but that it should all remain in the possession of those who now held it and that all should pay a *vectigal*, fee, for it to the state and that this money should be available for distributions to the poor. The result was some relief for the poor because of the distributions, but no encouragement to an increase in population. The Gracchan legislation was thus now repealed by devices of this kind, despite the fact that it would have been wholly admirable in its consequences if it could have been carried out; not much later another tribune abolished the *vectigal*, fee, and the Roman people lost everything. So Rome was now even shorter of citizens and soldiers, and had lost revenue from the land along with the possibility of distributions . . . (Appian, *Civil Wars* 1, 27, 121–4)

The step which C. Marius took in 107 of enrolling the *capite censi*, those without property who were simply listed in the census, was a logical one; it was not wholly unprecedented (see Ennius, *Annales* line 183 V, on the Pyrrhic War, 'the *proletarius* (another word for a *capite census*) is equipped with shield and fierce sword at public expense, and they watch over the walls and the city and the forum'); and the property qualification had become increasingly meaningless as the second century progressed. But the measure presumably made available for military service *some* men previously excluded; it also marked the abandonment of one of the three ways (pp. 168–9) in which the Roman citizen body had been articulated at least since the fourth century BC and excited controversy in retrospect; the hostile tradition asserted that C. Marius had changed the method of recruitment simply to court popularity or to provide a counterpart to his own humble origins;

his defenders asserted that the new system was more democratic and that propertied recruits were not available and even changed the occasion of his measure to 104, in order to justify it by reference to the threat posed by the Cimbri and Teutones, greater than that posed by Jugurtha.

At all events, the *proletarius*, who had hoped for land from the Gracchan legislation, was now encouraged to join the army; armed again at public expense, he no longer watched over the walls and the city and the forum, but over his own interest:

> Some claimed that C. Marius acted as he did because of a shortage of propertied recruits, others because of his wish as consul to court popularity, because he had been supported and raised up by the poor and the poorer a man was the better a follower he was of men greedy for power; his own property was not dear to him, since he had none, and anything would be justified if he was rewarded for doing it (Sallust, *Bellum Jugurthinum* 86, 3).

The desired reward, of course, was not simply the pay of a soldier, but an *ad hoc* grant of land at the end of the period of service:

> L. Appuleius Saturninus, a seditious tribune of the people, in order to win favour with the soldiers of C. Marius, passed a law that a hundred iugera of land in Africa should be assigned to each veteran; when his colleague M. (?) Baebius attempted to interpose his veto, he got him out of the way by a volley of stones from the mob (*de viris illustribus* 73).

A colonial law in 103 presumably encouraged further recruitment of *capite censi* and L. Saturninus proposed agrarian settlement and colonial settlement as tribune again in 100 (after murdering a competitor for office during the election); the former law was certainly passed by violence. C. Marius needed the laws for his veterans; but when the tribune turned to further murder to ensure the election of C. Servilius Glaucia as consul for 99, C. Marius was forced to bow to public opinion and act against the pair and their followers; they took to arms and fled to the Capitol, surrendered on the promise of safety and were in due course lynched.

In my view, C. Marius had extracted from the senatorial leadership before acting a promise that his veterans would be settled. Once again, the Roman oligarchy drew back from the brink of disaster, but their increasing ambition and decreasing scrupulousness were still at work. The Roman poor were now armed – and alienated from traditional patterns of behaviour, as the ready resort to violence in the years from 103 shows.[2]

Meanwhile, the consensus which held Roman Italy together, shaken by the events of 133–123, was also breaking down. Just as the poor fought increasingly for the benefit of the oligarchy, so Italians and Romans had fought side by side to create the Mediterranean empire, which Rome now possessed; but much of the tax revenue from it was spent in Rome. In Italy, the effects remained of a mixing process, which had allowed allies to join Latin colonies and Latins to join Roman colonies or to come to Rome, even if the process itself had come to an end (p. 104) and the barrier between Romans and others been made greater as a result; though infiltration of colonies by outsiders was a permanent feature of life in Italy. Ti. Gracchus had probably seen that the agrarian problems of Rome could not be treated in isolation from those of Italy (p. 115) and in 125 the notion of giving Roman citizenship to the Italians, in order to reconcile their upper classes to a loss of access to *ager publicus*, had been floated. It is hardly surprising that the Italians came to resent both their symbolic subjection to Rome, the fact that they had no vote at Rome and provided no magistrates at Rome, but were subject to the commands of Rome and of her magistrates, and what were undoubtedly abuses of power by Rome and Romans.

The major abuse of power by Rome was the calling up towards the end of the second century of an increasing proportion of allied troops. In Greece in 146 allies slightly outnumbered Romans in the army, in Spain in mid-century the numbers were more or less equal, in Illyria in 135 this was also the case. But the agrarian crisis deepened at Rome and the shortage of *assidui* worsened; when Ti. Gracchus failed to reverse the trend, the Roman reaction was to call up ever more allies, and in the wars against Jugurtha and

2. The seriousness of reforming purpose manifest in some of Saturninus' and Glaucia's legislation needs to be reconciled with this fact; both knew what had happened to Ti. and C. Gracchus.

against the Cimbri and Teutones the ratio of allies to Romans was about two to one. The enrolment of Roman *capite censi* by Marius made no difference to the burden on the allies. Velleius again preserves in P. A. Brunt's words, the 'indignant rhetoric' of contemporary polemic; the nature of the Italian perception of the situation is important:

> The fate of the Italians was as savage as their cause was truly just; for they were demanding citizenship in the state whose empire they defended with their arms. In every year and in every war they served with twice as many foot and horse as the Romans and yet were not given the right of citizenship in the very state which had reached through their efforts so high a position that it could look with contempt on men of the same race and blood as if they were outsiders and foreigners (ii, 15, 2).

A sombre reminder of the nature of agrarian developments in Italy was provided at the very end of the second century BC by the outbreak of another slave war in Sicily.

At the same time abuses of power by individual magistrates, highlighted by C. Gracchus, continued:

> For there was a certain Latin called Saunio, a comedian . . . but the Picentes, wishing to deprive the Romans (in the audience) of the pleasure and delight of watching him, resolved to kill him. He, seeing what was going to happen came onto the stage (and said) 'I am not a Roman, but like you am liable to be subjected to the floggings of Roman magistrates . . .' (Diodorus XXXVII, 12, 2–3, again a passage important for the Italian perception of the situation)

The story also illustrates another important fact, that the cultural developments which had taken place at Rome as a result of close and prolonged contact with the Greek world had also affected Italy. Beside an actor from Latium among the Picentes one can cite the distribution in Italy by L. Mummius of plundered works of art from Greece; in some respects indeed Italy was in advance of Rome. The tenth-rate Samnite town of Pompeii possessed a stone theatre from the late second century BC (see Fig. 7), planned as part

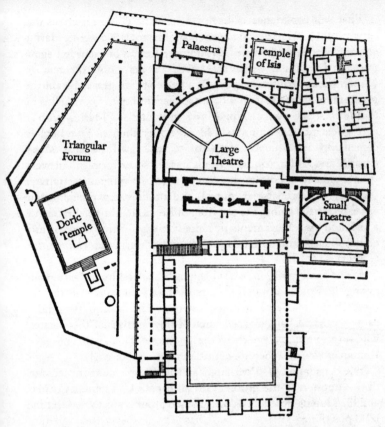

7 Plan of complex of public buldings at Pompeii (see. p. 128)

of an enormous monumental complex (perhaps not completed till
the Sullan age); the great sanctuary at Palestrina belongs also to
the late second century BC, as do monumental complexes at
Pietrabbondante and Vastogirardi, in the Samnite heartland. The
financial resources derived from the exploitation of the Greek east
by Italian men of business (as well as from such things as the export
of wine from Campania to Gaul) was being poured into
ostentatious projects in their home towns; the Social War is
unthinkable without the availability of those financial resources,
but the earlier purposes to which they were put are also a measure
of the self-confidence of the cities of Italy.

That self-confidence is likely to have been increased by the career of C. Marius, a *novus homo* from the recently (188) enfranchised community of Arpinum. After an unexciting beginning – the military tribunate with P. Scipio Aemilianus at Numantia, the tribunate (p. 123), a failure to win the aedileship, a praetorship achieved with difficulty, a legateship to Q. Metellus in Numidia – the consulship of 107 provided C. Marius with a springboard to a position held by no earlier Roman. Five further consulships in sequence, from 104 to 100, saw the defeat of the Cimbri and Teutones; as a result of this some form of cult was spontaneously offered to the victor (note that religious activity is slipping out of senatorial control) and a totally new phenomenon appeared in the coinage of the Roman Republic, the celebration of a man and his achievements by moneyers wholly unrelated to him; one moneyer went so far as to portray C. Marius as *triumphator* (Pl. 7b).

At the same time, C. Marius himself showed by his actions in giving the Roman franchise as a reward for valour in battle that he cared little for legal distinctions over citizenship. A similar carelessness perhaps marked some of the censuses of this period, with no attempt made to check the assertions of a man that he was a Roman citizen and therefore entitled to be registered.[3]

The censors of 97–6 perhaps had their suspicions aroused and drew attention to the problem; at all events L. Licinius Crassus and Q. Mucius Scaevola as consuls in 95 took steps to reassert the legal position:

For they passed during their consulate that law about which Cicero is here speaking, on the restoration of allies to their own citizenship. For since the peoples of Italy were gripped by an intense desire for the Roman citizenship and as a result a large number of them were behaving as if they were Roman citizens, a law seemed necessary to restore everyone to his own due citizenship. But the loyalties of the upper classes of the peoples of Italy were so alienated by that law that it was perhaps the chief cause of the Social War which broke out three years later (Asconius 67C).

3. There is no evidence that the colonial law of L. Saturninus went beyond the traditional provision allowing the enfranchisement of three men in each colony.

The outcry brought about at any rate a certain change of heart; in 91 L. Licinius Crassus was one of the chief supporters of M. Livius Drusus in his attempt to enfranchise the Italians; Drusus indeed enjoyed much support in the senate, though in the end not enough, whereas in 95 senatorial opinion was probably wholly in favour of the law of Crassus and Scaevola. A certain willingness to consider reform and a certain flexibility in the face of problems is still apparent within the Roman oligarchy; both can be documented also in the field of provincial affairs.

The Roman oligarchy after 121 was not only preoccupied with the fissures laid bare by the tribunates of Ti. and C. Gracchus and with the new possibilities for political activity provided by the emergence of the *popularis ratio*; they were also, for whatever reason, incapable of producing a quick solution to the problem posed by Jugurtha and, very shortly thereafter, faced with the cataclysm of the migration of the Cimbri and the Teutones. It is not surprising that the east was relatively neglected. The northern frontier of the province of Macedonia was continually under attack and was often penetrated; the piracy which in due course fed the Roman slave-trade was allowed to go unchecked:

It was Tryphon who was responsible for the Cilicians beginning to organize their gangs of pirates, together with the incompetence of the kings who then ruled in succession over Syria and also over Cilicia; for given the success of his revolutionary activity, others also took to starting revolutions and the quarrels of brothers with each other made their country liable to attack by anyone who wished. The exporting of slaves encouraged the Cilicians above all to take to piracy (as opposed, for instance, to demanding a ransom), for it was extremely profitable; the slaves were easily caught and there was a large and wealthy market not at all far away, Delos, which could receive and despatch tens of thousands of slaves on the same day . . . The reason was that when the Romans became rich after the destruction of Carthage and Corinth they used enormous numbers of slaves; and the pirates, seeing how easy it all was, flourished one and all, themselves going on raids and acting as slave dealers. And the kings of Cyprus and Egypt co-operated with them in all this, being enemies of the kings of Syria; nor were the Rhodians friendly to the kings of Syria, so that they did not help either. And at the same time the pirates pretended to be slave dealers and so were unhindered in their evil-doing. And at that time not even the Romans thought much about the areas beyond the Taurus; but they did send Scipio Aemilianus, to see what was going on in the tribes and the cities of the area, and after him others; and they decided that the piracy was the result of the incompetence of the kings, although they were too ashamed to take away the succession from the heir of Seleucus I Nicator since they had themselves confirmed him in his rule . . . Eventually the Romans were forced to put down the pirates by force and by means of an army, once they had grown powerful, although they had not taken any steps to stop them becoming powerful. Anyway, it is hard to condemn the Romans for negligence; for they were involved with other affairs nearer at hand and more urgent and so could not pay attention to affairs that were far away (Strabo XIV, 5, 2).

Perhaps most serious of all, extortion by governors and the exactions of *publicani*, tax-farmers, particularly in the province of Asia, were in the process of alienating the provincial populations from Rome. The wealth derived from the east in part of course returned to the east, in exchange for commodities which the east could provide, in order that the next round of tax, gubernatorial extortion and exactions by *publicani* could be met; the commodities involved were works of art to decorate the public places and private dwellings of Italy, land in the east, increasingly bought up by Romans and Italians, and slaves.

But much wealth of course came west, to feed the luxury of the upper classes:

Sergius Orata was the first person of all to invent oyster ponds, in the area of Baiae, in the time of L. Crassus the orator, before the Social War; he did not do this to satisfy his own taste, but to make money, and indeed earned enormous sums by his remarkable talent; he was also the first person to invent shower-baths and bought up villas in order to fit them out in this way and then immediately sell them (Pliny, *Naturalis Historia* ix, 168).

8   Roman building styles in *opus quasi-reticulatum* and *opus reticulatum*.

This picture of the emergence of speculative building for the rich at the turn of the century is corroborated by the observation of F. Coarelli that the spread at the same time of the style of building in *opus quasi-reticulatum* and *opus reticulatum* is the result of 'industrial' building, the large-scale production of similar units (Fig. 8).

The wealth which came west, however, also fed, through competition in display of wealth and through bribery in elections and trials, the internal conflict within the Roman oligarchy; further neglect of the east was thereby encouraged.

Yet as with Italy, an awareness of the problems and a willingness to attempt solutions are both in evidence. The Second Sicilian Slave War was provoked in 103 when C. Marius asked Nicomedes of Bithynia for troops to fight against the Cimbri and Teutones: Nicomedes replied that his subjects had been taken by slave-traders; the senate then proclaimed that no free ally might be a slave in a Roman province and disappointed expectations led to a rising of slaves in Sicily.

But Rome also set out to do something about piracy in the east and in 102 a praetor, M. Antonius, was sent against them; in 100 a law was passed which took wide-ranging measures relating to the government of the east (*Roman Statutes*, no. 12).

This law, a 'Law concerning the praetorian provinces', apart from announcing the Roman intention to deal with piracy, makes various arrangements for Macedonia and Asia, consequential upon the success of T. Didius and M. Antonius respectively, and regulates various aspects of a governor's status; it also refers to an earlier Lex

Porcia, which seems to be the first law to attempt to prescribe norms of conduct for a governor. Similarly, the extortion legislation of C. Servilius Glaucia of 104 or 101 goes beyond provisions designed to enable provincials to recover what has been extorted and again attempts to regulate the conduct of a governor. The three laws fit into a whole pattern at the turn of the century of reviving interest in the government of the provinces, particularly in the east.

It is likely that the decree of the senate adjudicating between the city of Pergamum and the *publicani*, in favour of the former, is to be dated to 101. Ephesus appealed successfully to the senate against the *publicani* in the same general period, similar appeals, also successful, from Priene and Ilium belong in the 90s and 80s. The renewal of a treaty between Rome and the small Aegean island community of Astypalaea in 105 and the granting of a treaty to Thyrrheium in Acarnania in western Greece in 94 are likewise to be seen as the result of successful attempts by provincial communities to safeguard their status. Also in 94 a decree of the senate enacted that loans (for the purpose of bribing powerful Romans) might not be made to envoys from provincial communities. A law of 68 relating to Termessus in south-western Asia Minor refers back to the year 91, clearly a year in which the status of Termessus underwent important regulation.

It is also extremely important to notice that the will to do something about the east appears both in measures of *popularis* origin such as the law of 100 and in senatorial measures; the central concern of those who affected the *popularis ratio* and of their opponents was after all the *res publica* and the former can be seen as moving into the field of policing the activity of the governing class; the consequent flood of *legislation* dealing with administrative details more suitable to senatorial decrees is in the same tradition. It is in this context interesting that E. Gabba has been able to delineate a group of *popularis* figures at the turn of the second and first centuries BC who were in the forefront of the development of Roman culture, at once the heirs and the competitors of the Hellenizing aristocracy of the early second century and later. On the other side of the coin it is symptomatic that L. Marcius Philippus, the future consul of 91, proposed in his tribunate an agrarian bill; an optimate also could attempt to steal the enemy's clothes.

(a)

(b)

(c)

(d)

(e)

(f)

The whole process of resumption of responsibility in the east culminated with the governorship of Asia by Q. Mucius Scaevola, probably in 94:

> When sent out to Asia as governor, he chose the best of his friends, Q. (a mistake for P.) Rutilius, as his adviser and sat with him in council, arranging everything and judging the cases which came up in the province. And he decided that his staff and he should pay all their expenses from their own pockets. Furthermore by the frugality and simplicity of his life-style and by his justice and incorruptibility he restored the province from its previous misfortunes. For his predecessors in Asia had taken the tax-farmers into partnership, the men who served as jurors for the *quaestiones* in Rome, and had filled the province with examples of lawlessness. But he was incorruptible and law-abiding in his jurisdiction and not only relieved those in the province from all fear of informers, but also curbed the lawless practices of the tax-farmers. For he ensured fair trials to those who had been wronged and in every case found the tax-farmers guilty, compelling them to reimburse their financial losses to those who had been wronged, while he ensured that charges involving a capital offence actually had a capital sentence passed. Indeed he prevented the manumission of the chief agent of the tax-farmers, who was prepared to offer a great deal of money for his freedom and had reached an agreement with his master, condemned him to death and had him crucified . . . So the pre-existing hatred of the empire was diminished as a result of his wisdom and virtue and the assistance he was able to give, and he received cult from those whom he had benefited and also gained full recognition of his achievements from his fellow-citizens (Diodorus XXXVII, 5 and 6).

The emphasis on the hostility of Scaevola to the *publicani* perhaps derives from Posidonius; they seem to have been one of his bêtes noires, along with the *equites* as a whole, no doubt in part deservedly. At all events P. Rutilius Rufus was condemned on his return under the now much more comprehensive law *de repetundis*, extortion law, perhaps on a charge of accepting bribes, in the context of trials of *publicani*.

Meanwhile, the inhabitants of Asia offered cult to Scaevola, perhaps as a new founder of their existence, the senate held up the edict in which Scaevola laid down the principles according to which he proposed to govern as an example to later governors of Asia; Cicero took it over when he went to Cilicia in 51.

Nor was Scaevola unique; in Sicily a governor who was perhaps L. Sempronius Asellio acquired a similar reputation to that of Scaevola:

(He), although only the son of a quaestor, himself became a praetor and was sent out as governor of Sicily; he found the province in ruins, but restored the island to prosperity by the best possible means. For like Scaevola he chose the best of his friends as legate and adviser, a man called Gaius (Sempronius) Longus, who affected a sober and old-fashioned life-style, and a man called Publius along with him, who had the best reputation of the *equites* living in Syracuse; the latter was a man of outstanding moral virtue, quite apart from being well-endowed by fortune with the good things of life (a characteristic Stoic viewpoint, presumably deriving from Posidonius) . . . (Diodorus XXXVII, 8, 1–2)

In 95 also, Sicily was the scene of Roman activity, which illustrates one of the fundamental principles which moved the Roman government when it had occasion to intervene in the affairs of the subject communities:

The inhabitants of Halaesa, in return for their own and their ancestors' many great services to our state of their own accord recently (in 95 – Cicero is speaking in 70) asked our senate to lay down rules for them, when they were in dispute over the choice of their senate. The senate decreed in complimentary terms that C. Claudius Ap.f. Pulcher, who was praetor, should draw up rules for them about the choice of the senate. C. Claudius Pulcher formed a *consilium* of all the Claudii Marcelli who were available (for the institution of the *consilium* see p. 25) and after consulting them laid down rules for the people of Halaesa, in which there were detailed regulations on the age of candidates, that no-one under 30 should be chosen, on 'trade', that no one who had been involved in it should be chosen, about the property qualification, and so on (Cicero, *II in Verrem* ii, 122).

Roman involvement in provincial affairs was motivated by self-interest as well as by a concern for justice; when she could she placed the landed gentry firmly in control and made sure they knew that their survival depended on the perpetuation of Roman rule. Rome chose her allies well; but not even they could save the province of Asia from Mithridates in 88, despite the passionate loyalty and self-sacrifice of many of them:

King Mithridates sends greetings to his satrap Leonippus. Chaeremon the son of Pythodorus has already entrusted for safety to the city of Rhodes those of the Romans who escaped, together with his sons, and now, learning of my approach, has himself fled to the temple of Artemis at Ephesus and from there sends letters to the Romans, the common enemies of mankind. The fact that he has got off scot-free for the wrongs he has already committed encourages him to further offences against us. See how best you can bring him to us or keep him in prison and under guard until I am free to deal with him (B. Welles, *Royal Correspondence*, no. 74).

XIII

The World Turned Upside Down

IN 91, THE ITALIAN ALLIES went to war with Rome; in 88 Mithridates VI Eupator of Pontus invaded the province of Asia. The war against the Italian allies was for all practical purposes a civil war and it was followed in 88 by the march on Rome of L. Cornelius Sulla. On that occasion he held power only briefly and then went off to deal with Mithridates, but he returned in 83 and in due course placed power in the hands of the group whose right it was, in his view, to control the *res publica*. A generation later, in 49, Caesar crossed the Rubicon; he left the *res publica* to be fought over by those who claimed to be his heirs, until his adopted son established a monarchy which lasted without interruption for as long as Rome herself.

After his death late in 91, in the year of his tribunate, M. Livius Drusus became a by-word for obsessive activity and consuming ambition; at the same time, the Roman world had to find an explanation for the cataclysm of the Social War. The optimate tradition, represented by Cicero and probably by Posidonius also, remembered Drusus as someone who made another attempt to break the stranglehold of the *equites* on the courts,[1] in fact as *senatus patronus*, patron of the senate. This tradition was prepared to forgive him a law on corn distribution and an agrarian law in an attempt to win support (another tribune in association with him also passed an agrarian law, a

---

1. Probably by constituting a mixed *album*, list, of senators and *equites* (Cicero, *pro Rabirio Postumo* 16; *pro Cluentio* 153); *equites* who served as jurors were now for the first time to be made liable to prosecution for judicial corruption. A mixed *album* was in fact created by the Lex Plautia of 89.

Lex Saufeia). An element of the tradition even saw the law to enfranchise the Italians as promulgated with the same end in view.

Another element in that tradition, however, saw Drusus as responsible for the Social War:

> Accordingly when the citizenship promised to the allies was not forthcoming, the Italians in their anger began to plot revolt. This book contains an account of their meetings, of their plots and of the speeches made in the gatherings of their leaders. As a result M. Livius Drusus, of whom even the senate had come to disapprove, as being the author of the Social War, was killed at home, no-one knows by whom (Livy, *Epitome* 71).

The legislation which Drusus *had* passed was invalidated. In due course, wild rumours circulated that the Italians had taken an oath to have the same friends and enemies as Drusus, that there had been a plot to kill the consuls and that the Italian leader Q. Poppaedius Silo had set out for Rome with 10,000 armed followers 'from among those who feared examination (under the Lex Licinia Mucia, p. 130)' with the intention of surrounding the senate and had only been dissuaded at the last moment. The rumours provide eloquent testimony of the timorousness of much of the Roman governing class. The reasons for that fearfulness perhaps emerge in part from the later characterization of the attitude to enfranchisement of the optimate tradition by the author of a political pamphlet attributed to Sallust ([Sallust], *ep. ad Caes.* II, 6, 1):

> A free state will become a monarchy, if a huge multitude attains the citizenship by virtue of the activity of one man.

The precise relationship of the different parts of the programme of Drusus is probably irrecoverable (according to Pliny *NH* XXXIII, 46 the programme had included a proposal to debase the silver coinage; Pliny has perhaps wrongly attributed a step which *was* taken a few years later.) But Drusus had enjoyed important support, that of M. Aemilius Scaurus, *princeps senatus*, and of L. Licinius Crassus, as is recorded by Cicero, in the best picture we possess of a senatorial debate:

It turned out that Crassus returned to Rome on the last day of
the dramatic festival, deeply disturbed by the speech which
Philippus was said to have delivered as an informal harangue;
everyone said that he had announced that he must devise some
other plan of action, that he could no longer transact the business
of the *res publica* (he was consul) with the senate as at present
constituted; early on 13 September 91 Crassus and a full senate
came to the senate house at the summons of Drusus. There
Drusus delivered a string of complaints against Philippus and
then made a formal report in the senate on the specific fact that a
consul in an informal harangue had made such a bitter attack on
the senate . . . Crassus bewailed the fate which had befallen the
senate, and its defencelessness; the inherited prestige of that
body was being plundered, as if by some lawless pirate, by a
consul, whose duty it was to behave as a good parent and a
faithful guardian towards it; nor indeed was it a matter for
surprise if someone who had squandered the resources of the *res
publica* as a result of his policy was now attempting to remove
the senate from any rôle in determining the policy of the *res
publica*.

Philippus was a man of violent temperament and a good orator
and readier than most to respond; Crassus as it were sparked him
off by his speech and it was more than he could stand; he flared
up and tried to put Crassus in his place by seizing some of his
property as security (for a proposed fine).

Particularly in response to this, the remarks of Crassus
seemed almost divinely inspired; he said that he did not regard
as a consul someone to whom he himself was not acceptable as a
senator. 'Do you, who treat the very authority of the entire
senate as a security and have made away with it in full sight of the
Roman people, do you imagine that I can be deterred by the
forfeit of any of my property? If you want to put Crassus in his
place you will have to deprive him of more than these; you must
cut out this tongue with which I speak; but even when that is
torn out I shall still be free to condemn your viciousness with my
breath.'

Everyone said that he spoke a great deal and used every ounce
of courage, intellect and strength and that he pronounced the
opinion which the full senate then endorsed, cast in elegant and

dignified terms, 'That the Roman people should be assured that neither the advice nor the loyalty of the senate had ever failed the *res publica*'; he also took care to be present when the decree was committed to writing (as is clear from the written codicil attached to it) (Cicero, *de oratore* III, 2–5).

A Lex Varia instituted a witch-hunt against those held to have encouraged the Italians; meanwhile, the war actually began with the assassination late in 91 of the Romans present at Asculum; Rome was still trying to preserve her hold by the traditional use of *clientelae*, as important in Italy as overseas (p. 136):

When the Romans realized what was happening, they sent round some of their own people to the cities, especially those who were close to any particular group in the cities, in order to find out inconspicuously what was happening. And one of these, seeing a young man being taken as a hostage from Asculum Picenum to another city informed the proconsul Q. Servilius, who was in the area . . . But Q. Servilius, rushing to Asculum on the spur of the moment and issuing harsh threats to the Asculani in assembly (according to Diodorus XXXVII, 13, 2, Servilius also treated the Asculani as slaves – note the theme of *libertas*), was killed in effect by people who supposed their plot was discovered. His legate Fonteius was killed with him . . . And when they fell, there was no mercy for the other Romans, but the Asculani fell on all those who were among them and killed them and plundered their belongings (Appian, *Civil Wars* I, 38, 170).

Apart from some coin legends (see Pl.7c), the Italians themselves have left no account of their motives in actually fighting against Rome after 91, in order to win the citizenship which we have already seen them seeking (pp. 114, 126); much of the difficulty in assessing those motives as reported by others lies in the ambiguity of the word *libertas*, freedom, closely linked in Roman thought with *civitas*, citizenship (the link is to be found also in Strabo V, 4, 2), but capable of covering both personal rights or political rights, within a Roman context, and outright independence. It is also important to remember that the aspirations of the allies down to 91 were not necessarily those which were dominant after 91.

Once the war had broken out, the Italians were in any case forced to organize a state, which of course also arrogated the right of a sovereign state to produce coinage:

The most important and at the same time the largest of the Italian cities was Corfinium, which had recently been designated as their common centre, in which they had established the other institutions appropriate to a large city and an imperial one and in particular a large forum and a senate-house; they also got together a good stock of everything necessary for the prosecution of the war, including a great deal of money and a plentiful supply of food. And they established a senate in opposition to the Roman senate, consisting of 500 men, from which those worthy of ruling the country and of taking counsel for the common safety of all were expected to emerge; they entrusted the management of the affairs connected with the war to them, giving the senators full powers. And they decided that two consuls and twelve praetors should be elected each year . . . Having thus organized everything carefully and having set up their own state for the most part along the same lines as the traditional Roman system, they looked confidently to the future and devoted themselves to the prosecution of the war, having given their common centre the additional name of Italia (Diodorus XXXVII, 2, 4–5).

Towards the end of the first year of the war, the Romans conceded the point of principle at issue by offering the citizenship to all communities which had remained loyal. Attempts were made (the details are obscure and there was further legislation in 89) to limit the number of tribes in which the new citizens could vote and hence their influence. But the offer of citizenship combined with

9   Map of Italy in 91
Roman and Latin territory in Italy is white (also tribal territory in the north), allied territory is shaded; the initial centres of the revolt were the two connected blocks of allied territory in the centre and the south; Asculum alone of the outlying areas joined the revolt at the outset; Latin Venusia was surrounded – and joined the rebels.

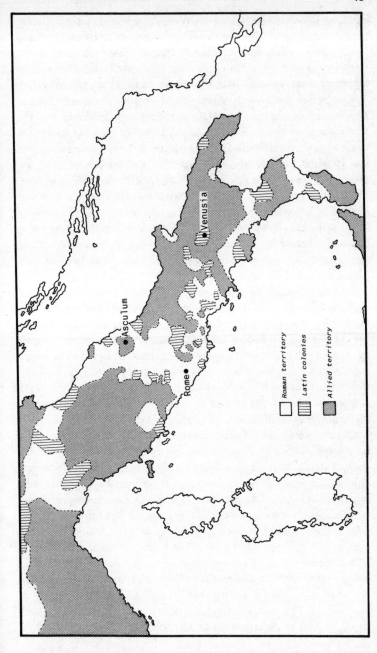

existing divisions (often of extreme bitterness) within Italian peoples and cities to hasten the end of the war. The Samnites and Lucanians continued fighting until 87 and were to be disaffected from Rome in 82; the Samnites even negotiated with Mithridates and produced a coinage with the ethnic SAFINIM (Samnium).

The Social War was effectively over, then, by the end of 89; but a grievance was left to be exploited, the limited distribution of the new citizens in the tribes. In addition, further violence had taken place at Rome itself, when in 89 the praetor A. Sempronius Asellio was lynched for attempting to alleviate the burden of debt, no doubt worsened by a fall in liquidity with the outbreak of war. Most serious of all, the fighting of what was effectively a civil war had led to a loss of scruple on the Roman side which mirrored the bitter strife on the Italian side; A. Postumius Albinus, a legate in 89, was lynched by the troops of Sulla, without their incurring retribution. It was in this atmosphere that news arrived that Mithridates had invaded Asia.

The kingdom of Mithridates VI of Pontus was one of a number in Asia Minor, some of which had emerged when the Seleucid monarchy was deprived of its territories west of the Taurus Mountains in 190 (p. 66), others of which had come into being as its control weakened in the areas east thereof (p. 131). Mithridates was undoubtedly anxious to extend his kingdom, though some of the evidence certainly derives from Posidonius, an opponent of his aggression and a supporter of Rome. It may be doubted whether Mithridates ever attempted to negotiate with the Cimbri, and it is unclear when he accepted that war with Rome was likely. But he does seem to have sailed close to the wind, strengthening his links with potential allies and tightening his control over his subjects around the coasts of the Black Sea, partitioning Paphlagonia with Nicomedes III of Bithynia, and seizing Galatia. A warning by C. Marius, on a tour of the east, apparently went unheeded and negotiations with Tigranes I of Armenia were followed by the acquisition of Cappadocia with his help. L. Sulla was able to restore Ariobarzanes I to Cappadocia, but he was expelled again in 91, along with Nicomedes IV of Bithynia; the two kings were restored in 89, and this time the Roman commanders chose to provoke outright war. One may surmise that the device which they used, leading to an attack on an ally, had often been used before (see, for instance, p. 103), but the adoption of the device was favoured by a factor which was probably new. It is an amazing incident, and this time Mithridates fought back:

> At the urging of the legates,[2] Nicomedes, who had agreed to pay large sums to the general and the legates in return for their assistance and had not paid, and who had in addition borrowed further large sums from other Romans on the spot, and who was being pressed to pay, unwillingly invaded the territory of Mithridates. And he plundered on as far as the city of Amastris, since no-one hindered him or came out to meet him. For Mithridates, although he had an army ready, nonetheless withdrew, (encouraging Nicomedes to go on and thereby) giving himself full and ample justification for beginning the war (Appian, *Mithridatic Wars* II, 41).

Mithridates, thus provoked, invaded the province of Asia and ordered a general massacre of all Romans, to the number, it was alleged, of 80,000. The command against him, as was to be expected, fell to one of the two consuls for 88, L. Cornelius Sulla (his colleague, Q. Pompeius Rufus, was assigned to a command in Italy, but was in due course lynched, when he attempted to take over the army of Cn. Pompeius Strabo, the father of Cn. Pompeius Magnus; Strabo made no attempt to stop the lynching).

Unfortunately, things were not so simple. P. Sulpicius, who had been an associate of M. Livius Drusus, proposed as tribune in 88 to reverse the limited distribution of the new citizens in the tribes, a proposal, which, like that of L. Cinna in 87, presumably related only to those who had not gone on fighting against Rome. He also proposed to recall those exiled in the witch-hunt over the origins of the Social War and to take steps to alleviate the burden of debt. This was no doubt a comprehensive measure, but only one clause is known, ultimately from the hostile testimony of the *Memoirs* of Sulla: Sulpicius attempted to limit borrowing by senators, although himself deeply in debt. In any case, Sulpicius and C. Marius allied, the latter to have the command against

2. It is conceivable that some of these Romans on the spot hoped that they were doing a favour to C. Marius, by creating an emergency for him to deal with.

Mithridates transferred to himself, which was in due course achieved by the use of violence.

The reaction of Sulla was to march on Rome; his *dignitas* had of course suffered a serious affront; and it was in his own interest and in that of his army to march. The revolutionary nature of the step may be seen from the fact that only one of his officers followed him, L. Licinius Lucullus. But Sulla was also no doubt steeped in the ideology which proclaimed the duty of the individual to act against a tyrant (p. 24); behind him there stood an already long line of those who had in the recent past turned to force to implement their concept of *libertas*, exclusive and not to be compromised:

> Legates met him *en route* and asked why he was marching on his own country under arms; he replied that he was doing so in order to free it from those who were ruling it as tyrants (Appian, *Civil Wars* I, 57, 253).

It would be hard to think of a clearer example of a prevailing ideology permitting a justificatory description of a revolutionary act. The claim was used also by M. Lepidus, L. Catilina, Caesar and Octavianus, as well as again by Sulla before his return from the east. The title of defender of the liberty of Rome was applied indiscriminately as a compliment in the period after Sulla and used both for the Gracchi and for their opponents in later historiography; those who claimed to be defenders of the privileges of the upper orders and those who claimed to be defenders of the rights of the people both used it. It could justify anything, and eventually it justified monarchy – but not yet.

His enemies routed, Sulla had some killed, the rest outlawed; the command against Mithridates was restored to him. An attempt was made to legislate to prevent a recurrence of 'sedition'; another attempt was made to alleviate the burden of debt (presumably even Sulla recognized the threat to stability which it posed, but another measure was necessary in 86). The elections were held and when L. Cornelius Cinna was elected:

> he even pretended to be pleased at this, as if the people in doing what it wanted was enjoying its freedom because of him (Plutarch, *Sulla* 10).

The ideological stance is consistent – and looks forward to the rôle of Sulla on his return from the east, whither he now set off.

One of the consuls of the following year, L. Cornelius Cinna, revived the programme of P. Sulpicius, but was driven out by his colleague. Soon, however, Cinna joined up with C. Marius and the two recaptured Rome at the end of 87; they too killed some of their opponents and the First Civil War was over.

The course of events which followed was observed by Posidonius:

> So Marius was elected consul for the seventh time . . . And now, although worn out by his sufferings as well as being somewhat deranged and verging on senility, he could not control his thoughts as they turned in terror to the awful prospect of yet another war and further struggles and dangers, which loomed the more because of his great knowledge of such things, and unending toil; for he realized that it was not a question of fighting against Octavius and Merula, who had opposed him at the head of an emergency levy drawn from the urban rabble, but that the same Sulla was in the field against him, who had already once driven him into exile and now had an army which had driven Mithridates back into his kingdom. Oppressed by such thoughts, and constantly pondering his long wanderings and his narrow escapes and the dangers he had undergone as he was driven over land and sea, Marius suffered terrible crises and nocturnal hallucinations and wild dreams, and kept on thinking that he heard someone saying, 'Rest is impossible for one who fears the return of the lion to his intended prey'. So fearing most of all the prospect of lying awake, he turned to drink and to unseasonable and unsuitable debauchery, as if he were attempting to ensure sleep free of nightmares. And finally when a messenger came from overseas, new fears came upon him, partly from apprehension for the future, and partly as it were because he was quite unable to bear the present; a sudden crisis came upon him and he fell ill, as Posidonius the philosopher records, remarking that he himself came before him and spoke of the business on which Rhodes had sent him, when Marius was already sick (and in fact about to die) (Posidonius, Frag. 255 Edelstein-Kidd).

There followed three years of peace, in the course of which the *dediticii* of 87, who had perhaps initially been given the citizenship without the vote, were granted the vote; and then the return of Sulla:

> So Sulla wrote firmly to the senate, mentioning his earlier career, including his achievements still as a quaestor in Africa against Jugurtha of Numidia and as a legate in the Cimbrian War and as a commander in Cilicia and in the Social War and as a consul; he particularly emphasized his recent achievements against Mithridates and listed *en bloc* for the senate the many nations which had belonged to Mithridates and which he had recovered for Rome; he also remarked that he had received those who had been driven out of Rome by Cinna and had fled to him in despair and that he had succoured them in their distress. His reward for all this, he claimed, was to be declared an enemy of the state by his opponents and have his house destroyed and his friends killed; his wife and children had barely been able to escape to him. So he was now coming to take vengeance on the guilty parties on behalf of those who had been wronged and on behalf of Rome itself. But he made it clear to the citizen body as a whole and to the new citizens in particular that he had no complaint against any of them (Appian, *Civil Wars* 1, 77, 350–2).

The emphasis on services to the state as a justification for what Sulla proposed to do is at first sight remarkable, but he knew that he was appealing to a central element in the Roman system of values and others were not slow to respond to his call. Q. Caecilius Metellus Pius, Cn. Pompeius, and M. Licinius Crassus all raised armies privately and joined his cause (for a favourable view of the rôle of Cn. Pompeius see [Caesar], *de bello Africo* 22).

Sulla in fact had come to identify his own fate with that of the *res publica*; the claim that while in Greece he had with him virtually a senate (Plutarch, *Sulla* 22, deriving from his *Memoirs*), even if designed to obscure the fact that massive support for Sulla only emerged among the upper orders when it was clear that he was winning, is indicative of the way his mind was working. His coinage moves from types which are purely personal (see also Pl. 5–6):

Head of Venus; before, Cupid with palm-branch.
Symbols of augurate; on either side, trophy.

to types which symbolize a link with Rome:

Head of Roma.
Sulla in triumphal quadriga.

When Sulla negotiated with the opposing consul L. Cornelius
Scipio in 83, he did so over 'the authority of the senate, the powers
of the people, about the right of citizenship' (Cicero, *Philippica*
XII, 27), 'At that time, the prize of victory was the *res publica*
(Valerius Maximus VII, 6, 4).

Sulla was sensible enough to make it clear that he would not take
Roman citizenship away from the Italians or tinker with their right
to vote; when Roman resistance collapsed most Italians accepted
Sulla. Only the Samnites and the Lucanians saw that there was still
a chance of revenging the defeat of 90–87; the younger C. Marius
had taken refuge in Praeneste (Palestrina), where Pontius
Telesinus the Samnite and Marcus Lamponius the Lucanian
attempted to rescue him. Failing to do so, they marched on Rome:

But now Pontius Telesinus, the Samnite leader, a leading spirit
in government and in war and deeply hostile to Rome, got
together about 40,000 men from among the best fighters
available and the most dedicated to the struggle and on the First
of November in the consulship of Carbo and Marius a hundred
and nine years before my time engaged in battle with Sulla at the
Colline Gate; the battle was so close that his own fate and that of
the *res publica* (note the association) were in the balance; the *res
publica* had not faced a greater danger, even on the occasion
when the camp of Hannibal was pitched within the third
milestone from Rome, than she faced on that day; for Telesinus
went from unit to unit of his army and repeated again and again
that the Romans' last day was at hand and that the city must be
torn down and destroyed, adding that the wolves who were the
oppressors of the liberty of Italy would always be there unless
the forest in which they always took refuge was cut down . . .
Sulla commemorated the *felicitas* of the day on which the army
of the Samnites and Telesinus was defeated by the institution of

annual games in the circus,[3] which are still celebrated under the name they derived from him, Ludi Victoriae Sullanae (in fact they were only known as the Ludi Victoriae until they needed to be distinguished from the Ludi Victoriae Caesaris) (Velleius II, 27, 1–6).

Sulla also exacted a terrible vengeance:

He had the Samnites cut down fighting, giving orders that no prisoners should be taken; but some threw away their arms and they were confined to the Villa Publica on the Campus Martius, apparently to the number of 3000 or 4000. Three days later he sent his soldiers in and slaughtered them all and then began the proscriptions; these did not end until every Samnite of repute had been killed or driven out of Italy. To those who reproached him for allowing himself to be carried away by his anger, Sulla said that he knew from experience that no Roman would be able to live in peace, as long as the Samnites existed (the reference to the remark of Telesinus is explicit). So what were once cities in Samnium have become villages and some have disappeared completely, Boianum, Aesernia, Pinna, Telesia near Venafrum and a number of others, none of which deserve to be called cities . . . But Beneventum survived in a reasonable state and also Venusia (Strabo v, 4, 11).

The fate of Praeneste, which had been forced to harbour the younger C. Marius, was similar; of 138 families attested before the sack, at most 20 survived into the last generation of the Republic.

The proscriptions were similarly designed to eliminate all who were the enemies of Sulla, not just the Samnites. Those who were listed could be killed with impunity and their goods were confiscated by the state; their descendants were debarred for ever from holding office. Some no doubt escaped out of Italy; the rest were killed. Their property was for the most part sold at auction, at knock-down prices to supporters of Sulla, whose later fortunes were in some cases made thereby. Men were later to claim that they

3. Sulla also assumed the extra name Felix, and was thereafter known as L. Cornelius Sulla Felix.

had bid from fear; Sulla no doubt wished to ensure that the governing class to which he proposed to hand over control of the *res publica* both had a financial interest in the preservation of the Sullan system and was morally implicated in its birth-pangs.[4] Similarly, those members of the upper orders of England who acquired monastic lands were explicitly recognized as likely supporters of the preservation of the Henrician reformation.

At the same time, some cities in Italy which had opposed Sulla were deprived of their citizenship, more were fined and mulcted of land, land which was used to settle the veterans of Sulla; here too self-interest was intended to act towards the preservation of the Sullan system.

For the victory of Sulla was the victory of the *res publica*, as Cicero was careful to assert when in 80 he defended Sex. Roscius of Ameria against the machinations of a disreputable associate of Sulla. The next step was not so obvious.

Sulla's concern for legal forms in the midst of illegality was immediately made clear. A decree of the senate was passed conferring *ex post facto* validity on all his acts from 88 to 82; Sulla withdrew from the city while an *interrex* (p. 22, both consuls were dead) was appointed, L. Valerius Flaccus, and by the authorization of a consequent Lex Valeria named Sulla dictator. Despite his supreme power, Sulla in fact transacted much business through the assembly; he at first refused a triumph to Cn. Pompeius because of its irregularity; and he resigned his dictatorship at the end of 81, to hold the consulship of 80 with Q. Caecilius Metellus Pius.

The measures of Sulla are a curious blend of reaction to particular ills as perceived by Sulla, and systematic reorganization of areas of government. Despite the fact that we are now in the period of Cicero's maturity, much is ill-documented and obscure. We happen to possess one out of a probable nine bronze tablets on which his law increasing the number of quaestors to twenty was engraved; the law is otherwise known from a six-word sentence of Tacitus (*Annales* XI, 22).

Emergency action was of course necessary to replenish the

4. A smaller, but still interesting, group bound by self-interest to the preservation of the Sullan system were those slaves of the proscribed who were freed by Sulla and granted citizenship.

senate; but Sulla went further than mere replenishment of the senate and roughly doubled it in size. Too little is known for us to be able to say with any degree of certainty who his new senators were. They doubtless came in part from existing senatorial families; some apparently came from those areas of Italy which had remained loyal in 90. Overall, Sulla of course wished to reward his supporters; but he also created a senate of a size appropriate to the size of the empire of which it was the governing body and provided for its replenishment by means of the automatic entry of twenty quaestors every year.

Sulla certainly envisaged the continuing enrolment of new citizens; his legislation assumed the existence of the census (Cicero, *pro Cluentio* 148) and Cicero asserted:

> We had had (down to 58) the censorship, with its power of sitting in judgment and branding with infamy, for 400 years; the power which no-one however wildly irresponsible ever tried to diminish, of sitting in judgment on our characters every five years (the *cura morum*), that power was buried at the very beginning of your consulship, you assassin (*in Pisonem* 10).

In fact only one census was completed between Sulla and Augustus, that of 70/69, a remarkable symptom of the dissolution of the *res publica*.[5] Members of existing citizen families were no doubt inserted automatically onto the registers, but relatively few of the Italians were included even in 70/69 and the organization of the *comitia centuriata* became progressively more out-of-date; but since twenty quaestors a year were henceforth available and entitled to enter the senate automatically, the census could in fact be dispensed with. As politics gave way to war, it perhaps mattered little that the lists of voters were in disarray and that the *cura morum* had ceased. Looking back on the last generation of the functioning of free institutions, Cicero actually included a provision for the automatic recruitment of senators in his ideal constitution (*de legibus* iii, 27).

Much of Sulla's legislation was backward-looking, though not for that reason *necessarily* inappropriate. Sulla made a systematic

5. There was perhaps an attempt in 75 to find an alternative to the censorship, by entrusting the consuls with some of its functions.

attempt to render impossible the rôle which the tribunate had played since 133; a tribune's right of veto was limited, his rights to legislate and put someone on trial were removed, and he was debarred from any further office. The rules governing the succession of magistracies, which had been formulated in the second century BC (p. 72), were re-enacted; a sumptuary law, again recalling legislation of the second century BC (p. 75), was passed; the practice of co-opting priests, not electing them, was restored.

But in connection with this measure, another is attested which begins to reveal a different perspective; Sulla recognized that the empire needed a larger governing class and the post-Sullan senate was roughly twice the size of its predecessors; the number of quaestors was increased to twenty, the number of praetors was raised from six to ten.[6] One thing Sulla did not touch; there remained two consulships at the peak, to be competed for by a larger number of men of ambition.

This group Sulla attempted to curb; following the precedent set by the *popularis* legislation of the end of the second century BC, he legislated on the duties of provincial governors. He also, in the course of a major reform of the judicial system which included (predictably) the restoration of the courts to the senate, picked up some of that *popularis* legislation in a new law of treason. His judicial reforms remained influential into the second century AD; his political reforms fared less well.

The group to whom he had handed over control of the *res publica*, however, never wavered in their determination to retain control. Their fear of significant change emerges from Cicero's remark about his speech during his consulate against the restoration of the rights of the sons of the proscribed:

> I succeeded in keeping from access to the assembly a group of young men, who, while undoubtedly honourable and talented had been assigned a status which meant that it was clear that if they acquired office they would disturb the stability of the *res publica* (*in Pisonem* 4).

6. Sulla seems also in passing to have removed the distinction between plebeian and curule aediles, a hangover from the period when the distinction between plebeian officers and patrician magistrates was crucial.

XIV

The Embattled Oligarchy

SULLA DIED IN 78 and was cremated, the first of the patrician Cornelii to be so, to prevent his body being dishonoured after his death, as he had dishonoured that of C. Marius. Immediately after his death, the restored oligarchy was faced by an attempt by M. Aemilius Lepidus, one of the two consuls of that year, to undo the Sullan settlement. When he turned to armed revolution, he was suppressed without undue difficulty, but in the process a special command was conferred on the young Cn. Pompeius. Meanwhile in 80, the Marian governor Q. Sertorius had re-established himself in Spain, whither he had fled from the advance of Sulla and whence he had initially been ejected. He attempted with some success to organize an independent state, and Spain was effectively out of senatorial control from 80 to 73; in order to regain control another special command was conferred on Cn. Pompeius.

In 73, a major slave-war was begun in Italy under the leadership of an escaped gladiator, Spartacus, who was only finally defeated by M. Licinius Crassus in 71, again with a special command. Meanwhile, Mithridates, with whom Sulla had made peace in 85 and against whom L. Licinius Murena had fought briefly in 83–1, had negotiated with Q. Sertorius in 75 and declared war again in 74, in order to prevent the execution of the will of Nicomedes IV of Bithynia, which left his kingdom to Rome. Piracy continued to be rampant in the east, despite the campaign of P. Servilius Vàtia, named Isauricus for his victory, in 78–5.

The price of success abroad was the creation of a special command and the surrender of effective control by the senate. L. Licinius Lucullus was initially in 74 given the province of Cilicia, in order to fight Mithridates, and gradually acquired in addition Asia, Bithynia and Pontus. The framework is *de iure* constitutional, but *de facto* hardly so. Lucullus behaved in a way which looked forward to the autocratic behaviour of Pompeius:[1]

> On the other side of the river, there is a powerful fortress of the Cappadocians called Tomisa; this was sold originally to the ruler of Sophene for 600,000 denarii, but Lucullus later gave it to the ruler of the Cappadocians as a reward for bravery when he served with him in the war against Mithridates (Strabo XII, 2, 1).

In the case of the pirates a special command was actually conferred on M. Antonius as early as 74; a special command against the pirates was then revived for Cn. Pompeius in 67 and in 66 he was given a special command against Mithridates. Possessed of this, he ruled the east without reference to the senate until 62, annexing not only the kingdom of Mithridates after his defeat, but the territory of the moribund Seleucid monarchy as well. In the process, he raised the annual revenues of Rome probably from 50,000,000 to 135,000,000 denarii.

The provinces of Cisalpine Gaul and Illyricum were conferred on C. Iulius Caesar, consul in 59, by a Lex Vatinia of that year (the province of Transalpine Gaul was added by the senate). Between 58 and 50 he conquered the whole of Transalpine Gaul between the frontiers of the old province in the south and the Rhine, again without reference to the senate, making war on a friend of the Roman people in the process (see below). With the example of Caesar before him, Crassus casually provoked war with Parthia in 54.

There was of course justified opposition within the oligarchy to the principle of special commands (for some details on their juridical status see Appendix 4); in 67:

> (Q. Lutatius Catulus) speaking against the law (to confer the command against the pirates on Cn. Pompeius) said in an informal harangue that Pompeius was certainly an outstanding

---

1. Already probably in 77 on the way to Spain Pompeius had decreed the confiscation of lands belonging to the Volcae and Helvii; another man saw to the execution of the decree, but Pompeius was regarded as the author of the assignation of the lands to Massalia.

man, but that he was too eminent for comfort in a free *res publica* and that all power should not be placed in the hands of one man (Velleius II, 32, 1).

Only one senator voted for the proposal, C. Iulius Caesar.

Cicero, in delivering in 66 his speech *de imperio Cn. Pompei*, on the *imperium* of Cn. Pompeius, in order to urge that the command against Mithridates be conferred on Pompeius, had to meet the same sort of argument. L. Licinius Lucullus, who was thus superseded in that command, was able to persuade the senate in 61 and after to delay the ratification of the settlement of the east by discussing every clause in detail. (The formal ground no doubt was that Pompeius had dispensed with the normal senatorial committee of ten legates, p. 65.) But the settlement of course meanwhile remained in force and Pompeius in due course turned to an alliance with Caesar to achieve its ratification.

There was initially bitter opposition to the command proposed for Caesar, and the younger Cato even proposed that Caesar be handed over in chains in atonement for the attack on the German king Ariovistus. In 57, special measures were proposed in order to enable Pompeius to deal with the corn supply (the transference to the civilian sphere of an expedient devised in a military context is in itself remarkable):

> The next day there was a full meeting of the senate and all the consulars were present; they refused to Pompeius nothing of what he asked; when he asked for fifteen legates, he named me as his first choice and said that I should be a second Pompeius in the execution of all business. So the consuls drafted a law giving full control over the corn supply all over the world to Pompeius for a five year period; Messius drafted another law, in which he gives Pompeius control over all the financial resources of the state and adds a fleet and an army and *imperium* in the provinces greater than that of those who command them. The consular law which we had a hand in now seems moderate, the law of Messius is intolerable . . . (Cicero, *ad Atticum* IV, 1, 7)

But it would be a mistake to ignore the value which was placed on success abroad in the ideology of the Roman oligarchy. It was in part because of this that the creation of special commands eventually won widespread acceptance. This emerges very clearly both from the remarks of Cicero in 66 in the *de imperio Cn. Pompei* and from the speech *de provinciis consularibus*, on the consular provinces in 56, urging the retention by Caesar of his command:

Well, let men think whatever they wish; for I cannot be other than a friend to anyone who has served the *res publica* well . . . War has actually been waged against the Gauls by C. Caesar as general, whereas before they were merely warded off . . . It is clear that the approach of C. Caesar was quite different; for he did not suppose that it was merely his duty to wage war against those whom he saw actually to have taken up arms against the Roman people, but also that the whole of Gaul was to be brought under our sway (Cicero, *de provinciis consularibus* 24—32).

Augustus knew very well what he was doing when in due course he appealed to this strain among others in Roman thought to justify the autocracy which he had established.

The senate was no more in command of the situation at home than it was abroad. Overseas, for reasons which changed between the 70s and the 60s and 50s, it exercised only a rather tenuous control over the empire of which it was in theory the governing body. Equally, it was unable to ensure the orderly conduct of the political process at Rome and in Italy.

The sons of the proscribed were one obvious source of disaffection; men from communities in Italy penalized by Sulla were another. The population of Rome itself was large and variegated; in the late second century BC it numbered perhaps 375,000, having possibly doubled since the early third century BC. The bulk of this increase was the result of the influx of slaves to serve the great houses; many of these slaves, of many different nationalities, were freed during their careers and continued to live in Rome in varying degrees of dependence on their patrons.[2] Numerous foreigners came to live in Rome to provide one specialized service or another. The living conditions of the urban

2. The voting rights of freedmen were an intermittent source of contention among Roman politicians (see p. 78).

population were probably by modern standards appalling; even by ancient standards they were perhaps poor and no doubt provoked resentment.

None of the groups of which the urban population was made up, free, freed, slave and alien, either singly or in concert, provided a coherent focus of disloyalty or a systematic threat to the *res publica* and the *status quo*. But the native cults of the different foreign nationalities probably provided an elementary principle of organization. Certainly numerous foreign religions were represented in Rome in the first century BC and were apparently perceived, on the analogy of the Bacchanalian movement, as a threat; frequent, if unsystematic, attempts were made to suppress one sect or another. At the same time unofficial books of prophecy circulated widely, perhaps a symptom of a propensity to insurrection, as they were in seventeenth-century England. The authorities of the Roman Empire, from Augustus onwards, were able to burn unofficial books of prophecy.

Overall it is hard not to suppose that the difficulties of the ruling oligarchy were compounded by the composition and the wretchedness of the population of the city of Rome. That population of course provided a ready body of support to ambitious politicians; the relationship which developed is, in my view, one aspect of the link between individual members of the élite and those outside it which was, in a different sphere, responsible for the dissolution of the Republic. The violence of politics in Rome, while explicable both in terms of early traditions of self-help in a peasant community and in the light of recent developments, was also, I believe, a factor in the slackening of political scruple which eventually allowed Caesar and Pompeius to fight for the possession of a *res publica*, the essence of which was collective rule by a group.

The decade after Sulla was already turbulent enough; certainly the *concordia*, which he had apparently regarded as established (to judge from the allusions in the speeches of the 70s reported by Sallust), was conspicuously absent. Despite the fragmentary state of our documentation for the period, agitation for the resumption of distribution of corn, which Sulla had apparently allowed to fall into desuetude, is attested for 78, 75 and 73. Agitation over the position of the tribunate is attested for 76, 75 (when the bar on a further career was removed), 74, 73 and of course 70 (see below);

agitation over the composition of the juries of the *quaestiones* apparently only began towards the end of the decade and is attested for 71 and 70 (see below).[3]

In 70, after their victories in Spain and over Spartacus, Cn. Pompeius Magnus and M. Licinius Crassus came to the consulship, the former having held no previous elective office, the latter after an orthodox career. With their encouragement, censors were elected, who completed their task in the following year, the tribunate regained its rights, and the courts were assigned to a mixed panel composed of senators, *equites* and *tribuni aerarii*, the latter, like *equites*, an *ordo* within those who possessed the census which qualified, but did not entitle, a man to be an *eques* (see Appendix 3). At the same time, a Lex Plotia was passed permitting the return of those who had supported M. Lepidus (p. 154); in 70, the Sullan oligarchy seemed firmly in control and ready to make concessions.

But in the same year, although the senate had agreed (amazingly, in the light of its earlier attitude) that land should be provided for the veterans who had fought in Spain, a Lex Plotia to provide for this failed; the reason was apparently shortage of money. The next twenty years saw growing disarray at Rome, while the needs and opportunities of the empire raised first Cn. Pompeius and then C. Caesar to a dominating position and provided both with an army loyal to the individual and not to the state.

Sallust saw the political history of the late Republic in terms of an underlying conflict between the few and the many, unleashed by the disappearance of any external threat with the destruction of Carthage:

> For the nobility began to push to excess its claim to *dignitas*, the people its claim to *libertas*; everyone sought to draw or snatch everything to himself. And so everything fell to one side or the other, and the *res publica*, which was the bone of contention, was torn to pieces (*Bellum Jugurthinum* 41, 5).

It was hardly true that Rome faced no external threat after 146 and

---

3. The choice of priests by election rather than co-option was not restored till 63.

the absence of one is in any case hardly a sufficient explanation of the phenomenon which Sallust describes, but the emphasis on *dignitas* must stem from direct knowledge of the age of Cicero. *Libertas* had of course already by 70 often stood at the centre of political disputes. What characterizes the next twenty years is the unscrupulousness of political competition, the provision of leadership to the poor by members of the élite and the disaffection of the poor from the *res publica* as a whole.

The censors of 70/69 excluded 64 persons from the senate, including P. Cornelius Lentulus Sura, who had been consul in 71. Some of those excluded, like C. Antonius, began their careers again and pursued them satisfactorily; C. Antonius was colleague to Cicero in 63. Others, like Q. Curius, apparently never got started; he was a leading supporter of Catilina in 63 and so also was Sura, who had not got beyond a second praetorship, held in that year. The lengths to which such men were prepared to go are striking testimony of their desperation for tenure of office and restoration of *dignitas* (the aims of Catilina and his supporters were of course, *inter alia*, to secure the offices from which they felt unjustly excluded, see below).

Even without the exacerbation of competition provided by 64 additional candidates for office, competition within the governing class enlarged by Sulla was severe. Its principal effect was to encourage widespread and largely unchecked electoral bribery, as well as yet more conspicuous consumption; the corollary of this was the emergence of an attitude to usury unparalleled before or after in the ancient world; 'those employments are to be condemned which incur ill-will, as those of . . . moneylenders' (Cicero, *de officiis* i, 150). Yet, as Moses Finley has emphasized, many of the magnates of the age of Cicero engaged in money-lending as well as in their preferred occupations of politics and war; anything went.

The potential for turbulence of the city of Rome was no doubt increased by immigration from the countryside (Sallust, *Catilina* 37, 4–7):

But as for the plebs in the city, that was indeed ready for revolution for all sorts of reasons. In the first place . . . those whom disgrace or crime had forced to leave home had gathered in Rome as if in a cesspool . . . Furthermore, those in their prime who had in the past borne with poverty in the countryside and earned their living by their hands had been enticed to Rome by the prospect of private and public distributions (note the collocation) and had opted for idleness in the city instead of labour without proper reward.

Sallust here echoes a contemporary remark of Cicero; despite his distaste for distribution of land, he thought that a revised version of the Lex Flavia of 60 'could drain away the dregs of the city and repopulate the empty spaces of Italy' (Cicero, *ad Atticum* i, 19, 4; the original purpose of the law was of course to provide for the veterans of Pompeius). The drift to Rome was accelerated by the institution by P. Clodius of corn distributions free of charge.

Meanwhile, the corn-supply of the city of Rome was frequently threatened. It had been interrupted by piratical activity before 67, and despite the suppression of piracy by Pompeius continued to be a matter for concern. One of the praetors of 66 had to occupy himself with it. Cicero wrote to Atticus in 61 that he had been able to make much of the current cheapness of corn in a speech in the senate; but when he was exiled in 58 and restored in 57, both he and his opponents were able to claim that the corn-supply was affected; continuing concern must lie behind the claims and counter-claims. Pompeius was given a special command in 57 to deal with the corn-supply (without all the powers proposed by some of his supporters, p.156), but it was still felt necessary in 52 to attempt to reduce the number of recipients of the corn distributions.

Nor could conditions in Rome be isolated from those in Italy. There Sulla had left a legacy of expropriation and deprivation; the rising of Lepidus and the revolt of Spartacus no doubt inflicted suffering both on those who had been left unharmed by Sulla and on those of his veterans who had been settled by him. The number of coin-hoards buried and not recovered because of the deaths of their owners, presumably by violence, is higher for the 70s than it is for the 80s (Fig. 10). Conscription continued to make life difficult for the peasant farmer; violent dispossession was a feature of life in rural Italy.

The burden of debt both in Rome and in Italy continued to be oppressive and was perhaps exacerbated in the 70s and the 60s down

218–216	⬭⬭⬭⬭⬭⬭⬭⬭⬭⬭ 10
215–211	⬭⬭⬭⬭⬭⬭⬭⬭⬭⬭⬭⬭⬭⬭⬭ 15
210–206	⬭⬭⬭⬭⬭⬭⬭⬭⬭⬭⬭⬭⬭⬭⬭⬭⬭⬭⬭⬭⬭⬭⬭⬭⬭⬭⬭⬭ 28
205–201	⬭ 1
200–196	
195–191	⬭⬭⬭ 3
190–186	⬭ 1
185–181	
180–176	⬭⬭ 2
175–171	
170–166	⬭⬭ 2
165–161	⬭⬭ 2
160–156	
155–151	⬭⬭⬭⬭⬭⬭⬭⬭ 8
150–146	⬭ 1
145–141	⬭⬭⬭ 3
140–136	⬭⬭⬭ 3
135–131	⬭⬭⬭ 3
130–126	⬭⬭ 2
125–121	⬭⬭⬭ 3
120–116	⬭⬭⬭ 4
115–111	⬭⬭⬭ 6
110–106	⬭⬭ 2
105–101	⬭⬭⬭⬭ 7
100–96	⬭⬭⬭ 6
95–91	⬭⬭⬭ 5
90–86	⬭⬭⬭⬭⬭⬭⬭⬭⬭⬭⬭ 15
85–81	⬭⬭⬭⬭⬭⬭⬭⬭⬭⬭ 13
80–76	⬭⬭⬭⬭⬭⬭⬭⬭⬭⬭⬭ 16
75–71	⬭⬭⬭⬭⬭⬭⬭⬭⬭⬭⬭ 16
70–66	
65–61	⬭ 1
60–56	⬭ 2
55–51	⬭⬭ 5
50–46	⬭⬭⬭⬭⬭⬭⬭⬭⬭⬭ 14
45–41	⬭⬭⬭⬭⬭⬭⬭⬭⬭⬭⬭⬭⬭⬭⬭⬭ 22
40–36	⬭⬭⬭⬭⬭⬭⬭⬭⬭ 13
35–31	⬭⬭⬭⬭ 6
30–26	⬭⬭ 2
25–21	⬭⬭ 2
20–16	⬭⬭ 2
15–11	⬭⬭ 3
10–6	⬭⬭ 3
5–3	⬭ 1

10   Coin hoards from Italy, Corsica, Sardinia and Sicily. The table plots the closing dates of known coin hoards in five year periods; the correlation between concentrations of coin hoards not recovered by their owners and periods of war and disturbance is very close.

Papers of the British School at Rome 1969, 79

to 63 by a dearth of new issues of coinage (Rome was desperately short of revenue between Sulla's dictatorship and 63) and consequent shortage of liquidity. Their misery led some men to hire themselves out as gladiators; others probably sold themselves into slavery.

Before the cataclysmic decade of the 80s, the senate had enjoyed at least the passive consent of the governed. In 63 this was clearly no longer so:

> (L. Catilina) then indeed said that there were two bodies politic, one weak and with a poor head on its shoulders, the other strong and with no head; but, as long as he was alive, he would be its head (Cicero, *pro Murena* 51).

The career of L. Sergius Catilina was up to a point normal; he had reached the praetorship already in 68, two years before Cicero, but he failed repeatedly to reach the consulship and late in 63, the year in which Cicero was consul, he turned to serious advocacy of a programme of redistribution of land and cancellation of debts. The underlying threat to the established order was, in my view, real and was not overestimated by Cicero. Already in 64 the government had felt it necessary to suppress the *collegia*, trade guilds, which were used as a way of organizing popular discontent; earlier in 63 Cicero had ensured the defeat of a Lex Servilia proposing agrarian settlement, *inter alia* by using his oratorical gifts to secure the support of the urban population; he was now able to play on its fears of the arson which, he claimed, formed part of the plans of Catilina and his associates.

Catilina left Rome, turning or more likely driven to violence by Cicero's accusations, and with his small and largely rural band of supporters was brought to battle, defeated and killed near Pistoria (Pistoia). The established order had survived; and the enormous wealth which the conquests of Pompeius brought in no doubt helped to increase liquidity and alleviate the burden of debt (it also of course helped to speed the dissolution of the Republic, see p. 171).

Sallust preserves a letter alleged to be from Catilina to Q. Lutatius Catulus, remarkable, even if forged, as evidence for what the upper orders of the period regarded as plausible motivation for armed revolt:

L. Catilina to Q. Catulus . . . So I have determined to offer no
defence of my revolutionary decision; I have determined to offer
some account of it from no feeling of guilt; you may easily see its
cogency. Provoked by injuries and insults, since I had been
robbed of the results of my toil and energy and had not achieved
a position of *dignitas*, I openly took up the cause of the
dispossessed, following my natural inclination . . . It is for this
reason that I have turned to plans for preserving what is left of
my *dignitas*, plans which are entirely honourable for someone in
my position (*Catilina* 35).

The next decade saw another member of the élite attempt to create
a power base for himself among the lower orders. Like Catilina a
patrician by birth, P. Clodius became a plebeian by having himself
adopted into a plebeian family and was elected tribune for 58; then
and in the following years he succeeded in building up a devoted
and powerful following among the urban population, restoring the
collegia suppressed in 64 and using them to organize the lower
orders. His opponents turned to the rural poor:

For Pompeius apparently knows, and has told me, that plots are
being laid against his life, that C. Cato is being supported by
Crassus, that money is being supplied to Clodius, that both Cato
and Clodius are being stiffened in their resolve by Crassus and
by Curio, Bibulus and his other enemies; he must take serious
steps to prevent his own demise, now that the people who once
thronged to hear him are almost wholly alienated from him, the
nobility is hostile, the senate is biased, the younger generation is
unsound. So he is making his preparations and summoning
men from the country; Clodius, however, is strengthening his
gangs; their strength is being built up for the occasion of the
festival of Quirinus. Meanwhile, we are much stronger with the
forces which Pompeius has to hand; but a large force is expected
from Picenum (family territory of Pompeius) and the Po valley
(partially enfranchised by the father of Pompeius), so that we
have enough in reserve to withstand the proposals of Cato about
Milo and Lentulus (Cicero, *ad Quintum fratrem* II, 3, 4, in 56).

Between bribery, violence and religious manipulation the government of the *res publica* was in a state of disarray. The classic case of religious manipulation occurred in 59, when M. Calpurnius Bibulus attempted to block the legislation of his colleague Caesar by announcing in advance that he was going to watch the skies for an unfavourable omen; its availability was not in doubt. Given the ways in which Roman religious belief could be manipulated, it is not surprising that there was intense competition in the late Republic for membership of one or other of the four main colleges of priests, the *pontifices, augures, septemviri* and *decemviri*; Caesar had himself elected Pontifex Maximus in 63 by massive bribery. The years 55, 53, and 52 started without the regular magistracies having been filled; lesser disruptions of the business of government were so common as to provoke no comment.

The incidence of violence may itself be taken as a mark of the desperation of the poor. The Roman mob perhaps included men of the middling sort, and the resentment which found expression in violence perhaps included resentment at the operation of the client economy. But the men who hired themselves out surely did so because deprived of any other means of livelihood. Growing unemployment in Spain before 1936 channelled men into the political gangs which plagued the Republic; similarly in Rome destitution provided material for the client bodyguards of the rich, a very different phenomenon from the *clientelae* of the early and middle Republic (see p. 27):

> But when men were increasingly driven from the fields and were deprived of the possibility of working and of their livelihood and forced to wander homeless, they began to covet the wealth of others and to sell their services along with their loyalty. So gradually a people, which had been a ruling people and governed the world, fell from its position and instead of ruling as a body bound itself as individuals to servitude ([Sallust],[4] *Epistula ad Caesarem* ii, 5, 4–5).

It would, however, be an error to suppose that Catilina and Clodius, Cicero and those who with Cicero opposed Clodius were merely engaged in the acquisition of support in order to further the

4. The work is a political pamphlet by an unknown author which masquerades as a letter to Caesar by Sallust.

cause of the groups whose interests they were advancing or defending. The various conflicts were possible precisely because both sides were able to appeal to powerful elements in the ideological tradition of the Roman Republic.

The emphasis laid by L. Catilina on his *dignitas* was wholly traditional even if the means adopted to enhance it were not; the rights and interests of the lower orders were things to which virtually all members of the upper orders claimed to be devoted even if their private feelings, which are here irrelevant, were rather different. In opposing Catilina, Cicero likewise appealed to both aristocratic and popular values.

In the case of Clodius, Cicero had affronted his *dignitas* by making it clear that he was guilty of being present at certain religious rites (those of the Bona Dea) to which only women were admitted, even though bribery secured his acquittal. But it was also a matter of political principle for Clodius to secure the exile of Cicero; the latter had been rash enough to have executed without trial some of the associates of Catilina, regarding them as self-declared enemies of the state; and he had thereby infringed one of the basic principles of the Roman political system, that no Roman could be put to death without a trial. The point of principle was put to Cicero already in 62, by Q. Caecilius Metellus Celer:

> As for those of your actions which have been neither moderate nor inspired by the clemency customary among our ancestors, it will not be surprising if you come to regret them ([Cicero],*ad familiares* v, 1).

It is also likely that the violation of the rites of the Bona Dea by Clodius was itself a political act, to proclaim opposition to the use which Cicero had made in 63 of a favourable omen from the Bona Dea. And serious political purpose can be seen in the attempt to introduce consistency into the procedure by which the censors marked a man with their *nota*, indication of disapproval, and in the legislation dealing with the allocation of consular provinces.

The memory of the Gracchi had been revered after their death and possession of their portraits was regarded as the mark of a *popularis* approach to politics; the proposal to erect a statue to Clodius in 47 shows that he was regarded as belonging to the same political tradition (Cicero, *ad Atticum* xi, 23, 3 – the text is emended).

Clodius had in fact been killed by T. Annius Milo in the course of a brawl, the aftermath of which finally persuaded majority opinion that there was nothing to do but entrust Cn. Pompeius with the restoration of order (see p. 180 and compare the position of C. Marius in 100, p. 126). Milo was put on trial and his guilt was so glaring that not even the oratorical skills of Cicero could save him; some of Cicero's peers, however, were quite clear about the nature of his justification:

> And so one approach seemed right to Cicero and another to Brutus in defending Milo; for Brutus by way of practice wrote a speech in which he went so far as to exult in the death of Clodius as a bad citizen, while Cicero said that he was rightly killed because he began the violence and was not of course deliberately killed by Milo (Quintilian iii, 6, 93).

The echoes of the stories about Ahala and of the justification for the murder of Ti. Gracchus are very clear (pp. 24 and 110); the killer of a would-be tyrant deserved the thanks of aristocracy and people alike.

In reflecting later on the tribunate of the Gracchi, Cicero borrowed the image of the two bodies politic (*de re publica* 1, 31, quoted on p. 110). The leaders of the two sides were of course in each case members of the upper orders; but the two approaches were not for that any the less real alternatives and their conflict was the more dangerous because both sides were able to appeal to aristocratic as well as to popular values. It was a gross delusion when in 56 Cicero attempted to persuade himself (and presumably his audience) that everyone was really a supporter of traditional aristocratic government, which was of course the real defender of popular interests:

> Who then counts as being one of the best citizens? As far as their number is concerned, they cannot be counted, nor indeed could we survive if it were otherwise. They include those who direct the counsels of the state and those who follow their lead; those of the upper orders, to whom membership of the senate is open; Romans who live in the townships of Italy and in the

countryside, men of business, even freedmen (*pro Sestio* 97).

Not only did Cicero delude himself about the degree of consensus which existed at Rome between the upper and the lower orders; he also failed to discuss either the traditional forms of *clientela* which had provided the power which the oligarchy as a group had once exercised or the new forms of *clientela* which gave urban demagogues or military dynasts their power.

The age of Cicero as a whole, however, was a period of investigation of and speculation about the characteristic institutions of Rome, in all of which Cicero himself participated. The full articulation of the system of census *classes* had probably only developed in the fourth century BC, in order to fund the pay of a Roman army increasingly called upon to fight at some distance from Rome (p. 39); ironically, pay itself at a uniform rate for all legionary soldiers already served to reduce the differentiation of the *classes*. In the classical form of the Republic, the *classes* articulated the citizen body as voters, tax-payers and soldiers. But as the Republic developed, the *comitia centuriata*, which was based on the *classes* (p. 194), became progressively less important in relation to the *comitia tributa*. After 167, the tax on citizens known as *tributum* and levied on the basis of the *classes* was not levied; in 107, C. Marius ignored the difference between those in the *classes* and those below in recruiting troops. By the first century, the disappearance of all the traditional structures of the Roman Republic was evident; E. Gabba is, in my view, right to argue that it was precisely this disappearance which led to investigation of what had gone and to speculation about a philosophical justification. The earliest coherent statement is provided by Cicero, remarkable for its blending of aristocratic and popular values:[5]

. . . eighteen (centuries within those) with the highest census rating. Then, having separated a large body of cavalry from the whole body of the people, he (Servius Tullius) distributed the rest of the people into five classes and divided the older men from

5. It must be remembered that this was written at a period when the censorship, on which the system depended, was in a state of disarray.

the younger men and so organized the classes that voting power was not in the hands of the multitude, but in the hands of the rich, and saw that the majority should not be the more powerful part, something which one must always guard against in a state. If the precise organization were unknown to you, I should explain it; as it is you are aware that the scheme is this: the centuries of cavalry and the first class, together with the *sex suffragia* (a further group of six centuries with the highest census rating, that of the first class), if one adds the century which was created for the master builders, to the great benefit of the city (Cicero here has to explain the apparent anomaly of a privileged position being given to craftsmen), produce a total of 89; if then only 8 centuries out of the 104 which remain join these 89, a majority is reached (89+8 = 97) and the entire people can be seen to have expressed its opinion; the rest of the people, much greater in number, but placed in only 96 centuries, is thus not excluded from voting, which could be an arrogant act, nor does it have too much power, which could be dangerous (*de re publica* II, 39–40).

An alternative current of thought is revealed by the proposal of C. Gracchus to determine the order of voting in the *comitia centuriata* by lot and by the revival of this proposal by the anonymous pamphleteer who wrote the *Epistula ad Caesarem* ii attributed to Sallust (p. 121).

Cicero participated in and encouraged the urban violence of his day (p. 165, note *pro Sestio* 86, a public speech of 56), while at the same time he dreamt of and theorized about a *res publica* of the past before everything had started to go wrong. But in the process he evolved a notion which was incompatible with the notion of the collective rule of the group; he postulated a *princeps* as disinterested supervisor of the political process. Cicero in fact was unable to resist the fascination of the charismatic leader of his day.

The ambition of the charismatic leader of the last generation of the Roman Republic, however, was hardly likely to be satisfied by the rôle which Cicero envisaged for him.

XV

The Military Dynasts

A PROVINCIAL IN the age of Cicero could be forgiven for wondering whether Rome was a state at all; it was not simply that in periods of civil war opposing sides came and went, each with demands which had to be met and which, when met, in due course provoked retribution; even in periods of outward stability in Rome, policy was subject to alarming reversal, as Strabo observed without a flicker of surprise or condemnation:

> (My maternal grandfather), receiving assurances from Lucullus, brought fifteen fortresses over to him. And although considerable promises were made in return for these services, when Pompeius came and took over the war from Lucullus, he treated as enemies all those who had ingratiated themselves with him because of the hostility which existed between Lucullus and himself. And when he had finished the war and returned home, he was able to ensure that the honours which Lucullus had promised to certain people from Pontus were not endorsed by the senate (xii, 3, 33).

Individual adventurers were able to pursue astonishing careers in the areas notionally ruled by Rome or under Roman tutelage:

> Now this Archelaus was the son of the Archelaus who was honoured by Sulla and the senate and he was a friend of A. Gabinius, a man who achieved the consulship. And when he was sent out to govern Syria, Archelaus came along also in the hope of sharing with him in his proposed war against the ruler of Parthia; but when the senate did not authorize it, Archelaus

abandoned this hope and turned to something better. For it happened that Ptolemy, the father of Cleopatra, had been expelled by the Egyptians and the throne was in the hands of his daughter, the elder sister of Cleopatra. And since they were looking for a husband of royal blood for her, he offered himself to those who were engaged in the job, pretending to be a son of Mithridates of Pontus, and was accepted and ruled for six months. He was killed by Gabinius in a pitched battle, fought while he was in the process of restoring Ptolemy (Strabo XII, 3, 34; compare XVII, 1, 11).

Opportunities for personal enrichment were enormous; in one sense little had changed since the early second century BC and Cicero in listing the sources of wealth of his day to a certain extent merely echoed the elder Cato (p. 73):

> For we recognize that those who seek wealth honourably by trading activity, building contracts or tax-farming need to make a profit; at your house one sees hordes of accusers and informers consorting together to make money, guilty and well-heeled defendants engaged in corrupting juries also with you as their manager, one sees the bargains you strike in order to make money as defending counsel, the guarantees of money in corrupt agreements between candidates, one sees the despatch of freedmen to lend money in the provinces and to plunder them, one sees the expulsion of neighbours from their lands, brigandage in the countryside, partnerships for gain with slaves and freedmen as clients, one sees the usurpation of possession in the case of empty properties, one remembers the proscriptions of the rich, the destruction of the townships of Italy, the well-known harvest of the time of Sulla, one remembers all those forged wills, all those people murdered, one realizes finally that everything is for sale ... (Cicero, *Paradoxa Stoicorum* VI, 2, 46, published in the 40s, but probably drafted earlier)

It was the first century which generated the *bon mot* that a provincial governor needed to make three fortunes, one to recoup his election expenses, another to bribe the jury at his expected trial for misgovernment, a third to live off thereafter. But the whole process was on such a vast scale that it was in effect qualitatively different from anything which had gone before. Before the 50s the greatest nabob of them all was Cn. Pompeius; his enrichment of the Roman treasury was balanced by his own. The capital which he acquired was spent in part in an attempt to control the political process at Rome, in part was put to generating yet further wealth. Much of it was out on loan in the provinces and client kingdoms of Rome; Cicero was horrified to discover that Pompeius had loaned money to Ariobarzanes III of Cappadocia at enormous rates of interest:

> First I argued with Ariobarzanes, getting him to agree to give him (Brutus, that is) the talents which were being promised to me. As long as the king was with me everything went very well; but later he began to come under pressure from the hundreds of agents of Pompeius. Now *he* can do more by himself than everyone else put together, partly for all sorts of reasons, partly because people here believe that he will come to deal with the war against Parthia. Anyway, he is now being paid at the rate of 198,000 denarii a month, and that out of taxes; nor is that enough to cover the monthly interest. But our friend Gnaeus is being very mild about it; he is getting nothing of the principal back and not even all the interest, but is content with what he is getting (Cicero, *ad Atticum* VI, 1, 3).

The rates of interest reflect to a certain extent of course the high risk involved and it may be that Pompeius never seriously expected to recover his capital or even to be paid the interest; return could be made in other ways, just as loans made between members of the Roman oligarchy often expected a political rather than a monetary return. Pompeius had kings in his pocket.

The problem of moneylending bedevilled the major issue of foreign policy which faced Rome in the 50s. Ptolemy XII Auletes of Egypt had been expelled by his subjects in 58 and resorted to massive borrowing and extensive bribery in order to secure a decree of the senate in favour of his restoration. The money was, however, irrecoverable unless he was actually restored; just as the Roman oligarchy was able to limit the powers conferred on Pompeius with the special command to deal with the corn supply in

57, so it was able to block every concrete proposal for the restoration of Auletes, from fear of the prestige and power likely to acrrue to whoever was successful. A. Gabinius, consul in 58, in 55 simply restored Auletes and was prosecuted and exiled for his pains (for the consequences in Egypt of Auletes' restoration see Fig. 11). The appearance of strength on the part of the oligarchy was an illusion; Caesar was engaged in Gaul in similar behaviour to that of Gabinius, but was quite clear when the time came that prosecution and exile were not to be contemplated.

Senators were of course not alone in enriching themselves from the provinces. When Caesar changed the method of collection of the tax of the province of Asia from collection by *publicani*, tax-farmers, to direct collection he reduced the amount due by a third; it is plausibly argued from this fact that the cut retained by the tax-farmers was precisely a third. There were in addition numerous opportunities for illegal exaction and the tax-farmers were also moneylenders on a large scale. It is likely that in addition to lending out their own capital they behaved as tax-farmers of later ages in the history of Europe and loaned out the money which they had collected before transmitting it to the government. Certainly it was they who provided the capital when Sulla imposed a levy of 20,000 talents (120,000,000 denarii) on the province of Asia; the consequences were disastrous:

Despite finding affairs in the cities in such a disastrous state, Lucullus in a short time relieved those who were being wronged of all their ills. For first of all he laid down that the maximum rate of interest was to be 12% per annum, secondly he disallowed all interest which exceeded the capital, thirdly and most important he decreed that the moneylender should take a quarter of the revenues of the debtor. And anyone who had added unpaid interest to the capital was deprived of the entire sum he was owed. As a result all debts were settled in less than a space of four years and property was returned unencumbered to its owners. The loan as a whole was the result of the fine of 120,000,000 denarii imposed on Asia by Sulla; those who had lent in fact recovered double what they had lent; as a result of the interest, the sum owed to them had reached 720,000,000 denarii. So they attacked Lucullus' reputation at Rome, regarding themselves as hard done by (Plutarch, *Lucullus* 20).

The ready cash available to the tax-farmers may also be inferred from the action of Pompeius in 49:

> Meanwhile, the money which had been demanded was being levied throughout the province with great brutality. In addition, all sorts of new ways of furthering the aims of rapacity were being devised; a poll-tax was levied on everyone, slave or free, column-taxes, door-taxes, corn, soldiers, arms, oarsmen, equipment, transport – all were demanded; anything whatever which could have a name attached to it provided an adequate excuse for levying money. Men with absolute power were placed in command not only of cities but even of villages and individual strong-points; whoever of these behaved with the greatest brutality and cruelty seemed most admirable and the most loyal citizen of Rome. The province was full of the attendants of magistrates and of the magistrates themselves, of officers and men in charge of the levies, who all saw that their own purse was filled as well as raising the money which had been demanded; for they kept saying that they had been driven out of their houses and exiled from their own country and lacked even the barest necessities, thus giving a good face to their shameful behaviour. In addition to all this, the burden of debt was very heavy, as often happens in times of war, when money has been demanded from everyone; in this context, if the moneylenders granted a stay of execution, they claimed that it was an act of the greatest generosity. As it was, the extent of debt in the province more than doubled in the course of those two years. Nor were the Roman citizens of the province spared in their need; a fixed amount was demanded from them by district and by city; in

11   Table showing silver content of coinage of Egypt.

The decline coincides with the attempt by Ptolemy XII Auletes to repay the loan which he had raised to fund his bribery of members of the Roman oligarchy.

D.R. Walker, *The metrology of the Roman silver coinage* i, Oxford, 1976, 151

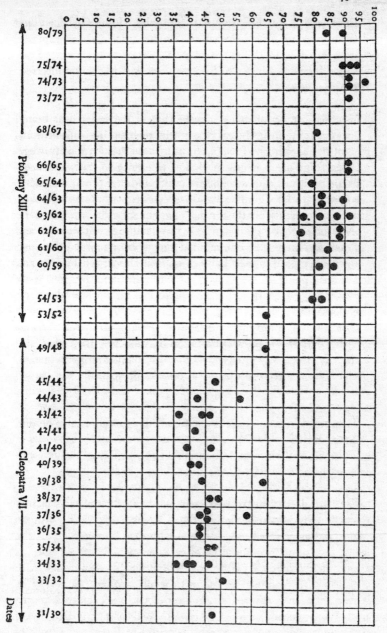

their case it was claimed that the money was being borrowed from them under a decree of the senate; finally, the Pompeians demanded from the tax-farmers a loan of the revenue of the following year, as they had done in Syria (Caesar, *de bello civili* III, 32, 1–6).

The defeat of Mithridates showed that in the last resort armed resistance to Rome in the east was futile; the Greek world turned to its cultural superiority in an attempt to win relief from its burdens or even to gain privileges. A chance reference to the west shows that the basic position was not dissimilar and that provincials there were prepared to contemplate association with Catilina in an attempt to escape from the burden of debt (Sallust, *Catilina* 40–1).

Provincial government not only provided men with wealth and connections on a scale unimagined a generation earlier; the great commands placed in their hands for a time almost regal power and led to their being showered with the symbolic honours appropriate to that power. Here again Pompeius by far surpassed all his predecessors.

Taking the extra name Magnus already after the African campaign of 82−1, in clear imitation of Alexander the Great, and using the title freely after the victory in Spain, Pompeius struck, perhaps for his triumph in 71, a remarkable special issue of gold coinage:

Head of Africa r.; on either side, symbols of augurate; behind MAGNUS.
Pompeius in triumphal quadriga r.; above, flying Victory with wreath; below PRO. COS.

He had already in the east been the recipient of a spectacular collection of honours. Before the 80s, cult of a living Roman magistrate is attested only for men who may be regarded as in a sense new founders of the cities or provinces which offered cult, M. Claudius Marcellus, T. Quinctius Flamininus, L. Mummius, Mn. Aquillius, M. Annius, Q. Mucius Scaevola; from the 80s onwards it was apparently offered as a matter of course, even to a notoriously bad governor such as C. Verres in Sicily. The trivialization of a considerable honour is the background to the extravagance of what was offered to Pompeius. Only a list can convey the number and scale of the honours conferred.

Apart from the usual honorific statues, cult is attested on Delos, at Athens and at Philadelphia: 'The people consecrated Cn. Pompeius Magnus *imperator*.' A month probably named after Pompeius appears at Mytilene; he is honoured as saviour at Samos, as saviour and founder after defeating the enemies of the world by land and sea at Mytilene, as saviour and benefactor of all Asia and guardian of land and sea at Miletopolis. Of the cities named after him, Pompeiopolis probably struck coinage in his lifetime with his portrait; Aristarchus of Colchis struck with his portrait in 52; at least four cities other than Pompeiopolis used a Pompeian era, each taking a moment during his presence in the east as the starting point of a new dating system.

What happend in the east was not without its counterpart in Rome. A moneyer connected with C. Marius had shown him as a *triumphator* (p. 130); L. Sulla had shown himself as a *triumphator* and had portrayed the equestrian statue of himself erected in Rome; with the portrayal of Cn. Pompeius on the coinages of the east, attitudes to portraiture on the mainstream coinage of the Roman Republic also shifted and Q. Pompeius Rufus, son of one of the consuls of 88, portrayed his father and his colleague in office, L. Sulla.

A small group of moneyers had celebrated C. Marius, and a few moneyers also L. Sulla; a large group showed by their types their attachment to Pompeius. The practice looks forward to the wearing by their supporters of gems with the portraits of the leaders of the Civil Wars from 49 onwards and to the wearing in all ages of the portrait of a monarch by his loyal followers.

In addition, Cn. Pompeius stood well along an extended line of leaders who claimed a personal link with a protecting deity. The practice began, as far as we can tell, with P. Scipio Africanus (p. 56); C. Marius dabbled in relationships with various eastern religions, L. Sulla claimed a special relationship with Venus and indeed conspicuously patronized a shrine of Aphrodite at Aphrodisias in Caria, whose priests were acute enough to realize the possibilities for enrichment open to them. The favour of Venus was claimed by a number of the contenders in the political struggle of the age of Cicero including Pompeius, claims which are mirrored in the coinage of the age of Cicero; our sources make much of the contest between Pompeius and Caesar for divine favour, clear evidence of the importance attached to this. The common people were indeed as ready to attribute divine characteristics to a victorious general as to a popular leader and clearly regarded evidence of divine favour as an important validation of a claim to power (see p. 185).

The development no doubt came easily enough in Rome, where first the patricians and then the mixed patrician-plebeian nobility had always claimed the right to guard and interpret the religious heritage of the state; it is not to be seen as a radical break (compare p. 130), but a development it undoubtedly was and it is interesting to note that it is accompanied by speculation about religion and in particular about the relationship between religion and society in an ideal state.

Ennius, a close contemporary of Africanus, had translated into Latin the work of Euhemerus, which discussed the view that great and mighty kings could become gods. In the first century BC, there was a great deal of interest in astrology as a science and the occult in general attracted much serious attention; Lucretius wrote the *de rerum natura*, a didactic poem in six books intended to introduce the philosophy of Epicurus to Roman readers and to disprove the existence of the gods as traditionally conceived; Cicero wrote the *de natura deorum* and devoted much space in the *de re publica* and the *de legibus* to religious matters; much of the extensive writings of Varro dealt with the Roman state religion, on which he held views analogous to those of Polybius in the second century BC (p. 93):

> For even Varro, the most learned of them all, virtually admits that all this (the divine descent of mortals) is false, although he is neither forthright nor confident in his admission. But he does say that it is expedient for a community that brave men should believe that they are descended from the gods, even though it may be false; for thus the human spirit, believing that it is of divine origin, will more readily undertake great tasks, will carry them out more energetically and thus finish the more successfully because of its faith (Augustine, *City of God* III, 4).

In the course of the decade which stretched from 59 to the outbreak of war in 49, Caesar came to surpass Pompeius and it is hard not to suppose that the result was intended. The two had combined with M. Crassus in 60 in order to ensure the election of Caesar to the consulship for 59, the first year in which he was legally entitled to hold it, and thereby to secure the revision of the contract between the state and the tax-farmers for Asia, in which Crassus had an interest, and the settlement of the veterans of Pompeius. The combination is now described as the First Triumvirate (cf. p. 190), but involved for the three participants only a vague undertaking to support each other once the original programme had been achieved.

Once in Gaul, Caesar set out to conquer the area (p. 155). His account of Pompeius' reasons for going to war in 49 is of course mere speculation about Pompeius; but it admits with dazzling clarity the actual effect on the balance of influence in Rome of the years in Gaul:

> Pompeius, urged on by the enemies of Caesar and because he wished no-one to be his equal in *dignitas* . . . (Caesar, *de bello civili* I, 4, 4)

It is interesting that while in Gaul Caesar tried to bid against Pompeius for the friendship of Massalia, by attributing to her the territory of the Sallyes (compare p. 154); certainly he acquired enormous wealth, which probably surpassed that of Pompeius. It provided a gift of 50 talents to Athens in direct competition with an earlier gift of Pompeius and in particular went to pay troops over and above the quota allowed for by the state, and to fund lavish bribery in Rome. Apart from the privately raised armies of the period 84–1, Crassus had probably paid for some of the troops which he used against Spartacus, and Pompeius had done the same in Spain; the *bon mot* had emerged that no-one was rich unless he could pay a legion out of his income, a revealing choice of criterion.

Above all, Caesar acquired an army in Gaul. Conscription from among those with land was of course still used to raise the armies of the age of Cicero, but the volunteer element was large and formed the characteristic element of a client army; I doubt if those who had been conscripted were much less dependent on their general.

Certainly the disparity between the pay of a legionary, still 108 denarii a year, and the income of his commander was even greater than it had been in the second century BC; for supplementation of the pitiful sum which was his due any soldier looked necessarily to the booty which accrued from a successful campaign, to the generosity of his commander in distributing it and to the willingness of that commander to connive at the spoliation of foreign, but not hostile, peoples. It has often been remarked that the threat of mutiny was frequent in the first century BC; it is also my impression that desertion to the enemy occurred regularly down to the 80s, but relatively little thereafter. The potential rewards of service with the legions were now enormous; with perseverance and pressure where necessary everything was possible.

The ultimate aim of a legionary was the acquisition of a plot of land; given the rôle of Caesar in providing for the settlement in 59 of the veterans of Pompeius, it was clearly a reasonable expectation that he would do the same in due course for his own, whereas it was not a reasonable expectation that the senate would do anything. The Roman empire could not survive without its armies, and they could not survive without their generals. The army of Caesar turned out to be superior to that which Pompeius could raise.

Strains in the combination between Caesar, Pompeius and Crassus led to a meeting at Luca and to the election of Pompeius and Crassus to a second consulship for 55. Caesar had his command in Gaul renewed for a further five years, while Pompeius and Crassus also acquired provincial commands, their need for which is clear evidence of their jittery insecurity. Pompeius acquired Spain, which he governed *in absentia* through legates, thus unconsciously pre-figuring the method by which Augustus was to govern his *provincia*. Caesar was also later to complain with much plausibility:

A command of a new kind had been created in order to threaten him, where one and the same man saw to the affairs of the city from outside the gates and governed in absence over a period of years two provinces with large armies (*de bello civili* 1, 85, 8).

The rioting which followed the death of Clodius brought

Pompeius to a sole consulship in 52 (p. 167); in the course of 52 his command in Spain was renewed for a further five years. For the moment Caesar expressed admiration for his success in curbing disorder (Caesar, *de bello Gallico* VII, 6):

> When news of all this reached Caesar in Italy (that is, north Italy, Cisalpine Gaul), since he had now heard that the affairs of the city had been put in better order by the efforts of Cn. Pompeius, he set out for Transalpine Gaul.

But as the end of Caesar's second term approached, it became clear that he expected to pass direct to a consulship and thence to another provincial command. It is a curious irony that in 52 Pompeius had also passed a law imposing a gap of five years between holding a magistracy in Rome and governing a province, a law which if passed earlier and enforced could have weakened the dangerous link between political competition at Rome and extortion in the provinces (p. 171). Meanwhile Pompeius and the core of the oligarchy under the leadership of the younger Cato moved closer to each other. The latter met, however, with a total lack of success in his attempt to impose the will of the oligarchy on Caesar; rather than risk a return to private life and the certainty of prosecution, at the beginning of 49 he led his army across the Rubicon, the boundary between his province and Italy, thereby beginning the civil wars which lasted until Octavianus gained sole power with the death of M. Antonius in Egypt in 30:

> Others say that he feared lest he be forced to give an account of everything which he had done in his first consulate against the sanctions of religion and of the laws and against tribunician vetoes; for M. Cato often said and even swore on oath that he would bring Caesar to trial, as soon as he had disbanded his army; and it was widely asserted that if he returned as a private individual he would like Milo have to plead his case before the jurors with troops stationed round about (to secure a conviction by intimidation). Asinius Pollio (a contemporary) lends weight to this view by reporting that when he saw his enemies dead or scattered at the battle of Pharsalus he said in these very words. 'This was their will; I, C. Caesar, should have been condemned

> despite my great achievements, if I had not sought *auxilium*,
> protection, from my army.' (Suetonius, *Divus Julius* 30)

Caesar's emphasis on his great achievements is certainly authentic
(see p. 157). The use of the word *auxilium* is also significant; when
a plebeian threatened by a magistrate appealed to a tribune he
sought *auxilium, auxilium* which was ultimately guaranteed by the
oath of the plebs to kill the man who defied it. The violence built
into the Roman political system had come to fruition.

Who was legally in the right was clearly a matter of dispute at the
time and it is an illusion to suppose that this can now be
established; to judge from the surviving evidence, little attention
was paid to the problem when men gave reasons for their actions.
Caesar was able to emphasize the fact that he was a defender of
libertas, a champion of the tribunes who had attempted to protect
his alleged rights; he also emphasized the defence of his *dignitas*, as
L. Catilina had done, and his services to the *res publica*; all are
familiar themes:

> When he heard of these preparations, Caesar harangued his
> soldiers; he reminded them of the wrongs done to him by his
> enemies over the years; he complained that Pompeius had been
> drawn away from him and corrupted by them through envious
> denigration of his reputation, although he had always subscribed
> to the reputation and *dignitas* of Pompeius and been his
> supporter. He complained that a revolutionary change had taken
> place in the government of the state, with the deployment of a
> military response to the tribunician veto, an institution which a
> generation earlier had been restored by force of arms (Caesar
> alludes to its restoration in 70 by Pompeius and Crassus as
> consuls; to say that they extorted their consulships by force of
> arms is an exaggeration). Sulla, in depriving the tribunate of all
> its other powers, had nonetheless left the veto (in protection of
> an individual) untouched; Pompeius, who had the reputation of
> having restored something which had been lost, had in fact taken
> away something which the tribunes had had before his
> restoration.
>
> Whenever in the past the *senatus consultum ultimum* had
> been passed, decreeing that the magistrates should see that the

res publica suffered no damage, a decree which issued a clarion call to arms to the Roman people, it had been done in a situation when dangerous legislation was in the process of being passed, when the tribunes were engaged in violence, the people had become disloyal, the temples and the strong points of the city had been seized . . . None of these things had now taken place or even been thought of.

Caesar also urged his soldiers to defend from his enemies the reputation and *dignitas* of someone under whose leadership as a general they had for nine years served the *res publica* with outstanding success and won numerous victories, and had conquered the whole of Gaul and Germany.

The soldiers of the thirteenth legion, which was on the spot, for Caesar had summoned it at the first sign of trouble, the others had not yet arrived, shouted in reply that they were ready to defend the injuries done to their general and to the tribunes of the plebs (Caesar, *de bello civili* 1, 7).

Nor were the soldiers of the thirteenth legion alone in their attitude (Caesar, *de bello civili* 1, 13):

When they heard of Caesar's approach, the town councillors of Auximum came in a body to Attius Varus (the Pompeian commander) and explained that they were not free agents; neither they nor the other towns could allow C. Caesar, *imperator*, who had deserved well of the *res publica* and had such great achievements to his name, to be kept out of the town and its defences.

The horrors of the Sullan proscriptions, which still made Cicero shudder when he drafted the *Paradoxa Stoicorum* (p. 171), had probably helped to deter some men from a recourse to violence in the generation after Sulla; now that the war had begun, traditional restraints largely disappeared:

. . . I was horrified at the sort of war which Pompeius envisaged, cruel and all-embracing, of a kind which men do not yet comprehend. What threats against the townships of Italy, against men of repute by name, in fact against everyone who had

not followed him! How often he said, 'Sulla could do it, shall I
not be able to do it?'! . . . Sulla or Marius or Cinna have been
regarded as having been in the right; on the side of the law,
perhaps; but what have we ever witnessed more cruel or more
devastating than their victories? (Cicero, *ad Atticum* IX, 10, 2–3)

Nor was it only the soldiers of Caesar who followed him into Italy;
when L. Sulla had marched on Rome, only one of his officers had
followed him; in 49, Caesar was deserted only by T. Labienus,
owing earlier allegiance to Pompeius and guessing him the likely
victor. It is hard to avoid the conclusion that the growing use of
violence in Roman politics had helped to make the step which
Caesar took natural and acceptable. Competition within the
oligarchy had finally reached the point where it destroyed the
framework which alone made competition meaningful; the armies
which fought for the various dynasts between 49 and 30 were
finally brought under control by an autocrat.

Many were uneasy in 49; no-one, so far as we know, displayed
the perceptiveness which emerges from the remarks of John
Hotham in 1642:

> . . . no man that hath any reasonable share in the commonwealth
> can desire that either side shall be absolute conquerors, for it will
> be then as it was betwixt Caesar and Pompey . . . the necessitous
> people of the whole kingdom will presently rise in mighty
> numbers, and whosoever they pretend for at first, within a while
> they will set up for themselves to the utter ruin of all the Nobility
> and Gentry of the kingdom.

In the case of England, those who had benefited from the
revolution were able to ally with the old order to stop it. In the case
of Rome, the collective power of the oligarchy as a whole was
already powerless in 49 against the core under the leadership of the
younger Cato which was determined to bend Caesar to its will. The
senate voted by 370 to 22 that Caesar and Pompeius should *both*
disband their armies. The vote was ignored; but perhaps it
mattered little that a compromise solution did not emerge. A *res
publica* in which Pompeius held the consulship in 55, then
acquired a province for 5 years, then held the consulship along

with it in 52, then had his province renewed for another 5 years, in which Caesar held the consulship in 59, then governed Gaul for 10 years, then held the consulship again, then acquired another province, such was only in name a *res publica*.

A series of bloody battles across the length and breadth of the Mediterranean world followed. Pompeius was defeated at Pharsalus in 48 and assassinated in Egypt soon after. The war took on progressively the aspect of a feud between Caesar and the heirs of Pompeius. By 45 there were no more armies in the field against Caesar. Throughout (and his ultimate victory owed much to the fact) Caesar distanced himself in one important respect from his enemies. Unlike them, he made a point of showing mercy to the defeated; for there were to be no proscriptions; but *clementia* was the characteristic virtue of the monarch.

A monarch *de facto* Caesar certainly became; he also acquired many of the symbolic rights appropriate to a monarch, such as his portrait on the coinage (Pl. 7f). Whether he wished to be called a king is unclear and it is attractive to suppose with Elizabeth Rawson that he wished rather to be seen to play with the notion and to have the *gloria recusandi*, the renown from rejecting the title. It is in any case unclear what being a king *de iure* actually meant to contemporary Romans; their ambiguous attitudes to their own kings in the past and to Hellenistic kings in the present are here no help.

Similarly, what was offered to Caesar went beyond even the divine honours conferred on Pompeius; Caesar was offered the position of a god at Rome (Cicero, *Philippica* II, 110):

So you who are so careful to foster the memory of Caesar, do you really love him now that he is dead? What honour did he achieve greater than the right to have a sacred couch, an image, a house like a temple, a priest? So just as there is a priest of Jupiter, of Mars, of Quirinus, is M. Antonius now the priest of the divine Julius? So why do you hesitate? . . .

Following earlier precedent, Caesar certainly made much of his descent from Venus and Aeneas (see also Pl. 4); he was also between 49 and 44 outstandingly imaginative and innovative in his exploitation of religious sentiment.[1] Still, it is unclear what being a god actually meant and in the event Caesar was not deified till after his assassination. For that futile gesture there was in the eyes of his assassins ample justification merely in the *de facto* power which he possessed; no institutional framework for a living monarchy had yet been created.

1. It is interesting to note again that religious development provoked speculation, in the shape of the *de gente populi Romani* of Varro, written in 43 and concerned *inter alia* with mortals who achieved deification.

Epilogue

THE MURDERERS OF Caesar were not greeted with the rapturous thanks which they had expected from a people restored to liberty; in all classes but their own a consensus capable of supporting a new kind of government was emerging and it was becoming possible to justify the establishment of an autocracy. The pattern was becoming apparent already in the lifetime of Caesar and became established during the fifteen appalling years when the murderers of Caesar and his avengers fought each other and the latter then fought amongst themselves. Between murderers and avengers there was little difference, for all were members of the Roman oligarchy and all fought for supreme power. The last issue of coinage of Brutus was an issue of denarii, bearing on one side two daggers and a *pileus* (a felt cap which was placed on the head of a Roman slave when he was freed in the ceremony of manumission) and the legend 'Eid(ibus) Mar(tiis)', to symbolize the freeing of the Roman state by the murder of Caesar on the Ides of March 44; on the other side was a portrait of Brutus, an overt symbol of monarchy.

Similarly, the precise means by which Octavianus, the adopted son, but not the designated political heir of Caesar, eventually achieved supreme power and became the first Augustus are secondary in importance to the fact that it was becoming possible to represent a monarchy as compatible with the Roman system of values and to the fact that almost all men were becoming increasingly receptive to such arguments. For central to the Roman revolution was not the replacement of one oligarchy by another, but the creation of a despotism supported by a very different consensus from that which had supported the collective rule of the Republican aristocracy.

It is natural for those such as Octavianus who have gained in power or wealth from a revolution to wish to fossilize its achievements and in the case of Rome the monetary stakes alone for which individuals played in the fight for supreme power after 44 were enormous. A hoard discovered at Brescello in north Italy in 1714 consisted of 80,000 gold pieces. It was lost in or after 38 and was presumably the treasure chest of a war lord; it was worth 2,000,000 denarii, in a period when a legionary was paid 250 denarii a year. It is also common for successful revolutionaries to entrench their position by the use of traditional institutions; but while it is true that in the case of the Roman revolution Republican forms survived, the old order was not restored when peace returned in 30 and political oratory died with the Republic (Tacitus, *Dialogus de oratoribus* 36).

The non-political upper classes had done well out of the functioning Republic, those wealthy men who refrained from entering the senate, but shared in organizing the exploitation of the provinces in their capacity as tax-farmers; a cynic might indeed suggest that the *concordia ordinum*, harmony among the different social orders, which Cicero vaunted as the determination of senate and *equites* alike to defend the *res publica*, was no more than an agreement to fleece the empire; and it was in fact a quarrel between senate and *equites* on precisely this subject which opened the way for Caesar in 59 (p. 179). But the non-political upper classes at Rome understandably became disenchanted with the way in which the aristocracy of the Republic governed or, increasingly, failed to govern; it is one of the ironies of history that the disenchantment appeared in a period when one of the principal causes of resentment had been removed by the law passed in 70, which shared the composition of the courts between *equites* and senate.

The disenchantment, however, is readily documented:

So I think that there are two ways in which the senate can be reformed, by increasing it in size and by introducing the secret ballot. The result of the latter will be that senators will be more inclined to vote according to their conscience. An increase in numbers will introduce a greater element of security and a wider range of experience. For particularly at the moment some senators are involved with the courts, while others are occupied

with their own business or that of their friends, with the result
that they have paid hardly any attention to affairs of state . . .
Thus individual nobles, with a few senators whom they treat as
makeweights added to their own power, approve, disapprove,
decree whatever they please; they have been able to act
according to their private whim ([Sallust], *Epistula ad
Caesarem* ii, 5—6).

The consequences of resentment of this kind emerge very clearly
from a remark of Cicero in 49:

Men from the *municipia* and from the countryside have been
having long conversations with me; the only things they care
about at all are their fields, their houses, their money (*ad
Atticum* viii, 13, 2).

Cicero misunderstood and undervalued such men; one of their
number was C. Cartilius Poplicola of Ostia, who served regularly
as a magistrate of his community during the age of revolution and
perhaps led the resistance to a raid of Sex. Pompeius during the
wars which followed the murder of Caesar; at all events he became
a pillar of the new régime and was rewarded by Ostia with a nude
statue in heroic pose and a magnificent tomb for himself, his wife,
children and descendants.

Beside the evidence for the reaction of the non-political upper
classes to the arrogance and incapacity of the Republican oligarchy
may be set evidence for a general feeling of insecurity in the Italy of
the age of Cicero. There is no evidence that anyone actually
advocated a seizure of power by Pompeius in 62, but large numbers
of people nervously wondered about the possibility. A sense of
insecurity is conveyed also by the number of cities which built or
re-built their walls.

Contemporaries were also very well aware of many other things
which were not as they should be. Members of a state which ruled
the known world turned to barbarians for help in their struggles
with each other, following the example set when the Samnites,
understandably enough, sought help from Mithridates VI. Cicero
viewed the practice with disgust, citing it as one of his reasons for
abandoning the Pompeian cause in 48 (*ad Atticum* xi, 6, 2;

compare 7, 3). The values which lay behind such a viewpoint later formed an important part of the background to Augustus' justification of his position.

Augustus also knew that the wealthy of the age of revolution feared with good reason the undisciplined armies of the late Republic. We have already seen that the emergence of the army as a specialized institution was a major factor in the generation of conflict in the late Republic; its rôle did not go unperceived by contemporaries (Cornelius Nepos, *Eumenes* 8, 2):

> For the very phalanx of Alexander the Great, which had crossed Asia and conquered the Persians, accustomed both to success and to licence, demanded not that it should obey its leaders, but that it should command, as our veterans do now. So there is a danger lest these men now do what those men did, with the result that by their disobedience and excessive licence they may destroy everything, no less those on whose side they are fighting than those against whom they are ranged. For if anyone reads about the exploits of those veterans, he will realize that they are like the exploits of our veterans and that the two groups are dissimilar only in the time at which they have lived.

A similar viewpoint, preserved by Appian, probably goes back to contemporary sources (*Civil Wars* v, 17, 68−71).

Augustus of course took steps to neutralize the army as a political force and it is important that Caesar already showed signs of moving in that direction; his pay increase, from 108 to 250 denarii a year, was presumably designed in part to reduce the dependence of the professional soldier on an individual general, from whom he expected a land allotment at the end of his term of service. In fact, since the Roman world lapsed back into chaos after Caesar's death, his measures simply made the struggle for power more expensive for his would-be successors and their exactions from the provinces correspondingly larger.

Insofar as the Roman world had a government at all after 44, it was provided by the triumvirate of M. Lepidus, M. Antonius and C. Iulius Caesar Octavianus, who divided the world between themselves in 43, until the first was forced into retirement and the last two were left to fight it out. The nature of their rule was clear:

> (P. Scipio Africanus) was unable to get his way in the senate, although indeed he was the leading citizen in the state, since at that time the *res publica* was ruled by law and not (as in the days of Nepos) by force (Cornelius Nepos, *Cato,* 2, 2).

Augustus again perceived the state of public opinion, in striking contrast to the miscalculation of the murderers of Caesar, and took care after his defeat of Antonius to dissociate himself from the illegal aspects of his early career and to emphasize his concern for legality. His *Res Gestae,* in which towards the end of his life he set out to justify his position, has been regarded as a misleading document; in a sense it is, but it is also a perfect mirror of the values to which Augustus could and did appeal. It begins with an account of his entry into public life, masking its unsavoury moments, and of his successes in the military and civilian spheres, in the service of the Roman people; an account of the consequent honours follows. Augustus then turns to his benefactions to the Roman people and to the successes of his foreign policy once he had been accepted as leader; again a list of consequent honours follows. No-one could accuse Augustus of *cum barbaris gentibus coniunctio*, the policy of close links with the barbarians, which was pilloried by Cicero. In the sphere of religion, also, Augustus' touch was sure; the élite of the late Republic had combined widespread enquiry and scepticism with a concern for ritual, reflected in the publication of books on religious practice, and Augustus knew very well what he was doing when he advertized his restoration of temples and cult observances.

The monarchy of Augustus and his successors, then, was supported by a very different kind of consensus from that which had supported the government of the Republic; the new régime, moreover, not only invited the participation – as its servants, needless to say – of those members of the upper classes who had played little part in the political life of the Republic, but also drew its personnel from a much wider geographical range. The cultural unification of Italy, following its political unification after 90, is indeed one of the most important elements in the history of the last generation of the Roman Republic (see Pl. 7d).

The final state of affairs was foreshadowed already by Cicero:

'. . . this is my and my brother's real country (*germana patria*)'
. . . 'But' replied Atticus 'what is it that you said just now, that
this place – for I take it that you mean Arpinum – is your real
country. For surely you do not have two countries; rather Rome
is the country of us all. Unless perhaps the country of Cato was
not Rome, but Tusculum.' 'But I do think that he and everyone
from a *municipium* has two countries, one by descent, one by
citizenship.' (*de legibus* II, 5).

It is hard now to imagine the sheer scale of the effort needed to
assimilate Italy after the Social War; it involved not merely the
creation of appropriate political institutions, but also the forging of
bonds in all areas of society. One important consequence of the
creation of new political units as part of a Roman framework was an
increase in the pace of urbanization in Italy; the universality of the
process of assimilation emerges from the fact that the Po valley
produced in the age of Cicero the poet Catullus, the historian
Cornelius Nepos and the Epicurean philosopher Catius.

The fluidity of Roman institutions in this period can also be
inferred from the groping and hesitant, not to say incompetent,
approach of inscriptions such as those from Tarentum and
Heraclea, which contain sets of municipal regulations, when
contrasted with the sure touch and stereotyped formulae of the
municipal charters of the period of the Principate, such as those for
Irni, Malaca and Salpensa, drawn up in the Flavian period.

A major rôle in the unification of Italy was of course played by
the army, which functioned also as an avenue of social mobility.
Already in the age of Cicero, M. Petreius, probably the son of a
centurion from Atina, reached the praetorship (and as propraetor
in 63 suppressed the revolt of Catilina). The turbulent years from
49 to 30 increased the effectiveness of the army as a vehicle of social
change and there appears under Augustus a particularly dramatic
example of the assimilation of an alien and his social advancement
alike, P. Otacilius, son of Arranes, now a municipal magistrate at
Casinum, the son of a Spanish cavalryman enfranchised by
Cn. Pompeius Strabo during the Social War. Such are the men
who chose for their grave monuments the 'fregi d'armi', friezes
with representations of arms and armour, which form so dominant
an element in the art of central Italy during the early Principate.

But the late Republic was more than a period of political innovation, with all its social and economic consequences; it was also a period of tremendous cultural advance. We have seen what happened in the early period of close contact between Rome and the Greek world after 200 and some of the developments which took place later. The result of a century of sometimes rather pell-mell borrowing from the Greek world was the achievement by the Roman élite as a whole of a remarkably high level of cultural awareness. This awareness then provided a background to and springboard for a number of astonishing individual achievements in the field of high culture. In the field of politics, individuals increasingly sought and achieved dominance at the expense of the group; John North acutely points out that this development is symbolized by the fact that in the first century BC priesthoods with obligations which conflicted with a political career could sometimes no longer be filled; thus there was no Flamen Dialis, priest of Jupiter, between 87 and 11. But just as the strivings of individuals in the field of politics form a collective phenomenon, so do they in the field of culture; the last generation of the Republic produced poets such as Lucretius, an antiquarian such as Varro, an orator such as Cicero, historians such as Caesar and Sallust, together with a host of lesser figures. An unknown artist produced the frieze portraying a Roman census from the so-called 'Altar of Domitius Ahenobarbus' (Pl. 3, 4), a variety of unknown artists, Italian as well as Roman, created brilliantly imaginative coin types (Pl. 7c–e). Latin literature and Roman art have arrived, and arrived in a period which was still devoting a vast amount of energy to the acquisition of an empire and to the exploitation of its resources, when legal innovation and religious experiment were the order of the day.

In the middle of it all, the poet Horace claimed to fear a conquest of Rome; but the Roman commonwealth was far too resilient for that and the empire passed undiminished from Republican to monarchic government. That change may indeed be seen as the greatest innovation of them all; but it carried with it the end of the will and the capacity to innovate further.

Appendix 1

The Roman Assemblies

THE MOST IMPORTANT single fact about the different Roman assemblies was that the men who composed them voted in groups. The earliest form of *comitia*, assembly, was the *comitia curiata*, which consisted of 30 *curiae*, ten from each of the three archaic tribes, Tities, Ramnes and Luceres; group voting was perhaps used because it was felt necessary for religious reasons to have the consent of every kin-group. In the middle and late Republic, the *comitia curiata* met only to transact such purely formal business as passing *leges curiatae*, which were technically necessary for some incoming magistrates, and ratifying adoptions; the *leges curiatae* apparently possessed religious significance and adoptions, which involved the transfer of family *sacra*, were likewise the concern of the gods.

Meanwhile, the notion of group voting had been transferred to the different new assemblies which developed as the state evolved. The first to emerge was the *comitia centuriata*, the people meeting as an assembly organized by *centuriae*, army units; just as a greater burden in fighting fell on the better armed, so they were given a greater say in the assembly. The better armed units voted first and the people were so assigned to *centuriae* that a unit of the better armed and therefore wealthy consisted of fewer men than a unit of the poorly armed and therefore indigent. Decisions were normally therefore taken by a relatively small number of men articulated in a relatively large number of voting units. As the Republic evolved, membership of a voting unit and of the *classis*, group to which it was assigned, came to be defined in terms of a property qualification, rather than in terms of quality of armour. The flagrantly undemocratic nature of the *comitia centuriata* was slightly modified, perhaps in 179, but not significantly.

In the course of the plebeian agitation of the fifth century BC, a parallel assembly of plebeians only emerged, the *concilium plebis*, organized by tribes, new regional units; of these units there were eventually 35. These 35 voting units were much more manageable than the 193 voting units of the *comitia centuriata* and the structure was taken over by a new *comitia*, the *comitia tributa*, which eventually came to transact much of the business which came before the Roman people. The composition of the *comitia tributa* was the same as that of the *concilium plebis*, with the addition of the small number of patricians. Since the two assemblies were virtually the same apart from their presidents, a Lex Hortensia of 287 recognized that decrees of the *concilium plebis, plebiscita*, although passed by only part of the people, were binding on all of it.

Although not overtly undemocratic, the *comitia tributa* and the *concilium plebis* were in their way just as unrepresentative as the *comitia centuriata*. In the middle Republic, a rural tribe was mostly represented in voting by those who were leisured and therefore wealthy enough to journey to Rome; in the late Republic, peasants who had migrated to Rome continued to vote in the rural tribes to which they had originally belonged. Decisions were therefore taken by those who were *de facto* the urban *plebs*.

In all Roman assemblies, speaking was only possible at the invitation of the presiding magistrate; there was thus no freedom of speech. It was also impossible to amend a proposal. The presiding magistrate asked the assembly to vote yes or no, a fact which meant that a proposal was called a *rogatio*; speeches were of course made on both sides, but simple acceptance or rejection were the only possibilities.

There are two views of the seriousness with which legislation was considered (Cicero, *pro Rabirio Postumo* 14):

Glaucia, a scoundrel of a man, but clever with it, was in the habit of advising the people to pay attention to the first line whenever a law was read out; if it was 'Any dictator, consul, praetor, master of horse . . .', the people were not to bother; but if it was 'Anyone who after the passage of this law . . .', the people should beware lest it become subject to some new court.

	Comitia Curiata	Comitia Centuriata	Comitia Tributa	Concilium Plebis
Voting units	30 *curiae*, 10 each from Tities, Ramnes, Luceres	193 centuries	35 tribes	35 tribes
Composition	One lictor to each *curia*	All citizens	All citizens	Plebs
Presiding officer	Consul, praetor, pontifex maximus	Consul, praetor, dictator, *interrex*	Consul, praetor, curule aedile	Tribune, plebeian aedile
Elections		Consuls, praetors, censors	Curule aediles, quaestors, lesser magistrates, special commissioners	Tribunes, plebeian aediles, special commissioners
Rogationes (legislative)	*Lex curiata*, adoptions	Declarations of war, treaties of peace and alliance, confirmation of power of censors, legislation	Legislation	Legislation (after 287, *plebiscita* had the validity of *leges*)
(judicial)		Capital charges (progressively transferred to *quaestiones*)	Crimes against the state punishable by a fine (progressively transferred to *quaestiones*)	
Place of meeting	*Comitium* or Capitol	Usually Campus Martius	For elections, usually Campus Martius For legislation, usually *Comitium* or Capitol	

12 Table showing functions of different Roman assemblies

On the other hand, Pompeius in 59 adopted a different approach with the agrarian law of Caesar (Dio XXXVIII, 5, 3):

> After this introduction, he went through each of the clauses and spoke in favour of them, so that the crowd was highly pleased.

Bibliographical Note
There is a good general account in E. S. Staveley, *Greek and Roman Voting and Elections,* London, 1972.

Appendix 2

The Roman Army

THE ROMAN READINESS to innovate is apparent not least in a military context, where indeed it was noticed by Polybius. In the fifth century BC and no doubt also at the end of the monarchy, the *assidui* who formed the Roman heavy infantry fought in a formation like that of the Greek and Macedonian phalanx, armed with thrusting-spears and round shields; the original legion of 6000 men was composed of 60 *centuriae* of 100 men each. When two consuls replaced the king, the legion was divided into two legions of 3000 men, but continued to be composed of 60 *'centuriae'*.

Perhaps towards the end of the fourth century BC a much more flexible formation began to appear, in which a legion was arranged in three lines; each line consisted of ten maniples, each of two *centuriae*; the men in the first line were known as *hastati*, those in the second line as *principes*, those in the third line as *triarii*; three maniples, one of each type, made up a cohort. At first, only the *hastati* had the new equipment of throwing-spear, sword and long shield (*pilum, gladius* and *scutum*); they appear as spear-throwers in Ennius, *Annales*, line 284 V, and perhaps owed their name to the fact that they were the first to throw spears. At the battle of Beneventum in 275, the *principes* apparently still fought as a phalanx with thrusting-spears and, presumably, round shields (Dionysius Hal. xx, 11); and Ennius, *Annales*, line 183 V, quoted on p. 125, is probably wrong to assume the long shield, *scutum*, as the norm for 281. The *principes* perhaps owed their name to the fact that the brunt of the battle fell on them. In Polybius' day, the third row, the *triarii*, alone retained thrusting-spears; a legion also included at that period 1200 *velites*, light-armed.

During the period when the infantry was developing, the

cavalry was also reformed, perhaps during the Second Punic War; the purpose of the reform was to make it better armed and less vulnerable.

Probably in response to conditions in Spain from the late third century BC onwards, the technique was adopted of *grouping* three maniples in a cohort; this became the normal tactical formation of the Roman army in the late second century BC. When Marius abandoned the property qualification for recruitment, he also probably removed the distinctions within a legion, which henceforth consisted of ten uniformly equipped cohorts. *Velites* also disappeared, as did Roman cavalrymen; both were replaced by foreign auxiliaries.

Bibliographical Note
I here largely resume, I hope correctly, the difficult article of E. Rawson, *PBSR* 1971, 13 = *Roman Culture and Society* (1991), 34–57.

Appendix 3

Equites

THE *equites equo publico* were in origin cavalry for whom a horse was provided by the state and for the upkeep of whose horse the state also provided. As Rome expanded overseas, she came increasingly to use auxiliary cavalry provided by friendly foreign powers and the status of *eques equo publico* came to be increasingly an honorific one. Down to 129 (see below) practically all senators were also *equites equo publico*; it was clearly exceptional when Cato as censor in 184 removed the public horse from L. Scipio on the grounds that he was not fit enough to ride it.

Meanwhile the growing complexity of Roman government led to the emergence of a group of wealthy men, who undertook contracts for the state, whether to put up a building or to collect a tax. (They were still landowners, like all wealthy men in Republican Italy, and had to give surety in land for the performance of their contract.) Senators were of course debarred from undertaking such contracts in their own names, since they were the body responsible for overseeing the contracts.

Public contractors, then, in the mid-second century BC, along with senators and sons of senators, as well as wealthy landowners who wished neither to enter the senate nor to undertake public contracts, and perhaps a few men of business made up the equestrian order, the *equites equo publico*. Pressure to enter the order may perhaps be inferred from the proposal by Cato to increase the number of *equites equo publico* from 1800 to 2200; but it is also possible that Cato wished to re-create a real Roman cavalry.

In 129, a *plebiscitum equorum reddendorum* was passed, a plebiscite compelling senators or men who became senators to surrender their public horse; the operation of the law may be observed in 70 (Plutarch, *Pompeius* 22):

> The censors Gellius and Lentulus were seated in public in their insignia of office and the parade of *equites* being examined was in progress, when Pompeius was seen coming down into the forum, wearing his insignia of office (he was now consul) and leading his horse by the hand (to surrender it). When he was near and his identity clearly visible, he ordered the lictors to stand aside and brought his horse up to the platform. The people were amazed and struck dumb, the magistrates wrestled with the mixed emotions of respect and joy at the sight. Then the older of the two asked, 'I enquire of you, Pompeius Magnus, whether you have undertaken all the campaigns which the law demands (as a qualification for elective office).' Pompeius replied in a loud voice, 'All – and all under my own command.' (Pompeius had held no elective office before the consulship, but a string of special commands.) On hearing this the people shouted out aloud in admiration . . .

The aim and result of the law of 129 was to free 300 public horses which could be conferred as an honorific mark of status on landowners, public contractors and men of business; there were clearly by now many men in these groups anxious for public recognition of their importance in the community. It is not surprising that the measure is described by Cicero (*de re publica* IV, 2) as a *nova largitio*, a new way of dispensing favours.

The senatorial and equestrian orders were thus separated, though it must be remembered that *sons* of senators continued to form a large part of the equestrian order (they were of course excluded when *equites* were recruited to the juries of the extortion court).

At some stage which is not known, there developed a further property qualification within the *prima classis*, which a man had to possess before he could be assigned a public horse; in the first century BC the figure was 400,000 sestertii (that for the *prima classis* was 100,000 sestertii). As a result, *equites* came to be used loosely to mean men who had over 400,000 sestertii rather than men with the public horse; but the latter, strict, definition remained valid in law and it was for instance these men who were recruited to the juries by C. Gracchus.

Bibliographical Note

Cl. Nicolet, *L'ordre équestre* I−II, Paris, 1966 (1974) and 1974, deals both with the definition of an *eques* and related juridical problems and with the social history of the equestrian order. A good brief account of the latter aspect is in P. A. Brunt, 'The Equites in the Late Republic' in II *Int. Conf. Ec. Hist.* Aix-en-Provence, 1962, I, 117 = R. Seager, ed., *The Crisis of the Roman Republic,* Cambridge, 1969, 83, much revised in *The Fall of the Roman Republic,* 1988, Ch. 3. T. P. Wiseman, *Historia* 1970, 67, = *Roman Studies* (1987), 57–73, resumes the debate on juridical problems. E. Badian, *Publicans and Sinners,* Oxford, 1972, Chapter 3 and 5, is quite unreliable on the definition of an *eques*, the law of 129 and the significance of the legislation of the Gracchan period, see the review by T. P. Wiseman, *Phoenix* 1973, 189 = *Roman Studies* (1987), 74–82.

Appendix 4

The Special Commands

THE LATE REPUBLIC was marked by the creation of a number of special commands overseas; their chief significance lies in the fact that normally they covered a wide area and were for a long period and that the procedure by which they came into being was independent of the routine assignation of provinces. But the actual powers which the different laws conferred on the recipients of the commands also have a certain importance; it is therefore extremely unfortunate that much of the evidence for the laws reflects above all the indignation of contemporary rhetoric – *imperium infinitum*, unlimited power, is a term of abuse, not a constitutional definition.

An important element in the traditional restrictions on the freedom of action of a Republican magistrate (apart from collegiality and limitation of tenure) was the designation of a *provincia,* initially simply a sphere of action, eventually an actual area assigned to a magistrate; this was in effect as true for a consul as it was for any other magistrate.

The earliest attested grants of special powers, as opposed to specially made grants of large *provinciae* for extended periods, were those made to M. Antonius in 74 and Cn. Pompeius in 67, in both cases to deal with the pirates; the two men were given 'equal power with that of the different provincial governors up to 50 miles from the sea' (Velleius ii, 31, 2). The purpose was presumably to relieve Antonius and Pompeius from the territorial restrictions which went with their *provinciae* and which might have prevented them engaging in hot pursuit of pirates. It had always been clear that the power of one consul was the same as that of the other consul and that the power of a pro-consul was the same as that of a consul and it no doubt seemed perfectly reasonable to give

Antonius and Pompeius power equal to that of a governor in his territory.

The result, however, was an indignified clash between the officers of Pompeius and Q. Caecilius Metellus, the governor of Crete, and between Pompeius and C. Calpurnius Piso, the governor of Gaul. For the moment the incidents provoked no reaction and the subsequent command conferred on Pompeius against Mithridates VI in 66 was merely one which was extended in space and in time. Finally, in 57, the notion emerged that, in order to deal with the corn-supply, Pompeius should be given power in the provinces *greater* than that of those who governed them (note that *imperium*, power, must be described as *maius*, greater, than some other power, not in isolation; there is no such thing as *imperium maius*); the proposal failed and it was left to Cicero in 43 to propose successfully that Brutus and Cassius be granted power overriding that of the other governors in the east and thereby provide – just in time – a precedent for the power conferred on Augustus in 23, although that of course had a number of special features and also overrode that of every other provincial governor.

1. Central Italy

2. Italy

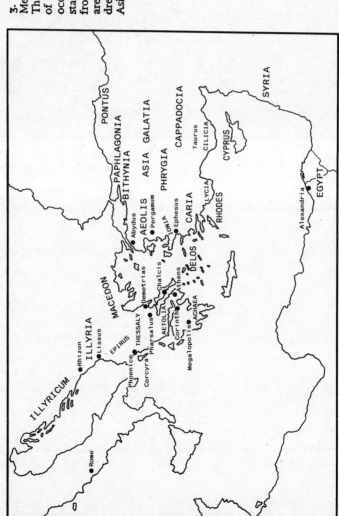

3. The eastern Mediterranean
The Roman provinces of Asia and Illyricum occupied areas substantially different from the geographical areas from which they drew their names, Asia Minor and Illyria.

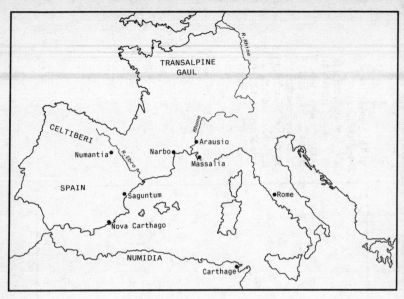

4. The western Mediterranean

Date Chart

753   Foundation of Rome
510   Institution of Republic

II – Italy and Rome

See IV

III – The Roman Governing Classes

509   Lex Valeria introducing *provocatio*, the right of appeal
        from a magistrate to the people; many historians have
        been sceptical as to whether the institution is so early, see
        on 449 and 300
494–493 The first secession of the *plebs*, winning the right to have
        five tribunes (ten from 457; see p. 25) and a legislative
        assembly known as the *concilium plebis*
        Creation of the plebeian aedileship
456   Lex Icilia distributing land on the Aventine to plebeians
451–450 Promulgation of the Twelve Tables by the *decemviri
        legibus scribundis*, board of ten for writing down the
        laws
449   Lex Valeria Horatia renewing or introducing *provocatio*,
        see on 509 and 300
        Lex Valeria Horatia making *plebiscita*, decisions of the
        plebs, binding on the whole people; many historians
        have been sceptical as to whether the measure is so early,
        see on 339 and 289

445	Lex Canuleia ending the ban on intermarriage between patricians and plebeians enshrined in the Twelve Tables
	Introduction of the military tribunate with consular power, open to plebeians, as an alternative to opening the consulate to plebeians
443	Creation of the censorship
439	Sp. Maelius killed by C. Servilius Ahala for allegedly aiming at tyranny.
421	Quaestorship opened to plebeians (Livy IV, 43, 10–44, 3)
409	First plebeian quaestors
400	Plebeian breakthrough with four out of six plebeian military tribunes with consular power; there had hitherto only been one in 444 and one in 442
367	Leges Liciniae Sextiae restraining usury, limiting the amount of public land which could be held by the rich, opening the priesthood of the *decemviri sacris faciundis*, board of ten for conducting sacrifices, to plebeians, and reserving one consulate for a plebeian; the last measure was only regularly observed from 342 onwards
	Creation of the praetorship
	Creation of the curule aedileship, at first not open to plebeians
364	First plebeian curule aediles
356	First plebeian dictator, C. Marcius Rutilus
351	First plebeian censor, C. Marcius Rutilus
342	See on 367
	Lex Genucia restraining usury
339	Leges Publiliae reserving one censorship for a plebeian, reducing the authorisation of the *patres* for legislation in the *comitia centuriata* to a formality by requiring that it be granted beforehand, and making *plebiscita*, decisions of the *plebs*, binding on the whole people, see on 449 and 289
336	First plebeian praetor
326	Lex Poetelia Papiria supposedly ending *nexum*, debt bondage.
300	Lex Valeria renewing or introducing *provocatio*, see on 509 and 449

Lex Ogulnia opening the priesthoods of the pontiffs and augurs to plebeians

289   Lex Hortensia making *plebiscita*, decisions of the *plebs*, binding on the whole people, see on 449 and 339

IV – The Conquest of Italy

504   Attus Clusus (Appius Claudius) migrates to Rome and is accepted as a patrician

449 or 496   Defeat of the Latins at the battle of Lake Regillus

406–396   War against and destruction of Veii

390   Capture of Rome by the Gauls

378   City wall of Rome built

348   Second treaty of Rome with Carthage

343   Adhesion of Capua to Rome

340–338   War against and defeat of the Latins

338   Grant of *civitas sine suffragio* to Capua

334   Foundation of Cales as the first Latin colony founded by Rome

328   Foundation of Fregellae

327   Outbreak of war with the Samnites; appeal of Neapolis to Rome

326   Treaty of Rome with Neapolis

321   Defeat of Rome at the Caudine Forks

312   Censorship of Ap. Claudius; building of the Via Appia from Rome to Campania; first issue of silver coinage by Rome

304   End of war with the Samnites

302   Intervention to suppress unrest at Arretium in Etruria and Carseoli among the Aequi

295   Defeat of Gauls, Etruscans, Umbrians and Samnites at Sentinum

280   Invasion of Italy by Pyrrhus

275   Defeat of Pyrrhus

265–264   Intervention to suppress unrest at Volsinii

241   Intervention to suppress unrest at Falerii

V – From Italian Power to Mediterranean Power

312	Censorship of A. Claudius (see above)
280	Invasion of Italy by Pyrrhus
279	Ap. Claudius prevents peace being made with Pyrrhus
275	Defeat of Pyrrhus at Beneventum
265–264	Intervention to suppress unrest at Volsinii
264	Outbreak of the First Punic War
260	Roman naval victory of C. Duilius at Mylae
259	Roman operations on Sardinia and Corsica
241	Defeat of Carthage at the Aegates Islands; end of the First Punic War
	Intervention to suppress unrest at Falerii
238	Seizure of Sardinia and probably also Corsica from Carthage
255	Last invasion of Italy by the Gauls
218	Outbreak of the Second Punic War
202	Defeat of Carthage at Zama in Africa; end of the Second Punic War
201	Peace treaty with Carthage

VI – The Conquest of the East

230	Roman ambassadors murdered by Illyrians
229	First Illyrian War; Demetrius left as Roman protégé
227	Two extra praetors in office for the first time to govern Sicily and Sardinia with Corsica
220	Demetrius becomes *persona non grata*
219	Second Illyrian War
218	Outbreak of the Second Punic War
215	Alliance between Philip V of Macedon and Carthage
212/211	Alliance between Rome and Aetolia
206	End of the First Macedonian War
200	Declaration of war against Philip V
197	Philip V defeated at Cynoscephalae
196	Declaration of the freedom of Greece at the Isthmian Games
192	Antiochus III of Syria invades Greece

190   Antiochus III defeated at Nagnesia in Asia

VII – The Consequences of Empire – the Governing Classes

197   Six praetors altogether in office for the first time
195   Consulate of the elder Cato
184   Censorship of the elder Cato
181   First law on bribery
           First law to limit conspicuous consumption
180   Lex Villia annalis regulating tenure of magistraces
149   Lex Calpurnia repetundarum on extortion
139   Lex Gabinia introducing the secret ballot for elections

VIII – The Imperial Power

195   Consulate of the elder Cato; governorship of Hither
           Spain
184   Censorship of the elder Cato
180–178   Governorship of Hither Spain of the elder Ti.
           Sempronius Gracchus
171   Outbreak of the Third Macedonian War
168   Perseus of Macedon defeated at Pydna
167   Abolition of the kingdom of Macedon
155–154   Outbreak of major hostilities in Hither and Further
           Spain
149   Outbreak of the Third Carthaginian War
148   Suppression of the revolt of Macedon
147   Achaea moves towards war with Rome
146   Sack of Carthage
           Sack of Corinth
137   Surrender of C. Hostilius Mancinus at Numantia in
           Spain
134   Second consulate of P. Cornelius Scipio Aemilianus
133   Sack of Numantia by Aemilianus

XI – The Consequences of Empire – the Governed

X – Reform and Revolution

XI – Rome and Italy

XII – The End of Consensus

91   Outbreak of the Social War
88   March of Sulla on Rome

XIII – The World Turned Upside Down

91   Tribunate of the younger M. Livius Drusus; outbreak
          of Social War
88   Invasion of the province of Asia by Mithridates VI of
          Pontus; command conferred on Sulla and then removed
          and given to Marius
          March of Sulla on Rome; command restored to Sulla
88–83   Sulla in the east
83   Return of Sulla to Italy at the head of an army
82   Defeat of the Samnites at the Colline Gate and death of
          the younger C. Marius
82–81   Sulla in office as dictator *rei publicae constituendae
          causae*, for reorganising the state
80   Second consulate of Sulla
78   Death of Sulla
78–77   Consulate and rising of M. Aemilius Lepidus

XIV – The Embattled Oligarchy

80–73   Q. Sertorius in control of Spain
74   Outbreak of the Third Mithridatic War
73–71   Slave revolt led by Spartacus
70   Consulate of Cn. Pompeius Magnus and M. Licinius
          Crassus
67   Lex Gabinia conferring the command against the
          pirates on Pompeius
66   Lex Manilia conferring the command against Mithri-
          dates VI on Pompeius
63   Consulate of Cicero and conspiracy of Catilina
          Settlement of the east by Pompeius and abolition of the
          kingdom of Syria
60   Formation of a political alliance between Pompeius,
          Crassus and Caesar, known to modern scholars as 'the

First Triumvirate', but not possessing any juridical status

59   First consulate of Caesar
58–49   Command of Caesar in Gaul
58   Tribunate of P. Clodius and exile of Cicero
57   Special command conferred on Pompeius to organise the corn supply

XV – The Military Dynasts

55   Second consulates of Pompeius and Crassus
52   Sole consulate of Pompeius
49–45   Civil war between Caesar and Pompeius and his followers and family
48   Defeat of Pompeius at Pharsalus in Greece
44   Assassination of Caesar

Epilogue

43   Lex Pedia creating Lepidus, Antonius and Octavianus as *tresviri rei publicae constituendae causae*, board of three for reorganising the state; beginning of the proscriptions and death of Cicero
42   Defeat of Brutus and Cassius at Philippi in Greece
36   Defeat of Sex. Pompeius in Sicily; attempted coup of Lepidus, followed by his expulsion from office
35   Death of Sex. Pompeius
31   Defeat of Antonius and Cleopatra at Actium

Further Reading

General

The standard large-scale account of the Roman Republic, with vast bibliographical apparatus, is now the second edition of the *Cambridge Ancient History*: VII, 2, 'The rise of Rome to 220 BC (1989); VII, 'Rome and the Mediterranean to 133 BC' (1989); IX, 'The Last Age of the Roman Republic, 146–43 BC', forthcoming. W.M. Beard and M.H. Crawford, *Rome in the Late Republic*, London, 1985, deals more provocatively with the same period as the last volume. A collaborative French work, Cl. Nicolet (ed.), *Rome et la conquête du monde méditerranéan* I. *Les structures de l'Italie romaine*, Paris, 1977, II. *Genèse d'un empire*. 2nd ed., Paris, 1989, contains much that is stimulating and important. See also R. Jenkyns (ed.), *The Legacy of Rome*, Oxford, 1992.

T.R.S. Broughton, *The Magistrates of the Roman Republic* I–II with Supplement, New York, 1960; III, Atlanta, 1986, provides a year by year list of magistrates with references to the sources and to modern discussions.

N. Lewis and M. Reinhold, *Roman Civilisation* I. *The Republic and the Augustan Age*, 2nd ed., New York, 1990, translate and comment on a selection of source material.

M.H. Crawford, *Coinage and Money under the Roman Republic, Italy and the Mediterranean Economy*, London, 1985, offers a historical analysis of the economic consequences of the Roman conquest of the Mediterranean.

P.A. Brunt, *Social Conflicts in the Roman Republic*, London, 1971, provides a brilliant synthesis; many of the themes are more fully worked out in a difficult, but rewarding, book, *The Fall of the Roman Republic*, Oxford, 1988.

Modern work on Roman Republican religion begins from J. A. North, *PBSR* 44, 1976, 1, 'Conservatism and change in Roman religion'; see also J.H.W.G. Liebeschuetz, *Continuity and Change in Roman Religion,* Oxford, 1979, mostly about the Roman Empire; J. A. North, in *CAH* VII, 2, and XI; W. M. Beard and J. A. North (edd.), *Pagan Priests*, London, 1990; W.M. Beard, J. A. North, S. R. F. Price, *A History of Roman Religion* I—II, Cambridge, forthcoming. For the suppression of Bacchanalian worship and its implications, see J. A. North, *Proc.Camb.Phil.Soc.* 1979, 85, 'Religious toleration in Republican Rome'.

For ways into the law of the Republic, see J. M. Kelly, *Roman Litigation*, Oxford, 1966; B. W. Frier, *The Rise of the Roman Jurists*, Princeton, 1985; D. Daube, *Roman Law, Linguistic, Social and Philosophical Aspects*, Cambridge, 1969, brilliant and witty. The most accessible work of reference for historians is H. F. Jolowicz and B. Nicholas, *Historical Introduction to the Study of Roman Law*, 3rd ed., Cambridge, 1972.

C. Wirszubski, Libertas *as a Political Idea at Rome during the Late Republic and Early Principate*, Cambridge, 1950, and Cl. Nicolet, *The World of the Citizen in Republican Rome*, London, 1980, are important treatments of the relationship between Republican political thought and practice. See also D. C. Earl, *The Moral and Political Tradition of Rome*, London, 1967; but now, above all, P. A. Brunt, *The Fall of the Roman Republic* (see above), Ch. 6, '*Libertas* in the Republic'.

E. Rawson, *Intellectual Life in the Late Roman Republic*, London, 1985, is a rich and interesting, if nervous and idiosyncratic, book, deliberately excluding both Cicero and poetry. The Republican chapters in E. J. Kenney and W. V. Clausen (edd.), *The Cambridge History of Classical Literature* II. *Latin Literature*, Cambridge, 1982, are on the whole good. See also R. Hunter, *The New Comedy of Greece and Rome*, Cambridge, 1985.

There is no treatment of Republican art which is satisfactory from a historical point of view; the most recent book is D. Strong, *Roman Art*, London, 1976.

There is a breathtakingly beautiful series of aerial photographs

in G. Schmidt, *Atlante aerofotografico delle sedi umane in Italia*
I–II, Florence, 1966–70; a smaller selection from a wider
geographical area may be found in J. S. P. Bradford, *Ancient
Landscapes*, London, 1957.

I – The Sources

See in general M.H. Crawford (ed.), *Sources for Ancient History*,
Cambridge, 1983.

A. Momigliano, *Studies in Historiography*, London, 1966, and
Essays in Ancient and Modern Historiography, Oxford, 1977, both
include a number of brilliant essays relevant to Republican history,
including ones on Timaeus, Fabius Pictor and Polybius; see also
The Classical Foundations of Modern Historiography, Berkeley
and Los Angeles, 1990).

Note also:

T. S. Brown, *Timaeus of Tauromenium*, Berkeley and Los
Angeles, 1958

L. Pearson, *The Greek Historians of the West. Timaeus and his
Predecessors*, Atlanta, 1987

F. W. Walbank, *Polybius*. Berkeley and Los Angeles, 1972

A. D. Nock, *JRS* 49, 1959, 1, 'Posidonius'

H. Strasburger, *JRS* 55, 1965, 'Posidonius on problems of the
Roman empire'

B. W. Frier, Libri annales pontificum maximorum: *the Origins of
the Annalistic Tradition*, Rome, 1979

P. G. Walsh, *Livy,* Cambridge, 1961

E. Gabba, *Dionysius and the History of Archaic Rome*, Berkeley
and Los Angeles, 1991

K. Sacks, *Diodorus Siculus and the First Century*, Princeton,
1990

B. Farrington, in *Head and Hand in Ancient Greece*, London,
1947, 55, 'Diodorus Siculus universal historian'

E. Gabba, *Appiano e la storia delle querre civili*, Florence, 1956

P. Stadter (ed.), *Plutarch and the Historical Tradition*, London,
1992

F. G. B. Millar, *A Study of Cassius Dio*, Oxford, 1964

R. Syme, *Sallust*, Berkeley and Los Angeles, 1964

The most determined assault on the repute of the Latin historical tradition has been made by T. P. Wiseman, *Clio's Cosmetics*, Leicester, 1979; the debate may be followed, for example, in his paper and that of T. J. Cornell, in I. S. Moxon, J. D. Smart, A. J. Woodman (edd.), *Past Perspectives, Cambridge,* 1986; it is less relevant to the material with which most of this book is concerned than to the early period, on which a prudent agnosticism may be maintained. The argument of A. J. Woodman, *Rhetoric in Classical Historiography*, London, 1988, is in my judgement based on a misconception of the nature of history.

An interesting use is made of the evidence of Plautus by A. Watson, *Roman Private Law around 200* bc, Edinburgh, 1971.

A. E. Douglas, *Cicero*, Oxford, 1968, is a sensitive account of his whole literary production, with bibliographical apparatus.

For the non-Roman tradition see T. J. Cornell, *Museum Helveticum* 1974, 193, 'Notes on the sources for Campanian history in the fifth century bc; *Annali della Scuola Normale di Pisa* 1976, 411, 'Etruscan historiography'.

The standard collection of Republican inscriptions in Latin is A. Degrassi, *Inscriptiones Latinae Liberae Rei Publicae* I–II, Florence, 1965, 1963, now to be supplemented by Part 2, Fasc,. 4 of Vol. 1, 2nd ed., of the *Corpus Inscriptionum Latinarum*, Berlin, 1986. Texts and translations of statute laws passed through the assemblies may be found in M. H. Crawford (ed.), *Roman Statutes*, forthcoming. Translations of selected Republican inscriptions in Latin may be found in E. H. Warmington,, *Remains of Old Latin* IV, London, 1940.

The standard handbook of Republican coins is M. H. Crawford, *Roman Republican Coinage* I–II, Cambridge, 1974.

The superb collection of recent syntheses of aspects of the archaeological evidence in P. Zanker (ed.), *Hellenismus in Mittelitalien*, Göttingen, 1976, has borne fruit in the fourteen volumes of the Guide Archeologiche Laterza, covering the whole of Italy.

II – Italy and Rome

There is a fuller account of the peoples of Italy in M. H. Crawford, *Coinage and Money* (see above), Ch. 1.

Note also:

M. Pallottino, *A History of Earliest Italy,* London, 1991

T. W. Potter, *Roman Italy*, London, 1987

E. T. Salmon, *Samnium and the Samnites*, Cambridge, 1967

J. Boardman, *The Greeks Overseas*, London, 1980

M. Pallottino, *The Etruscans*, London, 1975

E. Macnamara, *The Etruscans*, London, 1990

The most up to date material on the Celts is now to be found in the Venice exhibition catalogue, *I Celti*, Milan, 1991

III – The Roman Governing Classes

The most accessible and interesting account of the republican 'constitution' is that of W. Kunkel, *An Introduction to Roman Legal and Constitutional History*, 2nd ed., Oxford, 1973

The argument over the definition of a *nobilis* may be followed in M. Gelzer, *The Roman Nobility*, Oxford, 1969 (translation of *Die Nobilitat der romischen Republik*, 1912; and of 'Die Nobilitat der Kaiserzeit', 1915); P. A. Brunt, *JRS* 72, 1982, 1, '*Nobilitas* and *novitas*'; D.R. Shackleton Bailey, *American Journal of Philology* 107, 1986, 255,, '*Nobiles* and *novi* reconsidered'.

Current orthodoxy rejects 'analysis of the politics of the middle Republic in terms of groupings based on alliances between *gentes* or branches of *gentes*', e.g., F. G. B. Millar, *JRS* 74, 1984, 1, 'The political character of the classical Roman Republic' (the concomitant attempt to treat Rome as a democracy would have amazed Polybius); P. A. Brunt, *The Fall of the Roman Republic* (see above), Chs. 7 and 9; there is a rather wooden critique by J. Briscoe, in C. Deroux (ed.), *Studies in Latin Literature and Roman History* VI, Brussels, 1992, 'Political groupings in the middle Republic: a restatement', from whom the quotation above is drawn. A much more sophisticated approach is that of J. A. North, *Past and Present* 126, 1990, 3, 'Democratic politics in

Republican Rome: the formulation in the text here still seems to me on balance quite sensible.

P. A. Brunt, Ch. 8, is an assault on the importance of clientela in the structure of Republican politics: some babies have gone out with the bath water, see my review in *Athenaeum*, forthcoming.

For the relationship between Republican thought and practice, see above; and for the rhetoric of political persuasion, F. G. B. Millar, *JRS* 76, 1986, 1, 'Politics, persuasion and the people before the Social War (150–90 BC)'.

See also A. Watson, *Rome of the XII Tables,* Princeton, 1975; K. A. Raaflaub (ed.), *Social Struggles in Archaic Rome*, Berkeley and Los Angeles, 1986

IV – The Conquest of Italy

J. Heurgon, *The Rise of Rome*, London, 1973, is a useful general account of Roman history down to 264, with an accessible discussion of the treaties with Carthage; these are also well discussed in H.H. Scullard, *CAH* VII, 2, Ch.11.

R. M. Ogilvie, *Early Rome and the Etruscans*, London, 1976, takes an in my view unduly serious view of the capture of Rome by the Gauls.

The settlement of conquered land, the spread of Roman citizenship and the resulting military strength of Rome are the themes of an important trinity of books, E. T. Salmon, *Roman Colonisation*, London, 1969; A. N. Sherwin White, *Roman Citizenship*, 2nd ed., Oxford, 1973; P. A. Brunt, *Italian Manpower*, rev. ed., Oxford, 1987, the last a mine of information on a vast range of topics. There is a full discussion of Latin rights by Sherwin White, Chs. 1 and 3; of *cives sine suffragio* in M. Humbert, Municipium *et* civitas sine suffragio, Paris, 1978; the tribal system within the Roman citizen body is expounded by L. R. Taylor, *Voting Districts of the Roman Republic*, Rome, 1960. E. T. Salmon, *The Making of Roman Italy*, London, 1982, is thin and disappointing.

Narratives and analysis of the conquest of two areas are to be found in W.V. Harris, *Rome in Etruria and Umbria*, Oxford, 1971; E. T. Salmon, *Samnium and the Samnites* (see above); and

M. W. Frederiksen, *Campania*, London, 1984: the last work, published posthumously, is sadly disappointing; perhaps the best pages are those which attempt to understand what *civitas sine suffragio* felt like to a Capuan, 196–8.

For Cosa, see F. E. Brown, *Cosa. The Making of a Roman Town*, Ann Arbor, 1980. For the first issue of coinage by Rome, see M. H. Crawford, *Coinage and Money under the Roman Republic* (see above), Ch. 3, for the development of the census, Ch. 2.

V – From Italian Power to Mediterranean Power

R. M. Errington, *The Dawn of Empire*, London, 1971, remains a useful general account of Roman expansion. The major recent work on Roman imperialism is W. V. Harris, *War and Imperialism in Republican Rome,* 327–70 BC, Oxford, 1979; it is to be read with J. A. North, *JRS* 71, 1981, 1, 'The development of Roman imperialism'; and the papers in W. V. Harris (ed.), *The Imperialism of Mid-Republican Rome*, Rome 1984.

The most accessible up to date account of Carthage, important for its mastery of the new archaeological evidence, is to be found in M. Gros, P. Rouillard, J. Teixidor, *L'univers phénicien*, Paris, 1989.

A. J. Toynbee, *Hannibal's Legacy*, I–II, Oxford, 1965, is a wide ranging study of the First and Second Punic Wars and their consequences, which collects a vast amount of evidence and, in my view, almost completely misunderstands the Republic.

H. H. Scullard, *Scipio Africanus. Soldier and Politician,* London, 1970, lives up to its title.

E. Badian, *Foreign Clientelae*, Oxford, 1958, is a stimulating account of an important aspect of Roman rule and of the personal ties which underpinned it.

A. D. Momigliano, *Alien Wisdom*, Cambridge, 1975, is a brilliant account of the outside world, including the Romans, as seen by the Greeks.

For the internal developments in relation to expansion in Italy and overseas, the best approach to Ap. Claudius is probably via T. P. Wiseman, *Clio's Cosmetics* (see above); for developments in the ways in which Rome symbolized victory, see St. Weinstock,

Harvard Theological Review 1957, 211, '*Victor* and *invictus*'; E. Gabba, *Del buon uso della ricchezza*, Milan, 1988, 19–48 and 69–105, argues very interestingly for a consistent Roman attitude which aimed to prevent the governing classes engaging in activities which risked their impoverishment, interpreting the Lex Claudia in this context.

I have tried to write a *history* of Republican provincial government in *Storia di Roma* II, 1, Turin: Einaudi, 1990, 91–121, 'Origini e sviluppi del sistema provinciale romano'.

VI – The Conquest of the East

R. M. Errington, *A History of Macedonia*, Oxford, 1990, is a good introduction.

Ed. Will, *Histoire politique du monde helénistique* I–II, Nancy, 2nd ed., 1979–82, is an extremely well organised, topic by topic, account of the main problems, the sources and the modern bibliography.

E. S. Gruen, *The Hellenistic World and the Coming of Rome*, Berkeley and Los Angeles, 1984, sets out to minimise Roman interventionism in the east and its impact; I regard both methodology and conclusion as perverse and am in substantial agreement with the important reviews of J. W. Rich, *Liverpool Classical Monthly* 10, 1965, 90–6; E. Gabba, *Athenaeum* 65, 1987, 205–10.

J. W. Rich, *Proc.Camb.Phil.Soc.* 1984, 126, 'Roman aims in the First Macedonian War', also sorts out problems of chronology.

P. S. Derow, *JRS* 69, 1979, 1, 'Polybius, Rome and the east', is an important article on what Polybius understood Roman hegemony to mean.

VII – The Consequences of Empire – the Governing Classes

For the economic *shape* of the empire created by Rome, see M. H. Crawford, *Economic History Review* 1977, 52, 'Rome and the Greek world: economic relationships'; the argument is taken further in *Coinage and Money under the Roman Republic* (see above), Ch. 13.

For regulation of the *cursus honorum*, see A. E. Astin, *The* 'lex annalis' *before Sulla*, Brussels, 1958.

A. W. Lintott, *JRS* 80, 1990, 1, 'Electoral bribery in the Roman Republic', does not always succeed in distinguishing between bribery and canvassing.

On sumptuary laws, I follow the interpretation of D. Daube, *Roman Law* (see above), 117–28; see also the general view of E. Gabba (cited above).

J. S. Richardson, *JRS* 65, 1975, 50, 'The triumph, the praetors and the senate', documents the view followed in the text.

For Roman provincial government, see M. H. Crawford (cited above); F. W. Walbank, *JRS* 55, 1965, 1, 'Political morality and the friends of Scipio', discusses Roman attitudes to provincial government.

N. S. Rosenstein, *Imperatores Victi*, Berkeley and Los Angeles, 1990, is an important essay on the relation between military failure and aristocratic competition, the ancient debate on freedmen and citizenship may be studied in S. Treggiari, *Roman Freedmen during the Late Republic*, Oxford, 1969, 37–52; for the changes in the structures of the census classes in the second century BC, see M. H. Crawford, *Coinage and Money under the Roman Republic* (see above), Ch. 10; D. W. Rathbone, in De agri cultura. In memoriam *P. W. de Neeve*, forthcoming, 'The census qualifications of the *assidui* and the *prima classis*'.

VIII – The Imperial Power

Many of the social tensions and cultural developments of the second century can be followed in A.E. Astin, *Cato the Censor*, Oxford, 1978; *Scipio Aemilianus*, Oxford, 1967. There is a useful brief account in E. Rawson, *CAH* VIII, Ch. 12; but the major work in this field is now J.L. Cerrary, *Philhellénisme et impérialisme*, Rome, 1988.

For Rome and the east, see A. N. Sherwin White, *Roman Foreign Policy in the East, 168 BC to AD 1*, London, 1984.

For the wars in Spain, see A. E. Astin, *Scipio Aemilianus* (see above); and, above all, J. S. Richardson, *Hispaniae. Spain and the Development of Roman Imperialism, 218–82 BC*, Cambridge, 1986.

For C. Laelius, see A.E. Astin, *Scipio Aemilianus* (see above), 307–10.

For a satisfactory account of *provocatio*, we must wait for the forthcoming paper by J. D. Cloud.

For the religion of the Republic, see above.

IX – The Consequences of Empire – the Governed

The standard account of the economic and social transformation of Italy in the second century is now that of E. Gabba, inb *CAH* VIII, Ch. 7, building on earlier work by G. Tibiletti and of his own; J.-P. Morel, Ch.13, discussing the archaeological evidence, is the most accessible account in English of the advances represented by the three volumes published by the Instituto Gramsci, *Società romana e produzione schiavistica* I–III, Bari, 1981; there are also long reviews in English by D. W. Rathbone, *JRS* 73, 1983, 160; S. Spurr, *CR* 35, 1985, 123–31. M. W. Frederiksen, *Dialoghi di Archeologia* 4–5, 2–3, 1970–1, 330, 'The contribution of archaeology to the agrarian problem in the Gracchan period', remains salutary reading on the fragility of many of the inferences made. E. Gabba, *Republican Rome, the Army and the Allies*, Oxford, 1977, remains essential reading for the whole of the economic and social history of the Republic from this point on. The discussion in P. A. Brunt, *Italian Manpower* (see above), is equally fundamental. P. W. de Neeve, Colonus. *Private Farm-tenancy in Roman Italy during the Republic and the Early Principate,* Amsterdam, 1984, places an important aspect of the agrarian history of Italy on a new basis.

F. Coarelli, *PBSR* 45, 1977, 1, 'Public building at Rome between the Second Punic War and Sulla', refutes the view that there was an urban dimension to the Gracchan crisis.

The best account in English of the slave wars in Sicily is that of K. R. Bradley, *Slavery and Rebellion in the Roman World*, Bloomington, 1989; that of M. I. Finley, *Ancient Sicily*, London, 1979, Ch. 11, naturally remains worth reading.

X – Reform and Revolution

There is a functional account in D. Stockton, *The Gracchi*, Oxford, 1979.

L. R. Taylor, *JRS* 52, 1962, 19, 'Some forerunners of the Gracchi', explores the political antecedents for the Gracchan use of the tribunate.

A. Lintott, *Violence in Republican Rome*, Oxford, 1968 Ch. 12, is a fine evocation of the road to disaster at the end of the tribunate of Ti. Gracchus.

The attempt of J. W. Rich, *Historia* 1983, 287, 'The supposed Roman manpower shortage of the later second century BC', to unhook the programme of Ti. Gracchus from a concern with Roman military manpower founders irretrievably on Appian, *Civil Wars* I, 45.

XI – Rome and Italy

See in general D. Stockton (cited above); I hope to be able to write at greater length on the Italian dimension in Republican history in these years.

Much remains obscure in the history of the extortion and other courts in Rome; the best guide is P. A. Brunt, *The Fall of the Roman Republic* (see above), Ch. 4. A. N. Sherwin White, *JRS* 72, 1982, 18, 'The *lex repetundarum* and the political ideas of Gaius Gracchus', makes exciting use of a difficult text.

XII – The End of Consensus

For the settlement of Marian veterans, see P. A. Brunt, *The Fall of the Roman Republic* (see above), 278–80 (though the anecdote in Plutarch, of which I also earlier wrongly made use, probably relates to Manius Curius Dentatus). J. A. North, in *Apodosis*, London, forthcoming, 'Deconstructing stone theatres', unscrambles a number of vexing problems in the history of the late second century.

The best account of the aims of the Italians in 91 is by P. A. Brunt, Ch. 2.

For an attempt to insert some of the problems into a wider economic and social context, using above all archaeological evidence, see M. H. Crawford, *JRS*, 71, 1981, 153, 'Italy and Rome'.

XIII – The World Turned Upside Down

E. Badian, *Lucius Sulla, the Deadly Reformer*, Sydney, 1970, despite its sometimes mischievous approach, is much to be preferred to the full length biographies of Sulla on offer in a variety of European languages. There is now a massive study of the proscriptions, F. Hinard, *Les proscriptions de la Rome républicaine*, Rome, 1985.

XIV – The Embattled Oligarchy

P. A. Brunt, *JRS* 52, 1962, 69, 'The army and the land in the Roman revolution', revised as *The Fall of the Roman Repoublic* (see above), Ch. 5, remains one of the most important and original contributions to the history of the late Republic of our generation.

E. Badian, *Roman Imperialism in the Late Republic*, Oxford, 1968, documents the change of gear in the exploitation of the provinces in the late Republic.

The fundamental study of urbanisation in Italy after the Social War, on which all further work has built, is E. Gabba, *Studi Classici e Orientali* 21, 1972, 73, 'Urbanizzazione nell' Italia centro-meridionale del I secolo a.C.

For conditions in Rome, see Z. Yavetz, *Latomus* 17, 1958, 500 = R. Seager (ed.), *The Crisis of the Roman Republic*, Cambridge, 1969, 'The living conditions of the urban plebs'. For unrest in Rome, see P. A. Brunt, *Past and Present* 1966, 3, 'The Roman mob'; on P. Clodius see A. W. Lintott, *Greece and Rome* 1967, 157, 'P. Clodius Pulcher'; and in general M. W. Frederiksen, *JRS* 56, 1966, 128, 'Caesar, Cicero and the problem of debt'.

E. S. Gruen, *The Last Generation of the Roman Republic*, Berkeley and Los Angeles, 1974, is to be read with the review by M. H. Crawford, *JRS*, 66, 1976, 214, 'Hamlet without the prince'.

L. R. Taylor, *Party Politics in the Age of Caesar*, Berkeley and Los Angeles, 1949, is a modernising, but still interesting, account.

T. P. Wiseman, *The World of Catullus*, Cambridge, 1985, is a splendid evocation of late Republican society.

XV – The Military Dynasts

D. R. Shackleton Bailey, *CQ* 1960, 253, 'The Roman nobility in the Second Civil War', documents the extent to which families were split: fratricidal madness or an attempt to ensure the continuity of the family whoever won? P. A. Brunt, *JRS*, 76, 1986, 12, 'Cicero's *officium* in the Civil War', raises many of the ideological issues involved in the outbreak of the civil war.

For the religious and dynastic policy of Caesar, see St. Weinstock, *Divus Julius*, Oxford, 1971, and above all the review of J. A. North, *JRS*, 65, 1975, 171 '*Praesens Divus*'; E. D. Rawson, *JRS* 65, 1975, 148 = *Roman Culture and Society*, Oxford, 1991, 169, 'Caesar's heritage: Hellenistic kings and their roman equals'.

The picture in F. Millar, *JRS* 1973, 50, 'Triumvirate and principate', is redrawn by P. A. Brunt, in *La rivoluzione romana*, Naples, 1982, 236, '"Augustus" e la "respublica"' (in English).

Epilogue

R. Syme, *The Roman Revolution*, Oxford, 1939, is to be read with the review of A. D. Momigliano, *JRS*, 30, 1940, 74.

The title chapter of P. A. Brunt, *The Fall of the Roman Republic* (see above), is a concentrated and in my view largely right account; some of its themes are to be found in Momigliano's critique of Syme.

For the Italian elite, see R. Syme, *PBSR* 14, 1938, 1 = *Roman Papers* I, Oxford, 1979, 88, 'Caesar, the senate and Italy'; T. P. Wiseman, *New Men in the Roman Senate*, Oxford, 1971, is a sensitive study of a crucial aspect of the transition from Republic to Principate. I have attempted to understand the Romanisation of Italy between the Social War and Augustus in a chapter to be published in *CAH* X. For the military funerary monuments of the age of revolution, see *Studi Miscellanei* 10, 1963–4.

For the religious developments of the late Republic, see J. A. North, *JRS* 70, 1980, 186, 'Novelty and choice in Roman religion'.

For veteran settlement, see L. Keppie, *Colonisation and Veteran Settlement in Italy 47–14 BC*, London, 1985.

B. W. Bowersock, *Augustus and the Greek World,* Oxford, 1965, documents *inter alia* the emergence of a Greco-Roman governing class for the Roman empire.

Abbreviations

CAH	The Cambridge Ancient History
CQ	The Classical Quarterly
CR	The Classical Review
JRS	The Journal of Roman Studies
PBSR	The Papers of the British School at Rome

Index of Sources

(Each source is followed by a brief characterization or by a reference to such a characterization in the main text)

Inscriptions

Selective Index of Persons

Selective Index of Places

General Index and Glossary

The True Story of the Novel

Margaret Anne Doody

SHORTLISTED FOR THE
NATIONAL BOOK CRITICS CIRCLE AWARD

'Written with verve and wit, by any standard an extraordinary and idiosyncratic achievement . . . I find it difficult to give a fair idea of the
exuberance, intelligence and boldness of this book.'

FRANK KERMODE, *LRB*

'This book sets out to prove something worth proving, that the novel is
an ancient and protean form, and that criticism that takes no account
of this is both insular and misleading . . . If Doody's book should
become prescribed reading in the English departments of universities,
we might at least see a little more imagination in the novels of the next
century. If writers took to heart her lesson . . . the results could only be
beneficial . . . This is a fascinating and an entertaining book.'

ROBERT NYE, *The Scotsman*

'An elegant, learned and convincing book which deals a witty dispatch
to much of the nonsense talked about the history of the novel.'

MARY BEARD, *Independent*

'Doody's true story is a rich and imaginative attempt to overturn what
she sees as the 'official' history of the novel . . . She has a real case and
makes it with intelligence, width and great charm, radicalising the
history of the novel.'

JAMES WOOD, *Observer*

ISBN 0 00 686379 5

FontanaPress
An Imprint of HarperCollinsPublishers

Demanding the Impossible

A History of Anarchism

Peter Marshall

'To be governed means that at every move, operation or transaction one is noted, registered, entered in a census, taxed, stamped, priced, assessed, patented, licensed, authorized, recommended, admonished, reformed . . . exploited, monopolized, extorted, pressured, mystified, robbed; all in the name of public utility and the general good.'

So said Proudhon in 1851, and from the Ancient Chinese to today's rebel youth many have agreed – among their number Godwin and Kropotkin, Bakunin and Malatesta, Tolstoy and Gandhi, the Ranters and the Situationists, de Sade and Thoreau, Wilde and Chomsky, anarcho-syndicalists and anarcha-feminists. Peter Marshall, in his inclusive, inspirational survey, gives back to the anarchistic, undiluted and undistorted, their secret history.

'Reading about anarchism is stimulating and funny and sad. What more can you ask of a book?'   Isabel Colegate, *The Times*

'Massive, scholarly, genuinely internationalist and highly enjoyable . . . this is the book Johnny Rotten ought to have read.'
David Widgery, *Observer*

'Large, labyrinthine, tentative: for me these are all adjectives of praise when applied to works of history, and *Demanding the Impossible* meets all of them. I now have a book – Marshall's solid 700 pages and more – to which I can direct readers when they ask me how soon I intend to bring my *Anarchism* up to date.'   George Woodcock, *Independent*

'This is the most comprehensive account of anarchist thought ever written. Marshall's knowledge is formidable and his enthusiasm engaging . . . he organizes a mass of diverse material with great subtlety and skill, presenting a good-tempered critique of each position with straightforward lucidity.'   J. B. Pick, *Scotsman*

ISBN 0 00 686245 4

Fontana Press

Fontana History of the Ancient World
Series Editor: Oswyn Murray

The Roman Empire
Second Edition

Colin Wells

'Seldom has the government of the world been conducted for so long a term in an orderly sequence . . . In its sphere, which those who belonged to it were not far wrong in regarding as the world, it fostered the peace and prosperity of the many nations united under its sway longer and more completely than any other leading power has ever done.'   Theodor Mommsen

This sweeping history of the Roman Empire from 44 BC to AD 235 has three purposes: to describe what was happening in the central administration of the Empire and in the entourage of the Emperor; to indicate how life went on in Italy and the provinces, in the towns, in the countryside, and in the army camps; and to show how these two different worlds impinged on each other. It comprises a vivid account of the most intriguing period in ancient history.

'Wells is expert in the various aspects of Roman history, he reflects on issues independently and creatively, and he writes elegantly, and sometimes brilliantly.'   Eleanor Huzar, *Classical Outlook*

ISBN 0 00 686252 7

Fontana Press

Courtesans and Fishcakes

The Consuming Passions of Classical Athens

James Davidson

'The best thing to happen to ancient history writing for decades'
ANDREW ROBERTS, *Mail on Sunday*

'James Davidson's concern is with ancient appetites: food, drink and sex in classical Athens. At one level, he provides a guided tour from bordello to Billingsgate; at another, an essay on the politics of consumption. This is a book of many pleasures, both in analysis and in anecdote . . . Davidson's invigorating book paints the scene with polished scholarship and fine Hellenic gusto.'
PETER PARSONS, *London Review of Books*

'A most enjoyable book about enjoyment.'
PETER STOTHARD, *The Times*

'All students of antiquity will have to have this book.'
CHRISTOPHER STACE, *Daily Telegraph*

'If little boys are still being made to learn dead languages, and expected to enjoy *Everyday Life in Ancient Greece,* I hope their Greek master reads James Davidson's fascinating and witty book, and tells them the best stories from it. This certainly ought to wake them up at the back of the class.'
HUMPHREY CARPENTER, *Sunday Times*

'An excellent and learned exploration of a subject which for 50 years has crumbled to dust whenever touched. There are pleasures and authors who lie dormant for a century or more until a new kind of vividness, a super-freshness descends on them. James Davidson has that skill.'
PETER LEVI, *Spectator*

0-00-686343-4

FontanaPress
An Imprint of HarperCollinsPublishers

Caesar

Christian Meier

'Meier's is a compulsively readable, scholarly, imaginative, and almost poetic account.' PETER JONES, *Sunday Telegraph*

James Boswell called him 'the greatest man of any age'. As politician and diplomat, writer and lover, but above all as a military genius, Julius Caesar is one of the most perennially fascinating figures in history. Christian Meier's biography is the definitive, modern account of Caesar's life and career, and places him within the wider context of the crisis of the Roman republic. Written specifically for a general reader-ship, this authoritative, stimulating book serves, amongst other things, as a reminder to those who believe that men are mere servants of historical forces that the great individual still has an unarguably significant part to play.

'Meier's Caesar goes well beyond the confines of biography to present a radical analysis of a political system in decline, and the opportunities it afforded one of the most brilliant and unscrupulous individuals of all time.' JOAN SMITH, *Independent on Sunday*

ISBN 000 686349 3

FontanaPress
An Imprint of HarperCollins*Publishers*